D1206983

THE LETTERS OF
KING CHARLES II

UNIFORM WITH THIS VOLUME

THE LETTERS OF KING HENRY VIII
edited by M. St. Clare Byrne

THE LETTERS OF QUEEN ELIZABETH I
edited by G. B. Harrison

THE LETTERS OF KING CHARLES I
edited by Sir Charles Petrie

THE LETTERS OF QUEEN ANNE
edited by Beatrice Curtis Brown

THE LETTERS OF KING GEORGE III
edited by Bonamy Dobrée

King Charles II
By J. M. Wright

THE
LETTERS
SPEECHES AND DECLARATIONS
OF
KING
CHARLES II

Edited by

SIR ARTHUR BRYANT
C.B.E., M.A., F.R.Hist.S., F.R.S.L.

CASSELL · LONDON

CASSELL & COMPANY LTD
35 Red Lion Square, London WC1
Melbourne, Sydney, Toronto
Johannesburg, Auckland
S.B.N. 304 93172 1
First published 1935
This edition © Sir Arthur Bryant 1968
This edition first published 1968

Printed photolitho in Great Britain
by Ebenezer Baylis & Son Ltd
The Trinity Press, Worcester, and London
F.468

CONTENTS

INTRODUCTION TO THE FIRST EDITION

THE written utterances of Kings, however important politically, are seldom distinguished by literary style. It is hard to see why they should be, for style arises from an intense desire to make oneself understood, and Kings are easily understood; they have only to utter and subjects are bound to hear. Yet at least two English sovereigns, Elizabeth and Charles II, possessed the quality of literary personality: one could still read their letters and speeches even if they had not been penned in the Cabinet or delivered from the Throne.

That Charles possessed this gift is strange, for his life offered few opportunities for the pursuit of letters. Before his twelfth year he was tossed into a world of battle, exile and vagrant poverty, and only returned to a settled existence when his youth was over and his habits formed. Even in his brief period of untroubled childhood he was given little encouragement to read; ' Take heed,' wrote his first governor (husband of Lamb's ' thrice noble Margaret Newcastle '), ' of too much book.' And at the end of his life Dryden, who knew him well, testified that he understood men better than books :

> ' His conversation, wit and parts,
> His knowledge in the noblest, useful arts
> Were such dead authors could not give.
>
> .   .   .   .   .   .
>
> He drained from and all they knew;
> His apprehension quick, his judgement true :
> That the most learned with shame confess,
> His knowledge more, his reading only less.'

Yet turn to Charles's intimate letters—to his sister, ' Minette,' to Harry Bennet or Clarendon in the days of his exile, to his daughter, Lady Lichfield, in his old age,—and style, incisive, witty, unmistakable, is there. It is never in the conscious grand manner and verbal elegance of Elizabeth. Literary composition obviously never gave Charles the pleasure it gave her: ' You know my natural inclination to that exercise,' he wrote to Clarendon. But if style is the art of expressing meaning in the most forcible

ix

manner and in the fewest possible words, one cannot deny it to the man who wrote to his sister, ' We have the same disease of sermons that you complain of there, but I hope you have the same convenience that the rest of the family has of sleeping out most of the time, which is great ease to those who are bound to hear them,' or warned her against prophets : ' I give little credit to such kind of cattle, and the less you do it the better, for if they could tell anything 'tis inconvenient to know one's fortune before-hand, good or bad, and so my dearest sister, good night.'

Nor was it only when he laid aside the King that Charles could give the breath of life to words : often in his diplomatic correspondence he speaks for England, not in her more flamboy-ant manner—he is no Cromwell or Palmerston—but in her quiet confidence and moderation and matchless common sense. ' There is nobody,' he wrote on one occasion, ' desires more to have a strict friendship with the King of France than I do, but I will never buy it upon dishonourable terms. And I thank God my condition is not so ill, but that I can stand upon my own legs and believe that my friendship is as valuable to my neighbours as theirs is to me.'

This work is an attempt to comprise in a single volume all the most interesting of Charles's letters, political or personal, to which I have added a selection from his speeches and other official declarations of policy. The reader will find here, in whole or in part, the Declaration of Breda, the Declaration of Indulgence, and the great Declarations—almost invariably ignored by English historians—of 1681 and 1683. These have been printed before, but never within the compass of a single work, for up till now even the elementary student of the reign has had to consult an unusually large number of source books, mostly out of print. The reader will also find here a good many letters, copied from manuscripts in the British Museum, Public Record Office and Bodleian, and now printed for the first time. The most important of these are undoubtedly the letters written by the King to the Duke of York and Prince Rupert during the naval campaigns of 1672 and 1673. Several of these are misdated and misdirected in the manuscript volume (Lansdowne 1236) from which they are taken, but I have used the internal evidence they contain to allocate them to their proper dates and recipients. One only hopes that a reading of these brilliant and lucid letters of advice to his Admirals will dissipate for ever the old legend of Charles's idleness and incapacity.

I could wish that conditions of space had allowed me to use a larger number of Charles's unpublished letters, as well as many others which have already appeared before in print, but which I have been unable to include here. As it is I have had to strain the forbearance of my publishers to the utmost point in order to be able to make this, the first collection of Charles II's Letters and Speeches published, representative and comprehensive. To do so I have had to omit large portions of many letters and documents, though I have been careful to show where I have done so by dots. But I have done my best to present through the medium of those I have retained a balanced and unbroken story of Charles's life and reign. And in doing so I have found space for all the best extant examples of Charles's epistolary style —culled from his letters to Clarendon and Bennet and Elizabeth of Bohemia, and the famous correspondence with his sister so ably collected and arranged in his brilliant book, *Charles II and Madame,* by my friend Cyril Hartmann, to whom and Messrs. Heinemann, Ltd., I am indebted for permission to use them here. It is to be wished that this famous correspondence—probably the most momentous ever engaged in by an English king—had survived in its entirety; as it is, the one hundred and five letters printed by Mr. Hartmann from the archives of the Ministère des Affaires Etrangères are a mere fragment of the whole correspondence, which was returned to Charles (as he thought in its entirety) after Madame's death in 1670 and almost certainly destroyed.

One difficulty I have had: that apart from the letters to Madame, the first eleven years of Charles's reign, when he was a penniless *roi fainéant,* are for obvious reasons far richer in letters composed and written by himself than the far more important period between 1660 and 1685. After the Restoration the overwhelming press of business incumbent on that over-centralized monarchial administration necessitated that the great bulk of the royal correspondence should be composed by his Secretaries of State. For this reason and on account of ' the natural laziness I have towards writing ', as Charles himself put it, it was but seldom that any of his subjects could boast, as one did in 1670, of ' a most gracious letter from His Majesty, all writ with his own hand '. Fortunately I have been able to preserve the balance by using for the beginning of the reign those characteristic notes that were passed over the Council Table between King and Minister and were subsequently preserved among Lord Clarendon's manuscripts, and for the policy of its later years the royal speeches to Parliament. And if the earlier of these last bear unmistakable evidence of Clarendon's handiwork, the later speeches are full of touches that belong to Charles and Charles alone. ' I who will never use arbitrary government myself am resolved not to suffer it in any subject,' he told his last Parliament in 1681. It was not for nothing that Marvell immortalized King Charles's peculiar and informal style of oratory in the most brilliant political parody in the English language.

As this book is intended for general readers as well as students, I have modernized spelling and punctuation. For all letters written from England, I have used *old style* or English notation, while for those written from abroad during the exile I have shown both the *old* and *new style* dates.

To the Earl of Sandwich, who has allowed me to print two letters from his collection at Hinchingbrooke, to Mrs. Moorman (Mary Trevelyan), to the Hon. Charles Clifford and most of all to Cyril Hartmann I am under an obligation for their generous help. I would also acknowledge the courtesy of Messrs. Heinemann, Ltd., for permission to quote extracts from Mr. Hartmann's *Charles II and Madame,* and of Mr. John Murray for quotations from *Catherine of Braganza.* I should like also to take this opportunity of expressing my indebtedness to my former secretary, Miss Betty Robinson, and to others unnamed who have assisted in the task of preparing this book.

ARTHUR BRYANT.

CHAPTER I

THE PRINCE OF WALES

Charles II was born on May 29th, 1630, at St. James's, the first English-born heir to the throne since Elizabeth, and became at once the centre of controversy. His father, Charles I, a Scot, held views on the rights and sanctity of monarchy which, though largely justified by ancient law, ran counter to the growing Protestantism of his English subjects, and had already quarrelled with his Parliaments over their reluctance to grant him adequate revenue. His mother, Henrietta Maria, unpopular as a Frenchwoman and a Roman Catholic, had made herself more so by her imperious temper and hatred of compromise. From the first many suspected that the young Prince of Wales was being educated by his mother as a Catholic, though actually the King, a staunch Anglican, brought him and his brothers and sisters up strictly as members of the Episcopalian Church.

Charles's first extant letter, probably written at the age of nine, was addressed to his governor, the magnificent Earl of Newcastle.

1. To the Earl of Newcastle

Undated.

My Lord, I would not have you take too much physic, for it doth always make me worse, and I think it will do the like with you. I ride every day, and am ready to follow any other directions from you. Make haste to return to him that loves you.

Before his eleventh birthday, the courtly life of Whitehall and riverside Greenwich, where the young Prince was first bred, came to an end, and he became an unwilling witness of the fury of the people and of his father's humiliation, as he was forced by Long Parliament and London mob to yield concession after concession. The experience taught him the rudiments of two political lessons—the peril in a ruler alike of weakness and of open obstinacy—the one learnt from his mother's unceasing sermons and the other from a certain capacity of his own for shrewd observation, probably derived from his maternal grandfather, Henri IV of France. It was as well, for both faults were hereditary in his father's family.

3

In 1642 the King, leaving London in the power of his rebellious subjects, and taking his son with him, raised the royal standard in the provinces.   For the next three years Charles was living in his father's military court at Oxford, amid all its attendant laxity of discipline and morals.   Only one letter survives from the period written by him in his own hand to the Earl of Roxburgh.

ii. To the Earl of Roxburgh

Oxford, February 29, 1634/4.

My Lord, I understand by Sir William Ballantine that you have two horses ready to send me; it is a present which will be very welcome to me.   I shall desire you to take it into your care to consider of some way to convey them to me for which I shall give you many thanks, who am, Your affectionate friend.

CHARLES.

In the spring of 1645, the King, feeling his fortunes failing, sent his heir for safety into the west of England as nominal Commander of his forces there.   It proved a melancholy experience for the young prince, for he found the generals quarrelling, the exchequer empty and the Army hopelessly ill-disciplined.   As soon as it was attacked by the victorious Roundheads it fell back and melted away.

Prince Charles, having had no part in the quarrels that had brought about the war, was hastily put forward by his Council as a would-be pacificator.

iii. To Sir Thomas Fairfax, Commander-in-Chief of the Parliamentarian Army

September 15, 1645.

We have so deep a sense of the present miseries and calamities of this kingdom, that there is nothing that we more earnestly pray for to Almighty God than that He would be pleased to restore unto it a happy peace.   And we should think it a great blessing of God upon us if we might be so happy as to be an instrument in the advancing of it.   And therefore we have resolved to send two of our Council unto the King our father, with some such overtures as we are hopeful may much conduce thereunto; and do hereby desire you to send or procure from the Lords and Commons assembled in Parliament at Westminster a safe conduct for the Lord Hopton and Lord Culpepper, with twelve servants, to go to our royal father and to return to us. And we shall then manifest to the world our most earnest endeavours to stop this issue of blood, which must otherwise in a short time render this unhappy land most miserable.

It was in vain. In March 1646, as peace was only possible on terms of unconditional surrender, the Prince of Wales, with three hundred faithful followers, sailed from Pendennis Castle for the Scilly Islands. Driven thence to Jersey by the Parliamentarian cruisers, he joined his mother in June at the French Court —a step which his father had enjoined should only be taken in the last extremity and which the wisest man in his entourage, Sir Edward Hyde, held should never have been taken at all.

For the next two years Charles was a cipher at his mother's exiled Court, and was denied all part in public affairs. But in the spring of 1648 the English and Scottish Presbyterians, in a wave of reactionary feeling for the imprisoned King, united with their former foes, the Cavaliers, to throw off the yoke of the Army, which had subordinated every authority in the kingdom to the rule of force and reduced its former master Parliament to a tiny band of members of its own way of thinking. Risings took place all over the country, and a section of the Parliamentarian Fleet mutinying and sailing over to Holland, the Prince of Wales joined it at Helvoetsluys. Hence before hoisting his flag he addressed formal letters to his father's supporters in England.

IV. To the Mayor and Corporation of Kingston-upon-Hull

Helvoetsluys, July 17/27, 1648.

Trusty and well-beloved, we greet you well. We conceive it to be our duty to lay hold of all means that may probably conduce to the restoring of the King our royal father to his liberty and just rights, the redeeming of the whole kingdom from those heavy pressures which now lie upon it, and the settling of a well-grounded and happy peace. And it having pleased God to move the hearts of so many of the seamen to return to their natural obedience to the King, that now a great part of His Majesty's own navy royal . . . are under our command. . . . We have therefore thought fit to invite you to partake with us and all the well-affected people of the kingdom . . . in our undertaking . . . by a reasonable declaration of yourselves against that arbitrary and lawless power of the sword, which oppresses the whole kingdom.   Which, if you shall do, we assure you and the whole town of a full pardon and indemnity for all that is past, and our just protection of all your ships and goods. . . .

But as the risings in England were suppressed piecemeal by Cromwell and Fairfax, Charles was unable either to rescue his father from Carisbrooke, relieve the starving royalist garrison of Colchester, or bring the Parliamentary Fleet to action. For a short time he blockaded the mouth of the Thames, but was forced through shortage of victuals to return to Holland in September 1648.

Early in January 1649, while convalescing from smallpox at the Court of his brother-in-law, the Prince of Orange, Charles learnt of the military Council set up by the victorious Army for his father's trial. In haste he dispatched letters to the rulers of Europe, praying for their intercession, and, though it must have hurt his pride to do so, to his father's jailers.

v.To GENERAL FAIRFAX AND HIS COUNCIL OF WAR IN ENGLAND

The Hague, January 13/23, 1648/9.

We have no sources of information regarding the health and present condition of the King, our father, but the common gazettes which come into this country, our servant, Symons, whom we lately sent to present our humble respects to His Majesty, not having been able to obtain permission to do so, or to see him.   We have reason to believe that, at the end of the time assigned for the treaty made with His Majesty in the Isle of Wight, His Majesty has been withdrawn from that island to Hurst Castle, and thence conducted to Windsor, with some intention of proceeding against him with more rigour, or of deposing him from the royal dignity given him by God alone, who invested his person with it by a succession undisputed, or even of taking his life; the mere thought of which seems so horrible and incredible that it has moved us to address these presents to you, who now have power, for the last time, either to testify your fidelity, by reinstating your lawful King, and to restore peace to the kingdom—an honour never before given to so small a number as you—or to be the authors of misery unprecedented in this country, by contributing to an action which all Christians think repugnant to the principles of their religion, or any fashion of government whatever, and destructive of all security. I therefore conjure you to think seriously of the difference there is in the choice you make, and I doubt not you will choose what will be most honourable and most just, and preserve and defend the King, whereto you are by oath obliged. It is the only way in which any of you can promise himself peace of conscience, the favour and good will of His Majesty, the country, and all good men, and more particularly of your friend.

CHARLES P.

More eloquent was the blank sheet of paper, with Prince Charles's signature at its foot, which he sent them to fill up with any conditions they chose to impose upon him in return for his father's life. The appeal was in vain, and on January 30, 1649, Charles I ended his life on the scaffold and Charles II was King.

7

CHAPTER II

THE SCOTTISH ADVENTURE

Of the three kingdoms to which the eighteen-year-old exile succeeded, the largest, England, was under the heel of his father's murderers, who now declared a Commonwealth. In Scotland the ruling Presbyterians, though out of hatred for the English sectaries they proclaimed Charles King, were only prepared to receive him on terms incompatible with the very existence of the Anglican faith for which his father had died. Poverty-stricken Ireland alone remained, where the Lord Lieutenant, the chivalrous Marquis of Ormonde, was struggling at the same time to suppress the Catholic natives, who wanted political and religious independence, and to keep out invading Roundheads. At the time of the King's execution, he had just succeeded in negotiating a temporary treaty between the native chieftains, led by Lord Inchiquin, and the Protestant Anglo-Irish Cavaliers. Charles therefore decided to join him and wrote announcing his intention of doing so.

1. To the Marquis of Ormonde

The Hague, Feb. 27/March 9, 1648/9.

My Lord,

I have lately received from the Lord Byron a copy of the Articles of the Peace which you have made in Ireland, together with a copy of your letter to me, and am extremely well satisfied with both, and will confirm wholly and entirely all that is contained in the articles. . . .

I will make all the haste I can to come to you into Ireland, intending for my better security to pass over land through France, and to embark at Rochelle; and will use my best endeavours to procure supplies for you, and ever remain, Your loving friend. CHARLES R.

At her request, the King on his way to join Ormonde visited his mother at Paris. Here he was delayed for two months, partly by lack of money and partly by the entreaties of Henrietta, who having no faith in the Irish and no more repugnance to Presbyterians than to any other species of heretic, wished him to throw in his lot with the richer Scots. But Charles, respecting his father's last wishes, preferred to trust to the leader of the Scottish Cavaliers, the Marquis of Montrose, who was endeavouring to raise men in northern Europe for an invasion of Scotland.

II. TO THE MARQUIS OF MONTROSE

September 19/29, 1649.

I entreat you to go on courageously with your wonted courage and care in the prosecution of those trusts committed to you, and not to be frustrated by any reports you may hear as if I were otherwise inclined to the Presbyterians than I was before when I left you. I assure you I am still upon the same principles, and depend as much as ever upon your undertakings and endeavours for my business, being fully resolved to assist you and support you to the utmost of my power. . . .

In September, as news had arrived that Ormonde had been defeated at Rathmines and Cromwell had landed in Ireland, Charles moved to Jersey, which still flew the Royal Standard. Here he spent four penniless months, awaiting events and occupying his leisure in sailing and field sports. His difficulties did not prevent his unhappy followers from quarrelling and demanding favours which he was unable to grant. One letter survives which he wrote in reply to an ill-timed request from the Marquis of Worcester for a Dukedom and the Order of the Garter.

III. TO THE MARQUIS OF WORCESTER

Jersey, October 21/31, 1649.

My Lord Worcester, I am truly sensible of your great merit and sufferings in the service of the King my father, and I shall never be wanting to reward and encourage as well that kindness to his person as that zeal to his service which you have expressed in all your actions, and which I doubt not but you will still continue to me. I fear that in this conjuncture of time it will not be seasonable for me to grant, nor for you to receive the addition of honour you desire, neither can I at this time send the order you mention concerning the Garter. But be confident that I will in due time give you such satisfaction in these particulars, and in all other things that you can reasonably expect from me, as shall let you see with how much truth and kindness I am, Your affectionate friend. CHARLES R.

Ireland proved a broken reed. At the end of October came the news that Cromwell had stormed Drogheda, massacring 3,000 of Ormonde's stoutest troops. Charles had no money and nowhere to go, and the reduction of Jersey by the Common-wealth Fleet could not be long delayed. The Scottish Presby-terians, seizing their opportunity, at once dispatched an envoy to Jersey with orders to propose a conference in Holland between their Commissioners and the King. The King, having little other alternative, agreed, writing personally to their leader, the Marquis of Argyll, to urge that their demands should be made as moderate as possible.

IV. TO THE MARQUIS OF ARGYLL

Jersey, January 2/12, 1649/50.

My Lord of Argyll, I cannot but know how much you are able to contribute to the agreement between me and my subjects of Scotland : and desiring it so much as I do, I can much less forbear to entreat you to give all furtherance to the sending away Commissioners to Breda, and to the moderating of their instruc-tions as much as reasonably you may. It is now in your power to oblige me to a very great degree, and it shall be my care to remember, and to acknowledge that which you shall now (do) for my advantage, and to remain ever your affectionate friend. CHARLES R.

At the same time he wrote officially to the Marquis of Montrose, at that moment in distant Norway and about to embark on his desperate venture for Scotland, informing him of what he had done and privately assuring him that he would not abandon his interests.

v. To the Marquis of Montrose

Jersey, January 12/22, 1649/50.

. . . I will never fail in the effects of that friendship I have promised, . . . and that nothing can happen to me shall make me consent to anything to your prejudice. I conjure you, therefore, not to take alarm at any reports or messages from others; but to depend upon my kindness; and to proceed in your business with your usual courage and alacrity; which I am sure will bring great advantage to my affairs, and much honour to yourself. I wish you all good success in it, and shall ever remain your affectionate friend. CHARLES R.

The nineteen-year-old King was by nature sanguine, and possessed of splendid health and animal spirits. A few days after dispatching his solemn letters to Argyll and Montrose, he was writing cheerfully to his confidential servant, Edward Progers, then in Paris, ordering him to procure him clothes on the credit of his journey.

vi. To Edward Progers

Jersey, January 4/14, 1649/50.

I would have you (besides the embroidered suit) bring me a plain riding suit with an innocent coat, the suits I have for horse-back being so spotted and spoiled that they are not to be seen out of this island. The lining of the coat and the petit teies [*sic*] are referred to your great discretion, provided there want nothing when it comes to be put on. I do not remember there was a belt, or a hatband, in your directions for the embroidered suit, and those are so necessary as you must not forget them. . . .

In March Charles met the Commissioners at Breda. Though their speeches were long, their terms were short and unpalatable. Charles was to promise to enforce Presbyterian dogma and church discipline on his three kingdoms, and, by swearing to the Covenant, forswear the faith for which his father had died, repudiate Ormonde's treaty with the Catholic Irish and abandon

Montrose, who, as yet unknown to him, had now landed in the
north of Scotland with a handful of followers. A few, and those
the noblest, of his supporters urged Charles to starve sooner than
accept such terms. But the majority of his counsellors, anxious
for bread and contemptuous of abstract ideals, advised surrender.

Charles expressed willingness to accept Presbyterianism for
himself and Scotland, but held to the view that he could not
legally do so for either of his other kingdoms without their free
consent. In a letter to his host, the Prince of Orange, who had
reminded him that his grandfather, Henry of Navarre, had
declared a kingdom well worth a Mass, he explained his diffi-
culties and proposed a solution which foreshadowed that
actually achieved ten years later by the famous Declaration from
Breda.

VII. TO THE PRINCE OF ORANGE

Undated: circa April 11/21, 1650.

I have considered the several papers and propositions,
delivered to me by you, and do assure you, I desire nothing more
than that I may entirely unite the hearts and affections of all my
good subjects of Scotland to me. . . . And to the obtaining of
such a union I will consent to all that in conscience and honour
I may, without imposing on my other kingdoms.

I have not the least thought of violating . . . the established
laws of Scotland . . . or of altering the government, ecclesiastical or
civil, as it is settled there by law, but shall maintain, confirm and
defend all those laws, and particularly those concerning the
National Covenant, the confession of faith and presbyterial
government of that church. Touching that part of the League
and Covenant which concerneth my other kingdoms of England
and Ireland, it is not in my power justly to take any resolution
therein without the advice of my respective parliaments of those
kingdoms, by whose advice and consent only laws are to be made
or altered. Neither can I consent to anything which shall oppose
or disturb the peace lately concluded in Ireland. But I am very
willing to refer the full consideration of the said League and
Covenant and of all other particulars you mention (as to
England) to a free Parliament to be convened there by my writ,
as soon as the condition of that kingdom will permit me so to do,

by whose advice I am resolved wholly to govern myself therein. In the meantime, as I am very ready to do all that is in my power to the safe and quiet protection of my people of Scotland under the benefit of the laws of that kingdom . . . and for the burying all bitterness and animosities, which the former distractions and divisions may have produced . . . I am very willing and desirous to consent to an act of oblivion and indemnity to all persons of what condition soever of that kingdom of Scotland (excepting only such as had private confederacy with the murderers of their late sovereign, and with them did design, contrive, and consent to the same). . . .

In the end it was on these terms that Charles went to Scotland, though not before the Commissioners had induced him to agree to disown Ormonde's treaty with the Irish Catholics should the Scottish Parliament require him to do so, one of the Commissioners privately assuring him that once in Scotland his personal influence would ensure the achievement of all his ends. It was by clutching at such straws that the young man fell. The clear-sighted Hyde, absent on a hopeless embassy to raise money in Spain, wrote when he heard the news: ' Is it a king's condition or even the condition of a gentleman he can get. . . ? If there be a judgement from heaven, I can only pray that it may fall as light as may be.'

Such a judgement had already fallen on poor Montrose, to whom Charles now wrote, publicly ordering him to lay down his arms and privately imploring his forgiveness and offering money for his necessities. But Montrose had already been captured and, before Charles could learn of his fate or have time to intervene, was executed by his ruthless enemy Argyll.

After a voyage of sermons and humiliations, Charles landed in Scotland on July 1st, 1650. He found the country threatened with English invasion and groaning under the tyranny of Argyll and the Presbyterian Kirk, whose universal inquisition touched even the generals of the Army. Charles, remembering the Civil Wars in England, wrote in terms strangely shrewd for one of his years, imploring Argyll to keep the ministers and politicians from dictating to the soldiers.

VIII. To the Marquis of Argyll

Falkland, July 19, 1650.

My Lord of Argyll,—I received yours of this month just now, and I thank you for the care you had of that I writ to you about, which I find by the Committee's letter, which I am very well satisfied with. I will be at Dunfermline a' Tuesday night and a' Wednesday at Stirling; therefore I desire you to make provision accordingly.

The enemy being advanced so far, there is one thing I shall desire you to do; it is, not to let the Committee send any positive orders to David Leslie, either to fight or not to fight, but to leave it to his judgement what to do, for certainly he can tell upon the place best what is to be done. I have seen the sad experience of sending a general positive orders when one is not upon the place. I am, your most affectionate friend. CHARLES R.

Charles's advice in this as in everything else was completely ignored. He found himself subjected to the most humiliating supervision, lectured perpetually upon his sins and those of his family, and forced to dismiss his most trusted servants, who were stigmatized as ungodly. In a secret midnight interview he revealed his true situation to a messenger from Ormonde, whose affairs were going as badly as his own, and again a few weeks later in a letter to his father's old Secretary of State, Sir Edward Nicholas.

IX. To the Marquis of Ormonde in Ireland

St. Johnstone's, August 19, 1650.

My Lord of Ormonde, I have sent this bearer Dr. King expressly to acquaint you with my condition here. I desire you to believe him in what he shall say to you from me. I have commanded Robin Long to send you a particular account of what I have done concerning Ireland. I have received your letter by Daniel O'Neill, and he hath given me a full account of that kingdom and your condition there; which I find to be so ill, that I give you free leave to come from thence when you shall think it fit. For the way of it, I desire you to use the safest. I believe this bearer will tell you, that this country will not bid you welcome; for indeed they are not so kind to you as I could wish. Therefore I think France or Holland will be the fittest place for the present: but I shall leave that to your choice. I will only add this, that you have a care of yourself; which will be the greatest service you can do to your most affectionate friend.

x. To Sir Edward Nicholas

St. Johnstone's, September 3, 1650.

I have given this bearer his dispatch, and have signed all the commissions, with fifty-three blanks, which I desire you to fill up as you shall have occasion. . . . I have sent you here enclosed a letter of credence to the Prince of Orange, that if you should have occasion of his assistance you may use it. But pray have a care that you do not press him about money, for I have had so much from him already that it were a shame to seek more of him.

This bearer will acquaint you with my condition much better than I can do in a letter. I shall only say this to you, that you cannot imagine the villainy of the [illegible] and their party. Indeed it has done me a great deal of good, for nothing could have confirmed me more to the Church of England than being here seeing their hypocrisy. . . .

I had almost forgot a business of great importance. It is to speak to the Prince of Orange to send hither a smack or a herring buss with five or six men to lie here pretending it is to carry over a messenger when there is occasion: I being at the charge of keeping them when they are here. I would have the vessel come to Montrose. I would have you and Mr. Attorney to stay in Holland as being the place that is nearest to this kingdom and where I shall have occasion of your services. I have no more to say to you at the present but to assure you that I am and ever will be, Your most affectionate friend. CHARLES R.

The day that this last letter was written was the day of Cromwell's crowning mercy, the Scottish Army being delivered

*into his hands by the folly of the Presbyterian ministers, who
ordered their commander to abandon an impregnable position
and attack the English, who must otherwise have died from
starvation. The battle, by discrediting the rule of Argyll and
the Kirk, was almost as great a mercy for Charles as for Cromwell. The suppressed Scottish Cavaliers began to raise their
heads again and Charles entered into secret communication with
their leader, the Earl of Atholl, whom early in October Charles,
attempting to escape from Argyll's surveillance, tried to join.
The attempt, however, was a failure, Charles being ignominiously
captured before he could reach the Earl.*

XI. TO THE EARL OF ATHOLL

Cortachie, October 4, 1650.

My Lord, these are to certify you that I am now in Angus
this Friday at night and it is my express will and desire that your
lordship, with all your friends and followers, foot and horses,
repair to me with all imaginable diligence and come to the head
of Cloway. They shall receive further orders. Your very
loving friend. CHARLES R.

XII. TO THE EARL OF ATHOLL

Perth, October 6, 1650.

My Lord Atholl, I command you that, upon sight hereof,
you lay down arms, and let every man return to his own home,
and likewise all that are with you do the like. I am, Your affectionate friend. CHARLES R.

XIII. TO THE EARL OF AIRTH

Perth, November 10, 1650.

MY LORD,

I could not let this bearer, your son, return to you without
taking this occasion to let you know how sensible I am of your
affection to my service; and to assure you that there is nobody
more sensible of you and your family's sufferings (for my father
of ever blessed memory and myself) than I am. I make no
doubt but to be one day in a condition to make you better returns

than in paper, which [is] all for the present I can do.   I desire you to continue your affection to me, and to be ready upon all occasions, and you may be confident that I shall ever be Your loving friend.   CHARLES R.

But with the English in the capital, a strong tide of national feeling was running in favour of the King, who was at last within measurable distance of his dream of a united Scotland. At the end of the year he was crowned at Scone and allowed to take command of the Army.   Yet with half the country in the hands of the English, and famine and disease sweeping the remainder, the King's affairs were far from hopeful.

In November the news from Ireland had been so bad that Charles, fearful of losing another of his followers as he had lost Montrose, advised Ormonde to seek his own safety and take refuge in France.

XIV. TO THE MARQUIS OF ORMONDE

St. Johnstone's, November 11, 1650.

MY LORD OF ORMONDE,

The distracted and miserable condition of this kingdom and my affairs here, is so much fitter for a discourse than a letter, that I cannot be sorry I have not the means to give you a particular account of it but by this bearer, Mr. Digby, who is so well known to you, that I shall not labour much in his recommendation. . . .

The hazards and dangers (besides the trouble) I hear you do expose yourself unto upon all occasions, makes me take this to entreat and command you to have a care of your person; in the preservation of which I would have you believe I am so much concerned, both in my interest and affection, that I would not lose you for all I can get there.   If the affairs there be in such a condition, as it will be necessary for you to quit the country, and retire into France, then I do very earnestly desire and entreat you to repair to my brother the Duke of York,[1] to advise and assist him with your counsels, upon which I have such a

---

[1] Charles's second brother, James, at this time seventeen, was living in Paris with his mother.

confidence and reliance, that I have written and sent instructions to him to be advised by you upon all occasions. And I doubt not of his cheerful and ready compliance, and that you will find all good satisfaction from him.

If the Commissioners who treated to bring me hither had made good their undertakings, I had been in a condition to have helped my Lady, and had done it before now : but as they have not answered my expectation in all things, so they have much disappointed me in point of money. And the ill success of my affairs hath either so discredited me, or discouraged my friends elsewhere (who upon my coming hither promised to supply me) that I am not yet in a capacity of doing anything that way; which is indeed as much a grief to me as anything else I suffer. But if it please God to amend my condition, and give me the means, I will not fail to do it : nor do I desire anything with more passion, than that it may be in my power to acquit my obligations to you, and approve myself, Your most affectionate and constant friend. CHARLES R.

A further blow to Charles's cause was the death of his brother-in-law, the Prince of Orange, who had helped him with money and done much to counteract the leanings of the Dutch republicans towards their English brethren. Charles, full of sympathy for his widowed sister, wrote anxiously to Lady Stanhope, her lady-in-waiting.

xv. To Lady Stanhope

December 19, 1650.

I have been so long and am too well acquainted with you to believe you need be entreated to have a care of my sister, especially at this time when she hath so much need. Yet because there are not many things in my power by which I may make the affection and kindness I have for her appear, and this may be one, I cannot choose but tell you I shall put the services you do her upon my account. . . . How my sister does for her health, and with what discretion she bears her misfortune; whether my nephew[1] be lusty and strong, whom he is like, and a hundred

---

[1] Afterwards William III of England.

such questions I desire the answer of under your hand, because a less evidence will not satisfy the curiosity I have for those I am so much concerned in. What care the States take for the young General, and how kind and careful the Princess of Orange is of him, and what provision is made for my sister's present support I hope I shall hear from your husband. . . .

During the summer campaign of 1651, Charles was pitted against the greatest soldier of his time. Though out-numbered and out-manœuvred, he found himself in July between Cromwell and England, and resolved on a bold bid. With the loyal Duke of Hamilton and 16,000 of his staunchest troops, he marched at hot speed into England, trusting to the growing dislike of the republican government to cause a rising. A postscript, written in his own hand and added to a letter written on the frontier by the Duke of Hamilton to Progers, summoning him to join the gallant venture, shows Charles on the march. The letter is dated August 4, 1651.

XVI

. . . The Army being on their march I could not write to you myself. Pray make all the haste you can hither. . . .

C.R.

A few weeks later, on September 3rd, unsupported by the English, who were afraid to rise, Charles and his Scots were hemmed in and routed by Cromwell at Worcester. For six weeks the King was a fugitive in his native land, with a price on his head. Thanks to his own easy courage and the loyalty of the devoted men and women who, at the risk of their lives, smuggled him from one hiding place to another, he reached the coast and took boat to France, where he rejoined his mother's Court at Paris in October 1651.

CHAPTER III

IN EXILE

For the next two and a half years Charles was a refugee at the French Court, living on sufferance and scarcely knowing where to turn for bread for himself and his followers. His letters, of which there are many, dwell with some monotony on the unwelcome themes of begging from those weary of his importunity and appeasing the starving requests of those who had lost all through their loyalty. The following is to Sir Marmaduke Langdale, one of his father's generals, who, like others, had preferred proscription and exile to making terms with the usurping enemy in England.

I. To Sir Marmaduke Langdale

Paris, May 15/25, 1652.

I am as sensible of the ill condition I hear you are in, as I am fully satisfied with your merit in the King my father's and my service, nor does the present necessity I live under bring me any trouble so great as I find in the impossibility of relieving such persons as you are. But you may rest assured that when and in what proportion soever I shall be redeemed from this necessity, I shall proportionately help you, and always give you the most effectual testimonies I am able, that I am, your very loving friend.

Where the claims on Charles's generosity were personal, he felt bitterly the humiliation of his powerlessness to give generously. To Jane Lane, the Shropshire girl who had helped him to escape from England, and for whom he found a refuge as an attendant on his sister, Mary of Orange, he wrote on several occasions to apologize because he could not do more.

II. To Jane Lane

Paris, November 13/23, 1652.

I have hitherto deferred writing to you in hope to be able to send you somewhat else besides a letter; and I believe it troubles me more that I cannot yet do it, than it does you, though I do not take you to be in a good condition long to expect it. The truth is my necessities are greater than can be imagined. But I am promised they shall be shortly supplied. If they are, you shall be sure to receive a share, for it is impossible I can ever forget the great debt I owe you, which I hope I shall live to pay, in a degree that is worthy of me. In the meantime I am sure all who love me will be very kind to you, else I shall never think them so to, Your most affectionate friend.   CHARLES R.

From time to time the events of the outer world gave Charles a fleeting hope of bettering his fortunes. During the naval war between England and Holland, he offered his services to the Dutch Ambassador in Paris.

III. TO THE DUTCH AMBASSADOR IN PARIS, BOREEL

Paris, Jan. 27/Feb. 6, 1652/3.

Though I hope all the particulars which I have this day received from Rouen of the encounter between the Dutch fleet and my English rebels are not true, yet I fear the rebels have gained some notable advantage, and do for the present remain masters of the Channel; for which I am very heartily sorry. I am yet so confident that God will put it in my power to turn this success of theirs, and to prevent any greater, that if the States will assign me some ships, no more than they think may fitly serve under my standard, I will engage my own person with them in the company of their fleet, and either by God's blessing prevail with them, or perish in the attempt. I chose rather to impart this my wish to you, together with condoling for this misfortune, than to make a formal overture any other way, and if I may receive any intimation that it is acceptable, I will, with as little formality and without any conditions, make all imaginable haste thither and trust providence for the success.

The offer was not accepted, and Charles had to console himself with other hopes. The chief of these was a rising in the Highlands, of which grand prospects were constantly held out by over sanguine but not very active Scottish Royalists. Little or nothing, however, happened and Hyde at Charles's side wrote to

General Middleton, whom he was preparing to dispatch for Scotland, of the small results that attended so much talk.

IV. To General Middleton

March 11/21, 1652/3.

. . . Who would have thought, after so much discourse of an army in the Highlands that had taken Inverness and would quickly drive all the English out of the kingdom, that there should indeed be no men there but such who lodge in their own beds, and only project what they will do when they are able. . . .

Meanwhile the Highlanders were quarrelling among themselves.

V. To the Earl of Balcarres

Sept. 22/Oct. 2, 1653.

I have received yours of the 9th of August, and to my exceeding discomfort find the falling out, which I most feared, difference and unkindness amongst those whom I love and trust most. But since I am sure your jealousies of one another cannot make either of you less kind and just to me, I will hope that for my sake you will lay aside all misunderstandings, and join heartily together, that all other men, by your example, may be united in my service. . . . I do assure you I am so far from changing the good opinion you had reason to believe I had of you, when we parted, that my confidence in your affection is rather increased than diminished, nor hath ever any man endeavoured to do you any ill office with me; nor hath any man cause to think, that it is in his power to do it. And I must do Glencairn[1] the justice to tell you, that all his letters to me have been too full of commending you, that he always desired to proceed upon your counsel and advice; and I am sure Middleton looks upon you as one of his best friends, and by whom he desires principally to be guided. . . .

I will follow your advice in hastening Middleton as soon

---

[1] William, Earl of Glencairn, who was in command of the Highland Royalists and whom Balcarres, a Presbyterian supporter of the King, detested.

as is possible, who I know longs to be with you. In the meantime, I cannot desire anything more earnestly of you, than that you will lay aside the unhappy misunderstandings, that is of late grown, and assist Glencairn all you may, and remove all jealousies from others; and that the great work, which so much concerns us all, may be perfected without admitting any arguments or disputes. . . .

The possibility of a treaty between France and republican England made Charles increasingly anxious to remove from Paris, a wish shared by his chief advisers who deplored the effect that enforced inactivity was having upon his character. The difficulty was to find a country willing to receive him and the wherewithal to depart. At the end of 1653, when the decision had been made to move as soon as possible, the return of Prince Rupert from a Royalist buccaneering expedition offered some slight hopes of prize money, as well as the chance of raising the wind by the sale of his ship and cannon.

vi. To Prince Rupert

Paris, December 8/18, 1653.

If I had not thought you would have been here before this time, I would have written oftener and fuller to you. The truth is I do only defer the setting down the time of my going from hence and the resolving which way to go, till I speak with you.

You know what I am promised to receive from the French Court for my journey. In the meantime I am sure I am not only without money, but have been compelled to borrow all that I have spent near these three months so that you will easily judge how soon three thousand and six hundred pistols will be gone. And yet I must expect no more from hence, but depend upon what you shall bring me, for my ship, guns, and my share of the prize. I long to have you here. . . .

By the summer of 1654 Charles was able to move his little Court to Germany. For financial reasons it was decided that his brothers—the Duke of York, who was making a career for

himself in the French Army, and the little Duke of Gloucester—
should remain behind.   There was danger in this, for the Queen
Mother made no secret of her desire to proselytize Harry of
Gloucester.   Before leaving, Charles left careful instructions with
the Duke of York both on this point and others where his
mother's ceaseless interference in politics was likely to have
dangerous repercussions.

VII.PRIVATE INSTRUCTIONS TO THE DUKE OF YORK

July 3/13, 1654.

You know the model of my affairs in England, and therefore will not employ any persons to treat there.   When I go
myself for Scotland, I will transmit to you the business of
England, with all the particulars; in the meantime it must be
managed by myself, and in the way I have put it.

You must not employ or trust Bamfield[1] in anything, since
I am resolved to have nothing to do with him, and to forbid
all my friends to give credit to him in anything that concerns
me.

As soon as I think of making any general officers of an
army I will advertise you of it, and I pray do not make any
promises of such offices to any person whatsoever, without first
acquainting me with your thoughts.

Let nobody persuade you to engage your own person in any
attempt or enterprise without first imparting the whole design
to me, which will be easily done, whilst there is no sea between
us; and when that comes to be the case, assure yourself I will
desire nothing more, than either to have you with me, or in
action in some other place.   But, to deal freely with you, till I
am myself in action in some part of my Dominions, which I
will endeavour as soon as possible, I should be very sorry to see
you engaged before me. . . .

I have told you what the Queen hath promised me concerning my brother Harry in point of religion, and I have given
him charge to inform you if any attempt shall be made upon
him to the contrary; in which case you will take the best care

---

[1] A shifty adventurer, who had shown himself thoroughly unreliable
in negotiations with the Scottish Royalists, but had managed to ingratiate
himself with the Queen Mother.

you can to prevent his being wrought upon, since you cannot but know how much you and I are concerned in it.

You must be very kind to Harry Bennet,[1] and communicate freely with him; for as you are sure he is full of duty and integrity to you, so I must tell you, that I shall trust him more than any other about you. . . .

In July, 1654, Charles joined his sister, Mary of Orange, at Aix-la-Chapelle, where she was on holiday. In her beloved company he visited Cologne, where the burghers offered a sanctuary to him and his Court.

VIII. To Elizabeth, Queen of Bohemia[2]

Cologne, July 27/Aug. 6, 1654.

Madam,

I am just now beginning this letter in my sister's chamber, where there is such a noise that I never hope to end it, and much less write sense. For what concerns my sister's journey and the accidents that happened on the way, I leave to her to give Your Majesty an account of. I shall only tell Your Majesty that we are now thinking how to pass our time; and in the first place of dancing, in which we find two difficulties, the one for want of the fiddlers, the other for somebody both to teach and assist at the dancing the new dances. And I have got my sister to send for Silvius[3] as one that is able to perform both.

For the fideldedies my Lord Taafe[4] does promise to be their convoy, and in the meantime we must content ourselves with those that makes no difference between a hymn and a coranto. . . .

In October Mary returned to Holland. A month later Charles received letters from Paris reporting that his mother was using all her influence to have the fourteen-year-old Duke of Gloucester converted, and was planning his forcible removal to a Jesuit College. He at once acted with a decision and strength

[1] A confidential friend of Charles's whom he left behind as his brother's secretary: afterwards Earl of Arlington.
[2] Daughter of James I and aunt to Charles.
[3] Gabriel Silvius.
[4] Theobald, Viscount Taafe, a devoted Irish adherent.

of character which few had suspected in him, writing peremp-
torily to his mother, to Jermyn, her fat major-domo, with whom
he was particularly angry, to the Duke of York and to Gloucester
himself.

IX. TO THE QUEEN MOTHER

Cologne, Oct. 31/Nov. 10, 1654.

At the same time that I received Your Majesty's letter of the
23rd October, I received one from my brother Harry and another
from Mr. Lovell,[1] in which they give me an account of what Your
Majesty and Mr. Montagu[2] said to them concerning the change
of my brother's religion. And likewise I have other informations that there are lodgings providing for him in the Jesuits
College, which is quite contrary to the promise Your Majesty
made me before I came from Paris, which was that Mr. Lovell
should continue in his place about my brother, and that he should
have the free exercise of his religion in his chamber which I am
sure he can never have in the Jesuits College.

I must confess that this news does trouble me so much that
I cannot say all that I could at another time, but upon the whole
matter I must conclude that if Your Majesty does continue to
proceed in the change of my brother's religion, I cannot expect
Your Majesty does either believe or wish my return into
England. For you will force me to do that which must disoblige all Catholics, and on the other side all that I can say or
do will never make my Protestant subjects believe but it is done
with my consent, and that all that I say or do, is only a grimace.
Therefore if Your Majesty has the least kindness for me I beg
of you not to press him further in it. And remember the last
words of my dead father (whose memory I doubt not will work
upon you) which were to charge him upon his blessing never to
change his religion, whatsoever mischief shall fall either upon
me or my affairs, hereafter.

I beseech you consider this for your own sake and mine, for
(Christ's sake).

[1] Gloucester's tutor to whom Charles also wrote.
[2] Walter Montagu, Abbot of St. Martin's, Pontoise, and the Queen's
religious adviser.

31

x. To Lord Jermyn

Cologne, Oct. 31/*Nov.* 10, 1654.

I have received yours of the 24th and another of the 29th October both together, and I thank you for the news you send me. But I do very much wonder, that every letter that comes from Paris should mention the endeavours that is used to pervert my brother Harry in his religion, and you that have most reason of all others to do it makes not the least mention of it. I will not say to you much upon that subject in this letter because I have instructed my Lord of Ormonde (who will give you this letter) so fully in the point that I shall refer all to him. Only I must tell you this myself, that if you do not use all the means possible you can to prevent my brother from being seduced, and not only say, but give such testimonies of it that may satisfy me and all the world you do your best, you must never think to see me again, and that this shall be the last time you shall ever hear from me, being so full of passion that I cannot express myself.

Consider well of this, and if I have not my desire granted it will be such a breach between the Queen and me as can never be made up again.

xi. To the Duke of York at Paris

Cologne, Oct. 31/*Nov.* 10, 1654.

The news I have received from Paris of the endeavours that are used to change my brother Harry's religion does trouble me so much that if I have any things to answer to any of your letters, you must excuse me if I omit it this post. All that I can say at this time is I do conjure you as you love the memory of your father, and if you have any care of yourself, or kindness to me, to hinder all that lies in your power any such practices, without any consideration of any person whatsoever.

I have written very home both to the Queen and my brother about it, and I expect that you should second what I have said to them both, with all the arguments you can, for neither you nor I were ever so much concerned in all respects as we are in this.

XII. To the Duke of Gloucester

Cologne, Oct. 31/Nov. 10, 1654.

I have received yours without a date in which you mention that Mr. Montagu has endeavoured to pervert you in your religion. I do not doubt but you remember very well the commands I left with you concerning that point, and so am confident you will observe them. Yet the letters that come from Paris say that it is the Queen's purpose to do all she can to change your religion, which if you hearken to her or anybody else in that matter you must never think to see England or me again. And whatsoever mischief shall fall to me or my affairs from this time I must lay all upon you as being the sole cause of it. Therefore consider what it is not only to be the cause of the ruin of a brother that loves you so well, but also of your King and country, and do not let them persuade you either by force or fair promises. For the first they neither have nor will use, and for the second as soon as they have you, they have their end, and will care no more for you.

I hear also that there is a purpose to put you in the Jesuits College, which I command you upon the same grounds never to consent unto. And whensoever anybody shall go to dispute with you in religion do not answer them at all, for though you have the reason on your side, yet they, being prepared, will have the advantage of anybody that is not upon the same security that they are.

I have commanded this bearer, my Lord of Ormonde, to speak more at large to you upon this subject. Therefore give him credit in all that he shall say to you as if it were from myself. And if you do not consider what I say to you, remember the last words of your dead father, which were to be constant to your religion, and never to be shaken in it. . . .

The King's entreaties and commands did their work, and Gloucester, under the charge of the faithful Ormonde, left Paris to join the English Court.

Life at Cologne settled down to the usual routine of debts, faint hopes, rumours and enforced idleness. In a letter to his friend Bennet, at Paris, Charles described the way in which he and his fellow exiles beguiled the tedium of their days.

XIII.To Henry Bennet

Cologne, December 12/22, 1654.

Harry, you may easily believe that my approbation for your coming hither would not be very hard to get, and if you had no other business here than to give me an account how Arras was relieved, or who danced best in the mask at Paris, you should be as welcome as I can make you. I will not say any more to you now, because I hope it will not be many days before you will see how we pass our time at Cologne, which though it be not so well as I could wish, yet I think it is as well as some of you do at Paris; at least some that are here would not pass their time so well there as they do here, and it may be you will be one of that number.

One of the greatest alterations you will find here is, that my Lord Taafe is become one of the best dancers in the country, and is the chief man at all the balls. And I believe he is as good at it, as one of your friends at Paris is at making French verses. I have nothing to add to this, but to tell you you will find me still a true Bablon. CHARLES R.

All the while there was a ceaseless correspondence to be carried out with loyal supporters in England and Scotland, where at any moment some new disturbance might break out. Though he detested writing letters, Charles's epistolary style and cheerful good nature in this business of keeping up the spirits of remote supporters made him a great deal more than a mere signing machine to his indefatigable chief of staff, Hyde.

XIV.To Colonel Thomas Dalyell of Binns[1]

Cologne, December 20/30, 1654.

Tom Dalyell, though I need say nothing to you by this honest bearer, Captain Mewes, who can well tell you all that I

---

[1] A Scottish Cavalier, who had fought at Charles's side at Worcester, and had just been driven, with Middleton, from the Highlands. Many years later, as Charles's Commander-in-Chief in Scotland, he became the founder of the Scots Greys.

would have said, yet I am willing to give it you under my own hand that I am very much pleased to hear how constant you are in your affection to me, and in your endeavours to advance my service. We have all a hard work to do, yet I doubt not God will carry us through it and you can never doubt that I will forget the good part you have acted, which trust me shall be well rewarded whenever it shall be in the power of Your affectionate friend. CHARLES R.

xv. To the Earl of Lorne

Cologne, December 20/30, 1654.

I am very glad to hear from Middleton what affection and zeal you show to my service, how constantly you adhere to him in all his distresses, and what good service you have performed upon the rebels. I assure you you shall find me very just and kind to you in rewarding what you have done and suffered for me; and I hope you will have more credit and power with those of your kindred and dependants upon your family to engage them with you for me, than anybody else can have to seduce them against me. And I shall look upon all those who shall refuse to follow you as unworthy of any protection hereafter from me, which you will let them know. This honest bearer M. will inform you of my condition and purposes, to whom you will give credit, and he will tell you that I am very much Your very affectionate friend. CHARLES R.

In the early part of 1655, elaborate plans were made for a Royalist rising. The difficulty, as with all these attempts, was to synchronize the activities of the Cavaliers, for the eager were too eager, and the cautious too precautionary. To Ormonde, who strained at the leash to be gone, ' eager to try for a hanging,' Charles had to write warningly.

xvi. To the Marquis of Ormonde

Cologne, January 19/29, 1654/5.

You do not more wish to be in England than I do that you should be there, except you wish unreasonably. But I must tell you I will not venture you thither except something be first done, and in such case I will be ready to venture myself, so that you and I shall meet and speak together though it may be we shall part quickly. The truth is I cannot instruct you in the part you are to act nor well digest it with myself without conference together, and you will then see, it will be such a one as is worthy of the kindness I have for you.

I am not at all frighted with the news from England, from expecting the best I have expected, and am prepared to run away from hence upon an hour's warning, of which you shall have seasonable advertisement and know where to find me. The Chancellor[1] will say somewhat to you concerning the arms, in which Sir G. Hamilton is sufficiently instructed. . . .

The rising was timed to break out in March. In order to be near England Charles, under the pseudonym of Mr. Jackson, slipped away from Cologne with only Ormonde and a single groom, and rode across north Germany to the Friesian coast. On the way he wrote to Hyde, using the jargon of commercial correspondence and false names for greater secrecy.

XVII. TO SIR EDWARD HYDE

Dusseldorf, March 3/13, 1654/5.

SIR,

I believe you may think me lazy for not writing to you since my coming hither, but when you shall consider that I have neither stone nor closet, but must call for pen and ink every time I write, it will excuse me in some sort knowing my natural inclination to that exercise. And besides Mr. Pickering and Mr. Page has acquainted you with all we know here.

Yesterday in the afternoon I received a letter from Mr. Gorge at Harlem with one enclosed from Mr. Simonds . . . who is safely landed in Normandy, though he has run many dangers both by sea and land. For after having been like to be cast away was examined twice at his landing, but at last let go on his way to Cologne. He met with a factor just as he went ashore, that used to drive on our trade amongst the merchants of Normandy,

---

[1] Hyde.

who was just then a coming to me, but he went back again with Mr. Simonds, he resolving to send him or somebody else, when he shall be better informed of the state of our goods, which by the way of his writing is not so very ill as I was afraid it was. And last night as I was going to bed, I received another letter from Mr. Gorge . . . that assures me Mr. Brian has made his escape out of Dover Castle . . . which occasions their great severity to all passengers, which way soever they come, and is likewise the hindrance of a messenger that was coming hither, but has writ to Mr. Gorge that now my law suit in England is in far better condition than I had just reason to expect. . . . I must confess that the escape of that lucky fellow Brian pleases me very well, and think it a very good sign to see our factors have so good fortune as to escape the hands of my creditors, I am

Your servant,

W. JACKSON.

The rising was a complete failure. The disconsolate exiles therefore fell to the unprofitable business of reproaching one another for their lack of success, and Charles had need of all his optimism and tact to smooth over their differences and reanimate their spirits.

In a letter written that June to an unnamed supporter he gave his own view of the failure and its consequences.

XVIII. To 'M.N.'

Cologne, June 3/13, 1655.

. . . I pray do not give credit to those people, who take upon them to censure whatsoever I do, and have no way to appear wise but to find fault with whatsoever is done; the reason and ground whereof they do not in any degree understand, and hope to get information by finding fault. Trust me, however I have for the present been disappointed in my hopes in England, it hath not proceeded from any of the reasons you guess; nor could I have hastened anything there more than I did. They, who will not believe anything to be reasonably designed, except it be successfully executed, had need of a less difficult game to play than mine is. And I hope my friends will think that I am now too old, and have had too much experience of things and of persons, to be grossly imposed upon; and therefore they, who would seem to pity me for being often deceived, do upon the matter declare what opinion they have of my understanding and judgement. And I pray discountenance those kind of people, what affections soever they pretend, as men, who do me more hurt than my avowed enemies can do.

I hope we shall shortly see a turn, and that your dons will find they have mistaken their way; and (though it be deferred longer than I expected) that I shall live to bid you welcome to Whitehall.

In default of anything better, Charles occupied the rest of that year at Cologne in enjoying such distractions as the place afforded. A visit from his sister Mary lightened the late summer months, and he wrote charmingly to her attendant and his old ally, Jane Lane, to commiserate on the ill fortune that prevented her from accompanying her.

XIX. To Jane Lane

Cologne, June 20/30, 1655.

I did not think I should ever have begun a letter to you in chiding, but you give so just cause by telling me you fear you are wearing out of my memory, that I cannot choose but tell you I take it very unkindly, that after the obligations I have to you, 'tis possible for you to suspect I can ever be so wanting to myself as not to remember them on all occasions to your advantage. Which I assure you I shall, and hope before it be long I shall have it in power to give you those testimonies of my kindness to you which I desire.

I am very sorry to hear that your father and brother are in prison, but I hope it is upon no other score than the general clapping up of all persons who wish me well. And I am the more sorry for it, since it hath hindered you from coming along with my sister, that I might have assured you myself how truly I am, Your most affectionate friend. CHARLES R.

Of his hopes and pleasures that year, as well as of the changes in Europe that were drawing France and republican England

38

into alliance, and England and Spain towards war, Charles
wrote frequently to Bennet at Paris.

xx. To Henry Bennet

Cologne, June 25/July 5, 1655.

. . . I do not find by anything that Mr. Montagu has brought
from Court, that you are at all nearer knowing what the
Cardinal[1] will do for my brother.[2] Here you were two months
ago, and though my Lord Rochester[3] has not brought over with
him any particular design, or that I can say positively I shall be
able to employ my brother as soon as he comes, yet upon the
discourse I have had with him, and as things now stand, it will
be most necessary for my brother to come hither, still supposing
that he cannot stay in France. For I am confident we shall
have something to do, which I think is so little believed where
you are, that it were easier to persuade Sir John F—— he is no
good poet in French, than to make them think the other. All
that I can say to you at this distance, to make you believe, at
least to suspend your judgement, that I am not altogether
sanguine in this particular is, that when you and I have talked
together one half-hour, I am confident you will find that I am
not without some ground for being of this opinion.

My clothes are at last come, and I like them very well, all
but the sword, which is the worst that ever I saw. I suspect
very much that it was you made the choice. Therefore you
have no other way to recover your judgement in that particular,
but to make choice of a better, and if you go to the shop where
I bought mine, when I came out of Paris, you can hardly be
mistaken. My brother can tell you where it is. . . .

xxi. To Henry Bennet

Cologne, July 3/13, 1655.

I have little to say to you this week, only tell you that the
ambassador is at last arrived, and though he has not yet made

---

[1] Mazarin.
[2] The Duke of York.
[3] Henry Wilmot, first Earl of Rochester, had just returned from
England, where he had been conducting negotiations with the English
Royalists. He was the father of the Restoration wit and poet.

the proposition to me that is to do the business, he has enlarged himself so in his preamble, that without running the danger of being burnt for a witch, one may guess at it to that degree as to believe the contrivers mortal men.

I have written to my brother, that in case he goes to Landrecy, to have a care how he engages himself in the drawing of the Irish[1] from the service they are in, till he is assured whether his stay in France be certain or not. . . . You will . . . come in a very good time to Cologne, for my sister will be here the latter end of this month.   She tells me that the Queen has answered her letter, but I find it is but *cosi cosi* in point of kindness. . . .

XXII. To HENRY BENNET

Cologne, August 7/17, 1655.

. . . You must not expect to hear from me very often as long as my sister is here, for you may easily guess that I will be in her company as much as I can while she stays here.   And indeed Cologne is not a little altered, for from having very little company, and some of those worse than none, we have now as good as can be, and pass our time as well as people can do that have no more money, for we dance and play as if we had taken the Plate-Fleet, though I am confident our losses are not so great as Cromwell's is, who for certain has received a very considerable one at Hispaniola. . . .[2]

XXIII. To HENRY BENNET

Cologne, September, 1655.

I received three of yours the last week together, and one now of the 6th of this month.   I am very glad that my brother

---

[1] The Irish regiments serving in the French Army remained loyal to their lawful King, in whose right it lay, if he chose, to withdraw them from the service of their French paymasters.   With the growing likelihood of an Anglo-French alliance, Charles was already contemplating offering them to Spain, France's traditional enemy.

[2] The English Government, not without thoughts of the profitable joys of waylaying the Panama plate-fleet, had recently reverted to the Elizabethan tradition of a blue water war against Spain, and had sent an expedition under Penn and Venables to seize Hispaniola.   The attack

has given the Guidon's place to Schomberg's[1] son, but I cannot choose but think of the Irish footman that would needs leave his master to seek a better. His master asked him, *but what if you cannot find a better?* to which he answered very discreetly, *Why, Faith, then I will come to thee again.* I do not apply this now, only I cannot keep myself from believing but that Sir J. was offered very little or nothing at all, or else Schomberg would have gone without it. I hope you do not take yourself for one of the dispossessed, for I never pretended more than to be your croupier; indeed for Schomberg there is some reason, and if you, as secretary, did upon a good occasion give him a favourable dash with a pen, it could not at all be unjust.

You have heard before this time what changes there have been here of late: I believe O'Neill[2] has acquainted you with them, and therefore I will not say anything thereof. My sister and I go on Monday next to the Fair at Frankfort incognito; at our return you shall hear what has been done in the action. The doctor[3] is one, and, for my part, I think that O'Neill and he will lie together all the way, for they are buckle and thong.

It shall be hard, but I will find some business for you to come where we are this winter, which I hope will not be in this place.

XXIV. To Henry Bennet

Cologne, October 8/18, 1655.

We returned to this place on Tuesday last, and all our company very pleased with our voyage, for indeed it was as pleasant a journey as ever I saw, and some of us wished Whereas's company very often. You will hear by others how

was repulsed with loss, whereupon the raiders, with true English doggedness and acquisitiveness, seized Jamaica.

[1] Frederick Herman von Schomberg, many years later to be created an English duke, was serving as a lieutenant-general in the French Army, which the Duke of York was temporarily commanding in Turenne's absence. His eldest son, Otto, then sixteen, was killed in the following year.

[2] Colonel Daniel O'Neill, a devoted Irish adherent, much employed by Charles in confidential missions and after the Restoration made Postmaster General.

[3] Dr. Alexander Frazier, Charles's lifelong friend and physician.

my cousin the Elector[1] has behaved himself towards me; by which you will find he is not a whit changed. But at the same time I must tell you that I have been used with all the civility and kindness imaginable by the Elector of Mainz, who truly is one of the best and discreetest men that ever I saw. And I do assure you, our meeting has not been unuseful to me; the effects whereof I hope you will see when 'tis seasonable.

In the meantime I can say no more, but tell you, that when we meet, which I am resolved shall be this winter, for I will find out some embassy for you wheresoever I am, we will talk of that and many other things.

As for news from this place, I leave to others to write to you, only in general I must tell you, that we are in great hopes of the breach between Spain and England. . . .

PS.—I have given Buckley a note for you to keep the mill going; it should have been more if I had had it.

xxv. To Henry Bennet

Cologne, Oct. 30/Nov. 9, 1655.

The letters this week both from Flanders and England do confirm and augment my hopes of the breach with Spain, the particulars you will receive by others. And I think I may say it to a Bablonist, that I hope to see you in your master's company before many months past. And indeed if I had not that hope, I should be very melancholy to think of passing our winter here, my sister intending also to go for Holland some time next week.

If my brother can compass it, he will send you a letter this week of as many languages as Cologne can afford. We have here a very great intrigue between Sir A. H. and Mrs. P. which I believe will end in matrimony, and I conclude it the rather, because I have observed a cloud in his face any time these two months, which Giov. Battista della Porta in his *Physonomia* says, foretells misfortune.

I have many other letters to write, and therefore can say no more at this time. . . .

[1] Charles Louis of the Rhine, whose ingratitude towards his Stuart cousins was notorious.

XXVI. To HENRY BENNET

Cologne, Nov. 27/Dec. 7, 1655.

You will find by the letter I writ this week to my brother what I have directed him to do in case he cannot stay where he is. In the meantime I have again put him in mind to dispatch you hither as soon as he can, for I do not despair of having something for him to do, and I had rather send for him than have him sent out of France.

I can say no more to you now, having spent the time I should have been a writing in examining and discoursing one of the greatest villains[1] that ever was, which you will hear by others. Only I desire you to make haste hither, where you shall be very welcome.

In somewhat similar vein, Charles wrote to Ormonde. With him and his colleague, Hyde, the King was on terms of affectionate familiarity: they rebuked him frankly for his faults, and defended him with passionate loyalty against all others. He in his turn chaffed them to their faces and refused to listen to the constant insinuations brought against them by their rivals.

XXVII. To THE MARQUIS OF ORMONDE

Cologne, January 4/14, 1655/6.[2]

I have received yours of the 11th of this month, and am very well satisfied with the account you give me of the business you went about. The Chancellor does grumble and has sworn two or three half oaths at (as he calls it) your gadding. He will write to you more at large, though I think there is little to be said, but only to make what convenient haste you can hither, for there are some things necessary which cannot be done till you come. I have no more to say, only to wish that the wind may turn, for if it does not you will go near to lose the use of your face.

---

[1] Henry Manning, the spy, whose treachery in betraying their plans the exiles at Cologne had just discovered, and who was shortly afterwards shot by them.

[2] This letter is wrongly attributed in the Ormonde Papers (H.M.C. Rep. 14, appendix, part vii) to 1656/7.

*Early in 1656, open war breaking out between the Common-
wealth and Spain, Charles conceived high hopes of an official
recognition of his cause by the Spanish Government. At the
same time, with the closer relations between England and France,
the Duke of York's position in the latter country was becoming
increasingly embarrassing.*

XXVIII. TO THE DUKE OF YORK

Cologne, February 5/15, 1655/6.

. . . In my affairs I am able to send you some better hopes
than I could ever yet do. In Spain the war is declared against
Cromwell, and I look every day it should be so in Flanders.
The ministers there have it in their power to do it; and I am
assured they will presently show it. Besides this many discreet
persons, that are but lookers-on, believe as I do, that I shall find
my account very well in this change. I reserve the letting you
know what circumstances lead me into this belief till I send
H. Bennet to you, they being more proper for such a messenger
than a letter. In the meantime let me hear constantly from
you, for I confess the uncertainty of your condition gives me
much trouble. As any change happens in mine, I will write
it to you.

XXIX. TO THE DUKE OF YORK

Cologne, February 5/15, 1655/6.

Believing you might be obliged to show my other letter of
this same date, I write this to be seen by yourself only, to let
you know, that I have more particular assurances of the good
dispositions of Spain to my business than they are willing should
be yet public. Only to you I would not conceal it. The use I
would have you make of it is (without seeming to do so) to put
yourself in the best readiness you can to come away, when I
shall call for you, if at least you can be suffered to stay so long.
If you are sooner pressed, you know my mind.

One thing only you must suffer me to warn you of, to take
heed of obliging yourself to anything, or of entertaining any
propositions that you think may in any kind prejudice our public

business, which I believe will be presently put into a very fair way by a conjunction of our interests with those of Spain. Now considering what your dependence in France must be for the establishment of your present subsistence, they may possibly offer some conditions to you, and ask some promises from you, to which you may fairly answer, that not knowing the condition of my business, you cannot promise anything, for fear of doing it prejudice, or what else you think fit to this purpose.

If the things I look for fall out, our ill fortune will forsake us, and then we shall be happy together.

Before the end of February, Charles, impatient of waiting for an invitation from the slow-moving government of the Spanish Netherlands, precipitated matters by arriving in Brussels. The Spanish ministers there were much embarrassed by this breach of etiquette, but found it hard to resist Charles's insouciant wooing, and the latter was soon writing cheerfully to his ministers of his triumphs.

XXX. To the Marquis of Ormonde

Brussels, March 2/12, 1655/6.

I am just now come from·my first conference with F. and D.A.,[1] and though at first I found them dry, and expect that I should propose all, yet at last they began to be very free with me, and to that degree that, though it was not in matters of the last importance, I think (without being sanguine) I may hope that at our next meeting (which will be at five in the afternoon) we shall advance far in our business, and to all our satisfaction. . . .

XXXI. To the Marquis of Ormonde

March 9/19, 1655/6.

I think there can be no inconvenience in your speaking with the person you mention that is come from England, whoever it be. I return you the letter as you desire. . . .

[1] The principal Spanish ministers in the Netherlands, Alonzo Perez de Vivero, Conde de Fuensaldanha, and Don Alonzo de Cardenas.

45

Pray send us good news to-morrow, as the wine and mutton was to-day. God send you both better luck at picket than I have with H.B.[1] at cribbage. If you can find no other book in Italian worth sending, let me have by the first that comes *Pastor Fido.*

PS.—Pray get me a Spanish New Testament, for I hope we shall all have much need of that language.

XXXII. To Sir Edward Hyde

March 23/April 2, 1655/6.

My Lord Lieutenant has sent you word how long we have expected the articles the Spanish ministers promised to draw up; perhaps our friends at Brussels may receive them time enough to give you some account of them by the post that carries this letter. In the meantime, I send you the Father's letter I received to-day, which you see is full of good hopes. Whatever the success be of the whole matter, I mean to speak with the ministers in the end of it as I did in the beginning.

For the letters you send me, I shall not be able to judge of the fitness of them till I see the end of our Treaty; neither can I give you leave to go to Breda;[2] for, if it be resolved that I shall stay here, it will be necessary that you be by my brother when I give him orders concerning my family, and if I return to Cologne it will be as convenient for me to speak with you. This is a hard chapter, and I must ask my Lady's pardon for it.

Since I wrote this, I have yours of the 31st past, and with it the bill, which came in good time. I hope by my next I shall requite you with good news, and then I hope you will recover your accustomed greatness, which I find by yours to my Lord Lieutenant is much diminished since you say you can put on one of Harry's doublets, which I cannot understand to be anybody's but Harry Wilmot's.[3]

---

[1] Harry Bennet.
[2] Where Lady Hyde and her children were living.
[3] An allusion to Hyde's gout and wonted girth: Harry of Gloucester was a slim boy, while Harry Wilmot, Earl of Rochester, was very fat.

XXXIII. To Sir Edward Hyde

Brussels, March 31/*April* 10, 1656.

I have received yours of the 7th, and am sorry to find you are so unfit for a journey; for though I cannot tell you positively that I shall stay, yet I make little doubt of it. De Vic was last night with D.A. to desire him and the Count F. to appoint some time to-day, that I might speak with them, but as yet I have no answer: as soon as I have spoken with them, I believe I shall resolve you positively of what I am to do.

I will not fail to desire the ministers here to send directions to their ports in the Mediterranean, as you advise me, but I think the permission of my men-of-war[1] in these ports must first be granted before I move that, which is not yet done. Nic. Armourer[2] came this morning hither. I have spoken with him at large, and like what he brings. I will advise as many as can of those honest gentlemen that are at Paris to stay there till I may be able to send them more positive orders what they are to do, for I find that some of them will be forced to go over before that time, by reason of their passports that are limited to a time. Get yourself well as soon as you can, for I believe I shall send for you very quickly. . . .

XXXIV. To Sir Edward Hyde

Brussels, April 7/17, 1656.

I leave to my Lord Lieutenant to answer your long letter, and what my opinion is, and only tell you, that if you were here you would not be long of that melancholy opinion you are. And that which we have gotten already is more than I hoped for when I left Cologne; and which, if anybody could have assured us of two months since, would have made you caper in spite of the gout. . . . I am to meet the Archduke to-morrow morning: I believe our conference will be only general compliments and thanks on my part for his forwardness to oblige me in the Treaty.

[1] Prince Rupert's pirate ships which were sadly in need of a home.
[2] Nicholas Armourer, another faithful exile, later made one of the King's equerries.

47

I shall have a great care of my papers; I would you had given me the same caution for my keys, for I lost them on Good Friday seeing the procession; and therefore bid Tom Chiffinch[1] make up my cabinet in a canvas, and to bring it along with him.   It is suspected here by some that it is very possible that he may bring his wife along with him, and lest those conjectures should fall out, I thought not amiss to tell you that I think she will come time enough when the rest come; for I think the lighter my train be 'tis the better till I can bring all away.

Pray take order that all my books be put up carefully in such a trunk as you have for yours; and those that are in other people's hands let them be called for in, that they may be packed up all together, to be ready to be sent when I call for them.   It is Mr. O'Neill's opinion that the best way for my things that come from Cologne is, that when they come to port they go directly into Zealand, and so to Bruges by Sluys.

XXXV. To Sir Edward Hyde

Bruges, April 27/May 7, 1656.

I have yours of the first by the doctor who came hither on Friday last, and am glad to find you have so much hope that the money the Duke of Neuburg solicits will be so soon paid. I hope it may go a great way in discharging my family from Cologne.   I can give you little account as yet of what money I am to expect from France, not having received the account from my Lord Jermyn; by the next post I expect it. . . .

. . . I am sorry at this present to tell you, and I ask your wife's pardon for it, that it is most necessary for you to make as much haste as your gouty feet will give you leave to me, for many more reasons than are fit to be set down here. Your absence has been already inconvenient to me, and it does increase to be so every day more, and if it had not been for the consideration of my Lady, I had not permitted you to have played the truant so long.   I would you were besh-t for not letting me have a copy

---

[1] Charles's confidential gentleman and servant, brother to the better-known William Chiffinch, who succeeded him in 1666 as Royal Closet Keeper.

of your book of inscriptions, subscriptions and superscriptions,[1] for the want of it has made us speak ill of your person when our intentions were good enough towards it, and if by chance my Lord Lieutenant had not kept a letter that was intended for the Archduke, I could not now have written to Don Juan,[2] who looks to be treated in the same style. And therefore if you are to part in the afternoon, let your book set forth in the morning, that I be no more inconvenienced nor you no more cursed for want of it. I have bid my Lord Lieutenant answer all the other particulars of your letters. I have one thing to recommend principally to yourself, which is the getting, if it be possible, a set of coach horses, which at this present I had rather have than so much ready money.

Having extracted an informal recognition from the Spanish ministers, and a home for his Court at Bruges, Charles settled down to the old game of waiting. His letters to Bennet that summer reveal his interests—to obtain money and a promise of military help from his new allies, to withdraw the reluctant Duke of York and others of his followers from their embarrassing service in the army of Spain's enemy, France, and to extract as much personal entertainment as the unpromising resources of a little Flemish town could offer.

XXXVI. TO PRINCE RUPERT

Bruges, June 5/15, 1656.

Dear Cousin, Yours of the 17th of the last month came not to my hands till within these three days; so that I could not sooner return you an answer. I do thank you very kindly for your offer to assist me in such action as I may shortly be engaged in, towards the recovery of own. And to deal clearly with you, the condition of my affairs are such that I cannot make use of your offer in this occasion. Do not imagine my kindness

[1] A similar invaluable work for negotiating the shoals of seventeenth-century international court etiquette (and possibly the identical volume) was shown in the Charles II Exhibition in London in 1932.

[2] The new Spanish Viceroy of the Netherlands (an illegitimate son of King Philip IV) who was at this time taking over from his predecessor the Archduke Leopold.

will be the less to you, because I shall not have your company in this enterprise, but be confident if it shall please God to bless me and restore me to my own, you shall have a share in my good fortune, and find me always very kind to you. And in the meantime, I shall be very glad to hear that you have embraced any good command which this time is very like to offer you, and in which I shall wish you all imaginable good fortune, being very heartily, Dear Cousin, Your most affectionate Cousin.

CHARLES R.

XXXVII. To Henry Bennet

Bruges, June 27/July 7, 1656.

I am very glad to find by yours of the 10th of the last month that you have had so good a reception at the Palais Royal;[1] and though I see there was not so much danger of my brother's going into the field as I did imagine when you went from hence, yet I do not at all repent my sending of you at this time. For I do perceive there is not one there that has one leg a whit shorter than the other, and if it were not for the expectation of what we are like to have out of Spain, there might be nefritic motions made. I do now expect every day to hear out of Spain, and consequently to send you orders what you are to do.

I do not write this week either to my sister or brother,[2] for I believe when this comes to your hands, they will be both out of Paris; and besides I have nothing to say, therefore make my excuse to them. My Lord Lieutenant and O'Neill will let you know all the news here, so as I have nothing more to say, only that you bespeak six pair of shoes of my Paris shoemaker, such as he sent me last, and as many pair made by Dyke. But tell this latter that three pair must be black and the other coloured, and a little bigger than those he sent me last. Remember to bespeak my sword. . . .

---

[1] The Queen Mother's residence at Paris.
[2] Mary of Orange, then on a visit to her mother at Paris, and the Duke of York, who was still lingering in France.

XXXVIII. To Henry Bennet

Bruges, July 18/28, 1656.

. . . I received two days since a very civil letter from Don Juan by an express, to congratulate with me the ratification of the Treaty, and in his letter he mentions that there are orders come for *los medios cada mes* for me; the proportion I know not yet, nor have told anybody of it, but those that will let it go no farther.

I hope it will not now be very long before I shall be able to send you more positive orders than I can do at present. Pray make my excuse to my sister and brother for not writing now; for besides having nothing to say, I have had no letters from them these two posts. Remember me very kindly to my Lady S. and Monsieur H.[1] and tell them, I hope their journey to Bourbon will be prevented by one this way; for I assure you, theirs and their mistresses' presence in Holland were much more for all our good than the being where they are. I have nothing more to say, but to put you in mind that my clothes and other things be sent hither as soon as may be.

XXXIX. To Henry Bennet

August 1/11, 1656.

I have very little to say to you this week, having written to my brother all I could think of, to whose letter I refer you. Only I would have you omit no diligence to hasten my brother's journey all you can.

I have taken pills this morning, which hinders me from saying much more to you, but I believe my Lord Bristol[2] and the Chancellor will supply that defect. So as I shall add no more to this, only to tell you that I shall be in great impatience till I see you. For I am confident I shall tell you something when

---

[1] Lady Stanhope, lady-in-waiting to Charles's sister, Mary of Orange, and her Dutch husband, Baron van Heenvliet. Charles did not at all approve of his sister's untimely visit to his mother in France, since it was complicating his relations with Spain, and was anxious for her to return as soon as possible to Paris.

[2] George Digby, Earl of Bristol, a brilliant and erratic nobleman, who had just arrived at the King's Court from France.

you are here that will not displease you, and as yet you know nothing of.

I would have you bring me two beaver hats.   For my Lord Bristol's sword I do by no means like it, therefore do not bespeak mine of that fashion.

XL. To Henry Bennet

Bruges, August 8/18, 1656.

You will see by my last week's letters, that the resolution I have taken concerning my brother's coming hither does agree with what he has directed you to say in yours of the 11th upon that subject, so that I hope if this should find you still at Paris it will be the last that will do so.   I did believe that Gravelines would be the best way for you to take, which made me name it in my last to my brother, and I have sent to my Lord Lieutenant, who is not yet come from the Army, to take order that that pass you have already shall be sufficient.   I do see that your intelligence at the Palace Royal of what we do here is as nefritic as is uses to be, by what you say concerning the Presbyterians. . . .

. . . I will try whether Sir S. Compton be so much in love as you say, for I will name Mrs. Hyde[1] before him so by chance, that except he be very much smitten it shall not at all move him. Pray get me pricked down as many new corantos and sarabands and other little dances as you can, and bring them with you, for I have got a small fiddler that does not play ill on the fiddle.

XLI. To Henry Bennet

Bruges, Aug. 22/Sept. 1, 1656.

I don't write to my brother now, because I hope he will come away before this gets to Paris, but only venture this that in case you should be still there, to let my brother know that the reasons for hastening his journey do every day increase.   I did intend to have written thus much to himself, but having done the same thing so often, I thought that this was sufficient to let him see that my mind is not changed.

[1] Probably Sir Edward Hyde's pretty daughter, Anne, who four years later was to shock England by her marriage with the Duke of York.

You will find by my last, that though I am furnished with one small fiddler, yet I would have another to keep him company; and if you can get either he you mention, or another that plays well, I would have you do it.

By the end of the summer Charles had succeeded in withdrawing both his brother and his Irish regiments from the service of the French Crown, intending to use the latter from Bruges for a Royalist descent on England whenever the chance should offer. In the meantime his relations with Cardinal Mazarin and the French Government became very strained, and the small pension which he had hitherto drawn from his Bourbon cousins ceased.

XLII. PROBABLY TO LORD JERMYN

Bruges, September 19/29, 1656.

Being come to town late last night with my brother the Duke of York, and having very little to say, I desire you to make my excuses to the Queen and my sister, that I do not trouble them with my letters this post. I know not whether my brother has anything to say to me, from whence he comes. We have yet had so little leisure to speak together, yesterday being the day we met, that I have not spoke to him as yet one word of business; only according to his desire I have sent you the note for the nine hundred pistols, which I intend to be out of the arrears due to me; for I do not purpose to receive any pension for the time to come by the Cardinal's means, till I shall be better understood than I find I am.

XLIII. TO LORD JERMYN

Bruges, October 10/20, 1656.

I have received yours of the 13th, and am so far from being unsatisfied with the Cardinal's retrenching my pension, that I am sure I have told you before, if he had inclined to have continued it, I would absolutely have refused it. I pray therefore send me word to what time they have paid it, and so how much I have received from them, as likewise how much is in truth in arrear to that time, that I may be able as well to say how much they have failed of making good what they promised as to acknowledge what I have received.

You say the Cardinal preserves one equality towards me, that is, if there be anything attempted upon England, he shall complain of nothing that is done. And yet, whilst he hath much more reason to believe that will be the case than the contrary, he complains more than would become him whatever the case shall be, and in all companies talks of establishing Cromwell,[1] and uses other expressions than I expected from his discretion, when I gave over expecting anything from his kindness. I wish you should tell him, that a man who hath thought a necessity of his own making warrant enough for such proceedings against me as no necessity could in truth excuse, should allow a real visible necessity, which he cannot but discern, a good justification of my doing what all the world would laugh at me if I should not do; and you shall do well to put him in mind that I am not yet so low, but that I may return both the courtesies and the injuries I have received.

But Charles had scarcely gained by exchanging the friendship of France for that of Spain. The Spanish, with their dilatory formalities, were lavish with promises but exceedingly slow in performance: moreover they had very little money. To make matters worse, Charles had now not only an impecunious Court to support but an army of Swiss and Irish mercenaries, whom the Spaniards, though glad enough of their services against France, were maddeningly slow to provide with food, pay and quarters.

XLIV. To Don Alonzo[2]

Bruges, December 18/28, 1656.

I have seen your letter to the Chancellor, and am so full of indignation at the affront that is put upon me, that I have scarce patience to write this letter. I send this bearer, Blague, expressly

---

[1] Enmity to Spain and a certain similarity in their personal positions were drawing Cromwell and Mazarin steadily closer together. In the previous October they had signed a commercial treaty with a secret clause by which France promised to expel Charles from French soil should he re-enter it, and this was followed in March, 1657, by a military alliance.

[2] See p. 45n.

to let you know, that before I will suffer this affront to be put upon my regiment, which was never yet offered to any private Colonel whatsoever, I will break the regiment a thousand times over. I command you to tell Don Juan this from me, and that according to the usage I receive in this particular, so I shall judge what I am to expect from him in the rest of my affairs. Let me have without delay a positive answer of what I may trust to: for I cannot, nor will not, any longer be at the charges and trouble I am at.

For the exiles 1657 proved but another year of waiting. The habitual talk of a rising in England and of a joint Cavalier-Spanish descent on the English coast came to nothing, and the debts and shifts became so harassing that the King was forced to sell his coach horses. But in the spring the Earl of Bristol, who, by playing upon the easy susceptibilities of the bastard Viceroy, Don Juan, with astrological talk of crowns and sceptres had gained some concessions from the Spanish headquarters, won an unexpected success by persuading the Irish regiments in the French garrison of St. Guislain to betray the fortress to the Spaniards. Charles wrote of the incident to Ormonde, and in some amusement of Bristol's characteristic inability to achieve anything without marring it by his eccentricities.

XLV. TO THE MARQUIS OF ORMONDE

Bruges, March 16/26, 1656/7.

. . . Let me know by the first what are become of all the Irish that were in St. Guislain, for I have not heard a word spoken of them since the surrender of the place. But I hope my Lord Bristol has had that care I expect in order to my interest. I wish the stars would permit him to stay till I come to Brussels, or at least that we might see him before the second disapparition. Pray God that Taurus be as successful to him as Aries has been, and then I hope he will think a little more of terrestrial things, and not run himself and his friends into inconveniences, as you will see more at large by the Chancellor's letter.

For the rest no gleam of success lightened the gloom of that year, though Charles, taking advantage of the temporary rise in his stock effected by the St. Guislain episode, got permission from the Spaniards to move his residence to the more amusing milieu of Brussels. Here and at the Spanish Army head-quarters, where Bristol and Ormonde continued to argue with Don Juan, the struggle to draw money from the Spaniards continued, while the unhappy exiles and soldiers at Bruges begged and starved.

XLVI. To Sir Edward Hyde

Brussels, June 8/18, 1657.

I thought my Lord Lieutenant had from Ghent acquainted you with our condition here and the reason of his voyage, since which time there has been no alteration. He is not yet returned from the Army who are quartered all about Mons, though I expected him last night, as you will see by his letter here enclosed, and how likely I am to obtain a sum that will do me any good, when Don Juan tells me that others must be assisted out of that which I hoped to have had all to myself. The truth is, this scurvy usage puts me beyond my patience, and if I were with Don Juan I should follow your counsel, and swear two or three round oaths. But though I am in ill humour, me-thinks you are in worse, not to be more satisfied with Sir H. Bennet's letter than I find you are, for by it I cannot choose but conclude that in many particulars they have power here to give me satisfaction, if the spirit of Don Alonzo de Cardenas and his cautions do not spoil it. I expect my Lord Lieutenant every minute, and they call upon me for my letter so as I will say no more till to-morrow.

XLVII. To Sir Edward Hyde

Brussels, June 11/21, 1657.

I shall not give you an account of my Lord Lieutenant's journey to the Army, because he will do it at large himself. And the truth is I am so vexed with the delay I see is like to be in the obtaining of money, and consequently my not being able to get from hence till that be, that I have lost all patience, and give all men that have or shall have to do with money to the devil. . . .

XLVIII. TO THE EARL OF BRISTOL

July, 1657.

I need not put you in mind of the season of the year and how soon winter will be upon us, and you will easily believe I am in some pain for the preparations which ought to be ready against that time. Every week brings me letters from my friends in England, to know against what time I will expect them to be ready and what they may depend upon from me; and if this winter pass without any attempt on my part, I shall take very little pleasure in living till the next. I pray desire Don Juan to deal freely with me, what orders are come from Spain towards the making those provisions which are necessary for my enterprise, and what I may rely upon and in what time, that I may give directions in England accordingly. I shall with great impatience expect this account from you, which cannot be too particular.

Charles also had his difficulties with his family. His old ally, Mary of Orange, after her visit to Paris in the previous year, had become embarrassingly ready to fall in with the political intrigues of the Queen Mother, who, from the comfortable security of the Palais Royal, was as usual applying her surplus energy to untimely and unwanted interference in her son's affairs. Any one who, by intrigue or even downright disloyalty, got into disfavour at Charles's Court, was more or less certain of her encouragement; thus her dislike of Hyde and his Anglican friends had recently led her to patronize the Presbyterian Lord Balcarres, whom Charles had found to be untrustworthy. To his intense annoyance, Mary followed her mother's cue.

XLIX. TO MARY OF ORANGE

Brussels, September 10/20, 1657.

As I shall never be wanting in the least degree on my part to give you all sorts of assurances of my kindness to you, so I think the best way of continuing it, is using that clemency and freedom with you I have, and ever will do. And truly if I should tell you now that you have done nothing since we parted, which I might take unkindly of you, I should believe myself guilty in not dealing freely with you. I do not desire that you should prosecute all persons I am displeased with, but certainly I may expect from the kindness we have always had together, that those who are justly in my disfavour and who I have told you are so, should not be the better for it. . . . I shall for the present only name my Lord Balcarres, who I cannot choose but take notice of, that you have used him much better since I have been unsatisfied with him than ever you did before. Judge whether I have not reason to be troubled, when everybody must take notice of this to both our prejudices.

I will only add that this was not so two years ago, and I cannot accuse myself of being changed from what I was then. And now when I have said all this, I do assure you that neither anything you have done, nor anything you can do, shall ever change me from being with all the kindness imaginable. . . .

An even worse domestic embarrassment followed at the beginning of 1658, when the Duke of York, accompanied by young Harry Jermyn, nephew of the Queen Mother's major-domo, visited Mary of Orange at Breda. Almost at once rumours began to cross the frontier about Mary and Jermyn. When Charles, who had already learnt from his own experience how censorious the world can be, expostulated and ordered Jermyn to return to Brussels, Mary flew into a passion and demanded him back.

L. To Mary of Orange

February 1657/8.

I have instructed my brother so fully with my opinion and advice, as I shall not enter into those particulars which have given me so much trouble as this unhappy business hath done; though I must confess, I am sorry to see you take it as you do and think that my severity is the only thing to be satisfied, when I assure you, what I said and counselled you in the thing was merely out of kindness to you. . . . And it appears to me very strange that you should think that the continuing of that which is the cause of the report, should be a means of taking it away. I shall say no more, but refer all to my brother; and only add, that I hope you cannot imagine I am so little careful either of your honour or my own, as to show to the world I know anything of this business, much less to make any public discourse of it. And that what I advise you in this matter, proceeds purely out of that kindness which I will ever have for you. . . .

Meanwhile the exiles continued to wait for a change in their fortunes. There was the usual interminable correspondence with sympathizers in England, and as usual nothing followed it, for as long as Cromwell lived no one was prepared to rise.

LI. To John Mordaunt[1]

Brussels, May 6/16, 1658.

I am willing to believe those who assure me, that you are very willing to do me service, and that you do think that the only way to redeem your country from the misery and slavery it groans under is, by the blessing of God, to restore that which belongs to me, the detaining whereof must continue that misery, and subject the people to a continual succession of afflictions. I hope all good men will be of this opinion with you. And if you shall employ all your interest (which I know is considerable) to the advancing of mine, I doubt not but God will bless you in it. And, I do give you my word, I shall acknowledge it with all the real kindness you can expect. . . .

For the rest, the Spaniards remained as dilatory as ever, and Charles, in his familiar correspondence with Hyde, christened Don Juan, Don Devil.

LII. To Sir Edward Hyde

Brussels, May 26/June 5, 1658.

I have spoken with Don Alonzo since my Lord Lieutenant made an end of his letter, and do find there is no good to be

[1] A young English Cavalier who had opened negotiations with the King. In return for his services he was subsequently raised to the peerage.

done in the business of the clergy. But he proposed to me, in order to get money, that I would ask some office of Don Juan that might yield a reasonable sum, for he said there were places that one might get forty or fifty thousand florins for. I told him he was the best finder out of such a thing, and desired him as my friend to help me in it, which he promises me to do. What will come of it I cannot tell. As for my two months, I cannot say certainly when they will be paid, and, though I did not swear, I assure you I said all things that were necessary upon that subject. He promised to send for the pagador presently, to see what was possible to be done, saying it rested now absolutely upon him. I do intend to send for him to-morrow, and will try what my persuasions will do.

Sir J. came last night to town, and I have had a long discourse with him; if he will be but as good as his word he will do that which he ought to do. I hear just now that there is a considerable sum of money come by bills out of Spain, so that if I were not out of hope ever to see money again, one might expect some of this.

Pray give order to have a little cart made with two wheels to carry my bed, and let them make the cases that the bed is to be put in fit for that purpose. . . .

LIII. To Sir Edward Hyde

Brussels, June 18/28, 1658.

If you have not an answer to all particulars of your letters 'tis my Lord Lieutenant's fault, for I give them to him to answer and to keep. But you must excuse him if he hath not had leisure these two days past, for he hath had the charge of conducting my Lady Diana to see all the sights of this place.

I spake last night with the Nuncio, and do find that these people here have not acquainted him with anything at all. I did not enter into any particulars at all, but only in general, as you advise in one of your former. My Lord Lieutenant and I are of a mind to know of Don Alonzo what is done in their business, which I am confident is nothing, and if they have set nothing on foot, to desire leave to try what we can do ourselves. And truly I am more encouraged to have to do with this man here, because I find him reasonable, and especially in the point of my conversion, and does think the best way to that is, to do all that is possible to set me in England again, and leave the rest to God. I have dispatched Mr. E. and truly I hope there may come good of it; hurt there cannot.

I hope my Lord Lieutenant hath satisfied you in the matter of the bishops and abbots, by telling you it is impossible to be done, which was all the answer that Don Devil gave me, though I asked him why 'twas so twice or thrice, but could get no other answer. For our coming to you I think you do not expect any certainty till George Lane be returned from the Army, which I hope will be this week, which is all I have to say at present.

CHAPTER IV

THE RESTORATION

In September 1658 news reached the exiles that Cromwell was dead. For the first time restoration became a practical possibility. At first there was little change in the external appearance of English politics; Richard Cromwell succeeded his father as Lord Protector and the Army seemed as powerful as ever. But under the surface, the hatred felt by nine Englishmen out of ten for its rule, and the jealousies of the army leaders were working for the Royalists. Before the year ended Charles was authorizing his agents in England to approach General Monk, the republican Commander-in-Chief in Scotland.

1. To Lord Falconbridge, Lord Bellasis, and Sir John
    Grenville, or either of them

[*A rough draft by the Lord Chancellor Hyde.*]

1658.

I am confident that George Monk can have no malice in his heart against me, nor hath he done anything against me which I cannot very easily pardon; and it is in his power to do me so great service that I cannot easily reward, but I will do all I can. And I do authorize you, and either of you, with the advice of the rest, to treat with him, and not only to assure him of my kindness, but that I will very liberally reward him with such an estate in land, and such a title of honour, as himself shall desire, if he will declare for me and adhere to my interest. And whatever you shall promise to him on my behalf, or whatever he, or you by his advice, shall promise to any of his officers or the army, under his command, which command he shall still keep, I will make good and perform upon the word of a king. . . .

Though Monk, the most cautious man in the three kingdoms, returned no answer, Charles and his advisers continued to try to anticipate events in England. From Brussels and Bruges they maintained a ceaseless correspondence with their sympathizers in England, urging them to make friends with the Presbyterians, to get themselves chosen for the next republican

Parliament, and to do everything possible to swell the rising tide of discontent against the Government.

II. TO MRS. ELIZABETH MORDAUNT[1]

Brussels, March 2/12, 1658/9.

I have information enough how much I am beholding to you, which, considering all, shows more courage in you than I could expect.   I am persuaded I shall live to thank you when you shall need be less afraid to receive it.   In the meantime I send you the enclosed to borrow upon the person you think fittest to oblige, as an earnest of my kindness to you both, which shall be always constant to you upon the word of Your very affectionate friend.   CHARLES R.

III. TO PHILIP STANHOPE, SECOND EARL OF CHESTERFIELD

Brussels, March 23/April 2, 1658/9.

Yours of the 22nd February came not to my hand till within these three or four days.   And I do assure you, I have been very sorry for your misfortune, and am no less pleased to see the sense you have of it.   You may be confident of all that you desire from me, and that I have a just sense of the great affection and zeal you have upon all occasions expressed for the advancement of my service and interest.   I hope the time is at hand that will put an end to our calamities.   Therefore pull up your spirits to welcome that good time, and be assured I will be always very kind to you. . . .

By the summer the correspondence with England was taking the form of an elaborate plan for a concerted rising in every part of the country.

IV. TO JOHN MORDAUNT

March 11, 1658/9.

I have yours of the 25th of January, and I suppose you have since that time received others from me, in which I have said

---

[1] John Mordaunt's wife, whom Clarendon described as a young, beautiful lady, of a very loyal spirit.

all I could, and I am sure I need add nothing by this honest bearer, who will inform you of all things here. And if he doth not put all into your hands, which can fall out to be necessary upon all good accidents, it is not for want of foresight, for whatever we could think upon, that may prove useful, I have sent by him. I fear nothing more than too much wariness and want of confidence in my friends towards each other; as therefore I do not limit you to any number, so I wish you should proceed in anything upon conference with as many of them as you find at hand and well disposed, and take the rest in afterwards when they are willing. When you see the business is like to come to action, send me very particular advertisement by a messenger on purpose, and I will be as soon with you as I can, and it may be in a better posture than I dare promise. God send us a good meeting, when you will find me very kind to you.

At first Charles hoped to support the rising by an invasion of England with his ragged levies and a Spanish Army. But as usual the Spanish were dilatory, attributing their delay to a disbelief in Charles's ability to secure a port in England. Even more bankrupt than usual after the long war, they were now thinking of little else but peace with France. Charles therefore decided secretly to remove into French territory, ready either to cross to England should the rising succeed or to travel on to Fuenterrabia, where the rulers of France and Spain were to meet that autumn to conclude a peace and where he might be able to secure some new promise of help. Meanwhile the English rising must go forward without hope of Spanish support.

v. To John Mordaunt

June 10/20, 1659.

I have received yours of the 3rd of this month, and must in the first place desire you to commend me very heartily to all the good men who concurred with you in the sense of that letter. And I do assure you it is a great cordial to me to find so many such men of one mind, and who dare communicate so freely together. . . .

. . . I always see what the Chancellor writes to you, and therefore I shall say little to you of my own condition, which, if you well consider the present conjuncture, and the wants of this country, and the single port of Ostend, you cannot but make a good judgement of. And if some sober action in England, in opposition of the present visible power, doth not give me reputation, and by which they may see that the transporting two or three thousand men may very probably do my business, they will never contribute or consent that of myself I shall begin any enterprise with so small a force. For all I can say will not persuade them that my party is so considerable in England as I know it to be.

So that I must expect the issue of the conclusion and publishing the peace and the concurrence of both Crowns towards my assistance. Which, because it may take up some time . . . I do resolve, as soon as the meeting shall be between the Cardinal[1] and Don Lewis de Haro[2] which will be about the beginning of August (if in the meantime my friends in England do not give me an occasion to come to them) with a light train and incog. to go by post thither. . . . And this is the only way to come to a knowledge of what I may depend upon from them. . . .

I think it necessary that you and my friends should know this (without taking the least notice of my purpose till you hear I am gone from hence) that you may not be surprised when it is reported that I am gone from Brussels. And I cannot imagine that it can be a ground for my friends to delay the doing of anything there after they are ready for it, for if any such thing falls out the day before I set out, I will change my journey and make haste to you. If the news overtake me on the way, I will instantly return, and in that case shall find such assistance as I have mentioned ready to transport with myself, even out of France. And if the news come when I am there, it will give me that credit that all will be easy to me, and I shall find both sides strive which shall help me most. Therefore I hope this resolution of mine will rather incite my friends to lay hold on any reasonable opportunity for action than retard them.

I shall leave the Chancellor and Secretary Nicholas at

----

[1] Mazarin.
[2] The chief Spanish minister.

Brussels, who shall have direction to do all upon such occasion, to make ready my own troops here, as if I were here myself, and if any place be possessed on the sea side, to do all that is possible, and suddenly to throw over some men thither. And they will use all imaginable expedition to advertise me, and you shall find no time lost in what is to be performed by me. If the Army shall again dissolve the Parliament, methinks it should be a just and proper season for all men to betake themselves to their arms, and to defend themselves from violence, till some government be settled. . . .

VI. To John Mordaunt

June 24/July 4, 1659.

. . . Now you have given me an account of so particular preparations made, and resolutions taken by my friends, and that it is their concurrent opinion that my own presence or the presence of one of my brothers is necessary to the uniting and disposing my friends to take up arms for our common interests, and that they are fully resolved in that case to do so, I do very willingly accept the cheerful and affectionate invitation, and do promise you, that I, or one of my brothers, or both of us, will make all possible haste to you as soon as I receive an answer to this letter. It is very true, I have very good and particular assurance, that upon the conclusion of the treaty I shall receive very substantial assistance, to a degree that will enable me, with God's blessing, to protect my friends. . . . And that I might the more speedily make these inclinations to be effectual, I resolved by post to have found myself on the frontiers with two ministers, by which I hoped to have cut off many formalities which might have delayed those resolutions. But since it hath pleased God to raise the hearts of my friends to that courage, that they will undertake to put themselves into arms upon my own or brother's appearing with them, and since it appears to me that they have already communicated their purposes so freely that the delaying to put it in execution may very much endanger their safety and expose them to the rage and cruelty of a bloody and merciless enemy, I will look upon it as the dawning of God's wonderful mercy to us all, and a lively instance that He will cure the wound by the same hand that gave it, and make the English nation the means of removing that misery which it principally brought upon itself, without owning those great obligations to foreign princes, which they seldom yield without some advantage to their own interest. . . . This wonderful blessing I have daily begged of God Almighty, and the first appearance of it will, I doubt not, best dispose both the Crowns and all my other neighbours to give me any assistance I shall stand in need of. . . . I do therefore resolve that myself or one of my brothers, or both of us, will (with God's blessing) be with you as soon as you shall desire; in order whereunto, I wish and expect that you send over some fit person, that may let me know all the particulars of your advice, which way you think safest for us, and to what places we shall come, and who shall meet us, and everything else that is necessary for us to know; I making no kind of doubt, but if any ill accident shall befall us or either of us in the way, you will with the more vigour and consent pursue your resolutions of putting yourselves in arms.

If that sum of money be in readiness which you had hope of, I do not desire that it be sent over, but be kept there and sent to that place where you think it may be of most use upon our first appearance in arms.   Yet I cannot but tell you that I am above twelve months in arrear of that small assignation the King of Spain hath made me, so that my wants and debts are great, which you will easily believe will make my remove (in what manner soever) the more difficult, and leave my family the more distracted when they find I am gone.   Therefore if there could be 4 or 5,000 £ returned to me, it would make all things less difficult to me, which I do not say for delay.   For whether it come or not, as soon as your advice comes to me, I will make all the haste imaginable, being resolved to run all hazards myself, rather than expose my friends to the dangers which threaten them, and infinitely desiring to have no use of foreign force, if I can avoid it. . . .

To assist his friends in England, Charles made overtures to Sir Edward Montagu, the Admiral of the English Fleet in the Sound, believed to be at loggerheads with the Army chiefs and

*parliamentary republicans, who had recently compelled his friend
Richard Cromwell to resign the Protectorate.*

VII. To ADMIRAL SIR EDWARD MONTAGU

June 24/July 4, 1659.

I know not whether a letter sent lately by the Chancellor to
your cousin Montagu be come to his hands. However, you
will not be much surprised with receiving this from myself, since
you cannot but know how much it is in your power at present
with God's blessing to serve me, and that I cannot be without
a very earnest desire to dispose you to it, and a resolution to do
all that is in my power to gratify you for having done it.

I am persuaded that it is not hard for you to believe, that
if the Fleet, or a considerable part of it under your command
would return to its obedience to me, we should in a very short
time with God's blessing be possessed of a good port in
England, and quickly reduce the whole kingdom in the present
temper it is in, to that obedience which is due to me by the laws
of the land, which is all I desire, and restore the people to that
security and liberty which is due to them by the same laws, and
which I desire as much. And it would exceedingly affect them,
and all the world, as a method very agreeable to the divine
Providence, that as the revolt of the Navy was the first violent
introduction of the troubles which ensued, so the return of the
Navy to its loyalty and allegiance should be the preamble to the
peace and happiness of the kingdom. . . .

. . . How great your merit would be in this good change,
all the world would judge, and how great my obligation to you.
And if the honour and generosity of your own work, your affection and piety to God, your country, and to your King doth not
by the influence of God's grace incline you to this glorious enterprise, I cannot hope that any particular overtures made by me in
the condition I am in can make any impression in you. But if
those former considerations have wrought upon you, as I hope
they have, I am willing you should know, that I resolve to
gratify you to the utmost of my power, and will for the present
create you an Earl, and confer any office or command upon you,
that you shall affect. And will always have you very near me,

71

and trust you in my several concernments: and will oblige your friends and nearest relations in such a manner and to that degree as you shall propose on their behalf. . . .[1]

Having done all within his power Charles wrote to Mordaunt announcing his intention of setting out on the 21st July, and gave his final instructions to his brother, who was also to cross to England on news of the rising, and to Hyde who was to await events in Flanders.

VIII. To John Mordaunt

June 29/July 9, 1659.

I am fully satisfied, upon the representation that hath been made to me from several of my friends of the present distempers in England, that my presence with them is very necessary, and I am resolved by the blessing of God to set out from hence on Monday the 21st of this month this style, and to make what haste I can to them. And my brother will be about the same time likewise in England in some other place.

I do therefore desire my friends to put themselves into what readiness they can, and to give credit to what Mr. Mordaunt shall say to them from me, with whom I have conferred at large, and imparted my full resolution to him. And if my friends shall find it necessary for their preservation to put themselves in arms before my coming, I do promise them by God's help to pursue my resolution, and to find myself with some of them as soon as is possible.

IX. To the Duke of York

July 9/19, 1659.

Though I hope, after it shall be known that you and I are in England, we shall easily find a way of corresponding and communicating together, yet since we may for some time be restrained from that, and persons of all kinds may apply themselves to you to serve me, I think it necessary to tell you some

[1] Out of which promise arose in due season the appointment of Samuel Pepys to a seat on the Navy Board.

rules I have prescribed myself, which will be the best directions for you.

I shall endeavour to draw all persons whatsoever to serve me, and to that purpose in my declaration (which will be published at the time I appear) I offer a pardon to all men, except only those who sat actually upon the murder of our father, and voted for it : so that whoever shall apply himself to you, that is not of that number, you may freely promise him my pardon, which I will make good. Whatever rewards you shall think necessary to promise to any man who shall do signal service, I will make good; and I doubt not but all men where you come will obey you, and assure themselves of what you promise them as if I were present myself.

If any excepted person shall make offer to you of doing a very extraordinary service (which I do not expect that any of them will or can do) you may appoint some discreet person to treat with him, who may promise him that after he hath performed that service, he shall not be prosecuted by me, but shall have a time allowed to convey away his estate which shall not be seized by me, so that he withdraws out of my dominions, where he will never desire to live.

I require all persons to give you entire obedience in all things which may advance my service.

x. To Sir Edward Hyde

July 9/19, 1659.

As soon as you have any such clear advertisements of my being in England, that you can propose to yourself a probable way to get yourself to me, I would have you make what haste you can to me. And in the meantime, if your own affairs shall require you to make a short journey from this place, I give you leave.

If any money shall be returned from England for me and the disposal of it left to myself, you shall cause such of my debts to be paid with it as are most pressing; or such persons to be supplied with it as are most fit to be hastened into England after my embarkation. But such money as shall be designed by those who send it for the buying of arms and ammunition, shall be no otherwise employed. . . .

If upon hearing from the Fleet in the Sound, you find that Montagu or any other of the chief officers will be willing to confer and treat with you, I would have you go to them, and do all you can to satisfy them and dispose them to my service.

These preparations were brought to a sudden end on the eve of Charles's intended departure to Calais by a letter from Mordaunt, which showed that the Royalists in England were far from ready for the concerted rising they had promised, and worse still by proofs that their plans had been betrayed by one of their own members, Sir Thomas Willis.

XI. To John Mordaunt

July 18/28, 1659.

. . . I do assure you I have the same desire and impatience to be with my friends there, which I had when you parted from hence, but I cannot but observe that you say nothing of those particulars, which were the principal inducements to the resolutions we then agreed upon.   You do not mention any assurance of Bristol and Gloucester.   Major General Massey[1] in his letter to me of the same date with yours, though he seems to think the day to be too long put off, is far from being confident that he shall find all things in those parts so well as he left them.   And it seems by him Mr. Mansell is in no degree so forward as his friends here delivered him to be, nor doth he promise to engage. I do not find that you have any account from Mr. Popham, upon whose conjunction we absolutely depended, nor that Titus[2] hath yet spoken with him, which was the principal reason that you send your last express to stop my journey.   You say nothing of Lynn, nor of that association of Essex and Norfolk, upon which you know we depended for a body of above 1,000 horse, with whom I, or my brother resolved to be, and it doth not appear that any one of that party hath conferred with you, or agreed to the day.   You do not tell me that you have communicated this

---

[1] Sir Edward Massey, a strong Presbyterian, who since the second civil war had been trying to effect a restoration.

[2] Silius Titus, one of Charles's chief intermediaries in his dealings with the Presbyterian Party.

resolution with Sir William Waller,[1] and what he and his friends resolve upon it, nor do you inform me where yourself and the rest of the good men who have concurred with you, intend to be on the day appointed, and what forces you depend upon. Nor in the last place do you advise me whether to come myself, or who shall meet me. And I do not find the messenger instructed or able to enlarge upon any of those particulars; only he tells me, that if the Parliament be dissolved by the Army, you are resolved all immediately to betake yourselves to arms. In that case I confess I hope and believe it probable that all my friends will be of one mind, and make use of the present distractions and disorder to put themselves upon the defence . . . and I will do all I can to find myself with them. But if that doth not fall out, I do not see any great hopes of success. . . .

Therefore I must conjure you and the rest of my friends, if you do not find that there will be the general concurrence you expect, and that you are not sure to be possessed of Gloucester and Bristol or the other places upon which you have depended, that you do prevent any such engagements as may prove destructive to yourselves. . . . I presume you will give me a more particular account of all resolutions before you expect I should move from hence. . . . And therefore I pray make all possible haste to send me such advertisements that I may ground some resolutions upon, and that I may, in case it shall not be counsellable that I go to you, make all the possible haste to the frontiers. . . .

Until more certain news should arrive from England Charles left Brussels for Trevuren, ready to slip away to Calais at a moment's notice. Meanwhile his warning to Mordaunt was disregarded, and the unco-ordinated plans for the rising went forward. On August 3rd at four in the morning, with Ormonde and two faithful servants, he left for Calais, only to learn that Kent, where he was to have landed, had failed to rise. He therefore travelled on to Rouen, ready to take boat for a western port as soon as news of his supporters being in arms should reach him. On the 18th he wrote cheerfully to Hyde, announcing his intention of setting out next day for St. Malo.

[1] The old Parliamentary general, now wholeheartedly in favour of a restoration.

75

XII. To Sir Edward Hyde

August 18/28, 1659.

You will see by my companion's letter all that we know, and the resolution I have taken. To-morrow we set forth and do not doubt but by the help of God to get to our friends with less hazard than is imaginable in such a voyage. Upon the whole matter I am very cheerful and, though I am not altogether so plump, I begin to grow as sanguine as Mr. Skinner himself. . . . Sure never people went so cheerfully to venture our necks as we do. We have passed hitherto without so much as being suspected who we are, and hope we shall get to our journey's end with the like good fortune. God keep you.

But when he reached St. Malo, Charles learnt the truth— that everywhere the Royalists, betrayed and without certain orders, had failed to rise, save only in Cheshire where the Presbyterian magnate, Sir George Booth, had been almost immediately defeated and captured. There was nothing for it but to proceed to Fuenterrabia. A few weeks later Charles was writing from Saragossa to Hyde, who was fretting in Flanders for news of him, and describing the course of his leisurely and incognito journey through France.

XIII. To Sir Edward Hyde

Saragossa, October 5/15, 1659.

You will wonder to find me no farther advanced in my journey than this place where I arrived last night. For the truth is our greediness of getting into Spain with all haste, hath made us lose this time, and, as it falls out, more unluckily than could be imagined, for contrary to all expectation Don Lewis is still at St. Sebastian. And this unfortunate loss of time was by meeting a ship at Rochelle that was bound for San Sebastian and only stayed for a wind, which was so great a convenience both in respect of the hazard I might run of being known in so long a passage through France, as well as the quickness of the passage, made us stay there eight days in expectation of a wind that gave us every day hopes of turning fair. But at last, seeing no likelihood of it, on the contrary foul weather increasing, we were forced to take this way about, not daring to venture the straight way by Bordeaux, lest• by that time the French Court might have had notice of my motion this way, and so have received a check in our journey. . . . And because I will lose as little time as is possible in meeting with Don Lewis, I am sending O'Neill to-morrow to give him notice of my arrival here, and to adjust our meeting. Till which time I intend to stay here, and I hope to have an answer in ten days. This is all I can say to you yet, only I hope God hath directed all for the best.

Our journey hitherto hath been very lucky, having met with many pleasant accidents and not one ill one to any of our company, hardly as much as the fall of a horse. But I am very much deceived in the travelling in Spain, for by all reports I did expect ill cheer and worse lying, and hitherto we have found both the beds and especially the meat very good. The only thing I find troublesome is the dust, and particularly in this town, there having fallen no rain on this side the Perineans [Pyrenees] these four months. God keep you, and send you to eat as good mutton as we have every meal.

On October 28th (new style) Charles reached Fuenterrabia, to be received with great courtesy and even pomp by the Spanish ministers. From Mazarin, on the other hand, he could get nothing but a few cautious evasions; for the wily Cardinal had no intention of doing anything for a penniless prince until he could see some clear advantage for himself and France in such quixotry. None the less Charles remained sanguine.

xiv. To Sir Edward Hyde

Fuenterrabia, Oct. 24/Nov. 3, 1659.

You will receive by others the particular relation of my reception here. I shall only tell you that I am as much satisfied with Don Lewis's kindness and intention towards me as I can be. And if it were absolutely in his own power, I should not doubt but to return with the same satisfaction in the rest of my affairs. If you do not find that cheerfulness in my Lord Lieutenant's letter you might reasonably hope for, it proceeds from the mysterious proceedings of the Cardinal, which in truth is not yet to be understood, refusing absolutely to talk of England till the peace be signed, though Don Lewis did press him to it . . . though on the other side he takes pains to let me know underhand of his good inclinations and intentions towards me.

I cannot give you my particular reasons that make me more sanguine in my hopes than others, the motives proceeding from little circumstances on the place which are not easy to set down in writing. Nor, I believe, will you accuse me of being over sanguine in other matters. Yet upon the whole I think there is more to hope than to fear, and I am confident you would be of my mind if you were here. One convenience we have which is certain, that we shall not be kept long in suspense, but know what we are to trust to in few days.

I have written to both my brothers by the post that parted from hence two days since, but I believe this will come first to your hands. I have no more to add, only I think 'tis reasonable on our parts to prepare our friends to expect that there will be something done this winter, which God forbid there should not, and that they put themselves into the best readiness they can without noise to expect it. Which is all I have now to say. God keep you.

It all ended in nothing. Peace was concluded without France or Spain promising any concrete help to the English King, while his offer to marry Hortense Mancini, Mazarin's niece, was politely but firmly declined.

After a Christmas visit to his mother in Paris, Charles returned to Flanders to await what was really his best chance of restoration, the inevitable course of events in England, where soldiers, fanatics and republican politicians were at daggers drawn, and government was following government in crazy succession. By the New Year he was busy at his old employment of writing letters of encouragement to any one in England, Royalist, Presbyterian or discontented Republican, who might be prevailed upon to help him.

xv. To Major-General Browne[1]

January 4/14, 1659/60.

I cannot suffer this honest man, who knows us both so well, to return to you without telling you that how unhappily soever we have both been hitherto disappointed in what we have proposed, I hope the time is at hand that we shall have success according to our wish. And I shall look upon it as the most signal blessing God Almighty can confer upon me and the nation, if He please to make that place, which I love very well, most instrumental to my restoration and the happiness of the kingdom, which heretofore contributed so much to the miseries we have undergone. . . .

What my present resolutions are, this bearer will inform you, and how much I depend upon your assistance and activity, and how kind I am to you, which you shall find when I can make it evident in other expressions.

One thing of worth Charles had gained from his visit to Paris —the affection of his fifteen-year-old sister, Henriette-Anne, or Minette as he loved to call her. Henceforward, till the day of her death, he carried on a frequent and intimate correspondence with her.

xvi. To the Princess Henriette-Anne
[*Translated from the French.*]

Jan. 28/Feb. 7, 1659/60.

I begin this letter in French by assuring you that I do not mind your scolding me. I give in joyfully since you quarrel so charmingly with me, but I will never give up the friendship that I have for you. And you give me so many marks of yours that we shall never have any other quarrel but as to which of us shall love the other most, but in this I will never yield to you.

I send you this by the hands of Janton, who is the best girl in the world. We talk of you every day and wish a thousand times in the day to be with you. Her voice has almost entirely

[1] Richard Browne (afterwards knighted), one of the chief London Presbyterian leaders, who for a long time past had been in open dissatisfaction with the republican government.

come back and she sings very well. She has taught me ' *La Chanson de ma queue* '—' I prithee, sweet hart, come tell me and do not lie '—and a number of others. When you send me the scapulary, I promise you to wear it always for love of you.

Tell Madame des Bordes[1] that I will send her my portrait soon; at present the painter is not in this town, but he will return in a few days. Let me know, I pray, how you pass your time, for if you have been for some time at Chaillot[2] in this inclement weather you will have found it somewhat tedious. In future, I beg of you, do not treat me with so much ceremony in addressing me with so many ' Majesties,' for I do not wish that there should be anything between us two but friendship.

Meanwhile events in England moved more rapidly than Charles or any one else could have anticipated. On January 1st (old style) the silent Monk had marched across the Scottish border into England to restore the sovereignty of Parliament and save the country from the warring ambitions of his fellow generals. On reaching London he had gone farther and, after a suitable pause, had compelled the Rump, the corrupt remnant of the Long Parliament, to allow the majority, whom they had excluded for differing from them, to retake their seats. On March 16th (old style) the Long Parliament, further prompted by Monk and his soldiers, dissolved itself, and the whole country prepared for the first free general election for twenty years. In the tide of Royalist reaction now setting in, there could be little doubt of its result. To the exiles watching these events from Flanders it seemed unbelievable, and Charles wrote to Jermyn, whom during his Christmas visit to Paris he had forgivingly created Earl of St. Albans, of the wonderful rumours that were stirring their hearts.

XVII.To the Earl of St. Albans at Paris

Brussels, March 24/April 3, 1660.

I have little to say to you, the post being not yet arrived from England, which comes very unseasonably, for we did expect by these letters something of consequence, and the wind con-

---

[1] Henriette's *femme de chambre* and confidant.
[2] A rather tedious convent to which the Queen Mother paid frequent visits, taking her daughter with her.

tinues so full east as no ships can stir from thence. There is reports here that come from Calais as if they should have passed a vote in the House for King, Lords, and Commons, the truth of which you know by this time.

Pray hasten all you can my coming to you; for, besides the passion I have to wait on the Queen, I think it the properest place for my public concerns. There is a gun which I bespoke of the Turennes; if it be finished pray send it to me, and I [will] return you what it costs. God keep you.

All the while Charles continued to write urgently to England, pressing co-operation on his ever-growing and diverse sympathizers, who, though now at one in desiring a restoration, were divided from one another by the suspicions of twenty unhappy years.

.

XVIII. TO LORD MORDAUNT[1]

March 17/27, 1660.

My Lord, I have yours of the 10th, and your wife's of the day before, and I am very glad you have so good an opinion of Monk. And sure if he and the Parliament proceed as you seem to think they will, I do not knów how it is like to come to arms. However, I shall make as good preparations as I can.

I send you enclosed a letter to Mr. Morrice,[2] and do as often write such letters as I am desired by persons fit to be trusted. And upon that account I write many letters through those hands which are trusted by the persons who are most concerned, and I find good effects of them. But we must not discountenance anybody who may be made to do good service, to gratify any private jealousies or animosities amongst themselves, and therefore I shall not withdraw my good opinion and hopes of Clobery because he and Morrice do not love each other. I will hope for good service from them both, and it may be they may both do me the more service even from their jealousies and dislike of each other.

---

[1] Mordaunt had been given a peerage by Charles.
[2] A Devonshire gentleman and cousin to Monk.

I have never heard of Morrice before, and you shall do well in all such cases, to give me as large information as you can, and by what persons you have your assurance, that I may be sure to avoid clashing. For you must know that I do now very frequently receive addresses and propositions from many worthy men, who make propositions with reference to persons who will only trust whom they please, and I must not deny to gratify them in such particulars as cannot shock with the main carrying on my business. When anything of that nature is proposed I reject it from whomsoever it comes, except they will communicate to my Commissioner to whom I refer them. And I doubt not but by degrees all will come into one channel, and that all my friends will depart from unnecessary jealousies of each other. And I hope this intercourse that's begun between my Lord of Oxford and you will contribute much to it, and that you have showed him all the commissions, and all the instructions, that he may not only see the esteem had of him from the beginning, but the order and method in which my business is put. And I would have the same communication used towards all persons of quality and interest, who shall be willing to concur with you in the promoting of my interest. . . .

I am sorry to find that there is not that communication with Massey and Titus as I desire; and methinks nobody should make scruple of trusting them, when they know how much they are trusted by me. . . . For I am very sure that they are not only very honest and entire to me, but have very good interest in men of the best quality and consideration. I do all I can to promote the credit of all those who wish me well, and I doubt not you will do the same; all being little enough for the work in hand.

Commend me to your wife, and if anything can make you suspect my kindness to you, you are not so wise as I take you to be; you may be confident it shall never fail you.

Before the end of March Charles, waiting at Brussels, received secret advice from Monk which caused him to hurry away from the territory of a state still officially at war with England, and take up new quarters at Breda in Holland. Hence he wrote both to Monk and Montagu, now once more in command of the Fleet, and under Hyde's direction drew up the

famous document which under the name of the Declaration of
Breda laid down the lines on which Restoration, not only of
Monarchy, but of peace, personal liberty and legal government
might be effected in distracted England.

XIX. To General Monk

March 27/April 6, 1660.

If this be the first letter you have received from me, it is only
because some of your friends have not found a convenience of
delivering one to you, which they have had long in their hands.
And you cannot but believe, that I know too well the power you
have to do me good or harm, not to desire you should be my
friend. And I think I have the best ground of confidence that can
be that you will be so, in believing you to be a great lover of
your country and that you desire to secure the peace and happiness and to advance the honour of it, and knowing very well
that my heart is full of no other end, which I am sure you will
know yourself as soon as you know me. And whatever you have
heard to the contrary, you will find to be as false as if you had
been told that I have white hair or am crooked. And it is upon
this confidence only that I depend upon you and your assistance
to the bringing that to pass which I may say can only with God's
blessing bring peace and happiness to the nation and restore it
to its just reputation and honour, and secure all good men in the
possession of what belongs to them. As I know these ends
can only prevail with you, so I do not think you will be the less
zealous for them, because together with them you advance my
interest and oblige me, who can never be without that sense of
your prince, as the greatness of the obligation merits; and I
should enlarge upon that particular, if I did think it would be
acceptable to you. However, I cannot but say, that I will take
all the ways I can, to let the world see, and you and yours find,
that I have an entire trust in you, and as much kindness for you,
as can be expressed by Your affectionate friend. CHARLES R.

xx. Declaration to all Subjects

Breda, April 4/14, 1660.

Charles, by the grace of God, King of England, Scotland, France and Ireland, Defender of the Faith, etc. To all our loving subjects of what degree or quality soever, greeting. If the general distraction and confusion, which is spread over the whole kingdom, doth not awaken all men to a desire and long-ing that those wounds which have so many years together been kept bleeding may be bound up, all we can say will be to no purpose. However, after this long silence, we have thought it our duty to declare how much we desire to contribute there-unto : and that, as we can never give over the hope in good time to obtain the possession of that right, which God and Nature hath made our due : so we do make it our daily suit to the Divine Providence, that He will in compassion to us and our subjects, after so long misery and sufferings, remit and put us into a quiet and peaceable possession of that our right, with as little blood and damage to our people as is possible. Nor do we desire more to enjoy what is ours, than that all our subjects may enjoy what by Law is theirs, by a full and entire administration of justice throughout the land, and by extending our mercy where it is wanted and deserved.

And to the end that the fear of punishment may not engage any conscious to themselves of what is past to a perseverance in guilt for the future, by opposing the quiet and happiness of their country in the restoration both of King, peers, and people to their just, ancient and fundamental rights, we do by these presents declare that we do grant a free and general pardon . . . to all our subjects of what degree or quality soever who within forty days after the publishing hereof shall lay hold upon this our grace and favour, and shall by any public act declare their doing so, and that they return to the loyalty and obedience of good subjects; excepting only such as shall hereafter be excepted by Parliament. Those only excepted, let all our subjects, how faulty soever, rely upon the word of a King solemnly given by this present Declaration, that no crime whatsoever committed against us or our royal father before the publication of this shall ever rise in judgement or be brought in question against any of them to the least endamagement of them, either in their lives, liberties, or estates, or (as far forth as lies in our power) so much as to the prejudice of their reputations by any reproach or term of distinction from the rest of our best subjects : we desiring and ordaining that henceforward all notes of discord, separation, and difference of parties be utterly abolished among all our subjects, whom we invite and conjure to a perfect union among themselves under our protection, for the resettlement of our just rights and theirs, in a free Parliament, by which, upon the word of a King, we will be advised.

And because the passion and uncharitableness of the times have produced several opinions in religion, by which men are engaged in parties and animosities against each other, which when they shall hereafter unite in a freedom of conversation, will be composed or better understood, we do declare a liberty to tender consciences and that no man shall be disquieted, or called in question for differences of opinion in matter of religion, which do not disturb the peace of the kingdom, and that we shall be ready to consent to such an Act of Parliament,[1] as upon mature deliberation shall be offered to us, for the full granting that indulgence.

And because in the continued distractions of so many years, and so many and great revolutions, many grants and purchases of estates have been made to and by many officers, soldiers and others, who are now possessed of the same, and who may be liable to actions at law, upon several titles, we are likewise willing that all such differences, and all things relating to such grants, sales and purchases shall be determined in Parliament, which can best provide for the just satisfaction all men who are concerned.

And we do further declare, that we will be ready to consent to any Act or Acts of Parliament to the purposes aforesaid, and for the full satisfaction of all arrears due to the officers and soldiers of the Army under the command of General Monk, and that they shall be received into our service upon as good pay and conditions as they now enjoy.

[1] An Act which Parliament was to refuse the King the opportunity of passing.

At the same time Charles wrote formal letters to the Speakers of both Houses of Parliament, to the Lord Mayor of London and to General Monk. These he entrusted to Sir John Grenville (who had brought Monk's message to him and upon whom he now conferred an earldom) with instructions to deliver them as Monk should advise.

XXI. TO THE SPEAKER OF THE HOUSE OF COMMONS

April 4/14, 1660.

Trusty and well-beloved, we greet you well. In those great and insupportable afflictions and calamities under which the poor nation hath been so long exercised, and by which it is so near exhausted, we cannot think of a more natural and proper remedy than to resort to those for counsel and advice who have seen and observed the first beginning of our miseries, the progress from bad to worse, and the mistakes and misunderstandings which have produced and contributed to inconveniences which were not intended; and after so many revolutions, and the observation of what hath attended them, are now trusted by our good subjects to repair the breaches which are made and to provide proper remedies for those evils, and for the lasting peace, happiness and security of the kingdom.

We do assure you upon our royal word, that none of our predecessors have had a greater esteem for Parliaments than we have, in our judgement, as well as from our obligation. We do believe them to be so vital a part of the constitution of the kingdom, and so necessary for the government of it that we well know neither Prince nor people can be in any tolerable degree happy without them. And therefore you may be confident that we shall always look upon their counsels as the best we can receive, and shall be as tender of their privileges and as careful to preserve and protect them as of that which is most near to ourself and most necessary for our own preservation.

And as this is our opinion of Parliaments that their authority is most necessary for the government of the kingdom, so we are most confident that you believe and find that the preservation of the King's authority is as necessary for the preservation of Parliaments; and that it is not the name, but the right constitution of them, which can prepare and apply proper remedies for those evils which are grievous to the people and which can thereby establish their peace and security.   And therefore we have not the least doubt but that you will be as tender in and as jealous of anything that may infringe our honour or impair our authority as of your own liberty and property, which is best preserved by preserving the other.

How far we have trusted you in this great affair, and how much it is in your power to restore the nation to all that it hath lost and to redeem it from any infamy it hath undergone and to make King and people as happy as they ought to be, you will find by our enclosed Declaration, a copy of which we have like-wise sent to the house of peers.   And you will easily believe that we would not voluntarily, and of ourself, have reposed so great a trust in you, but upon an entire confidence that you will not abuse it. . . . We look upon you as wise and dispassionate men, and good patriots, who will raise up those banks and fences which have been cast down . . . nor can we apprehend that you will propose anything to us, or expect anything from us, but what we are as ready to give as you to receive.

If you desire the advancement and propagation of the Protestant religion, we have by our constant profession and practice of it given sufficient testimony to the world that neither the unkindness of those of the same faith towards us, nor the civilities and obligations from those of a contrary profession (of both which we have had abundant evidence), could in the least degree . . . make us swerve from it; and nothing can be proposed to manifest our zeal and affection for it to which we will not really consent.   And we hope in due time ourself to propose somewhat to you for the propagation of it that will satisfy the world that we have always made it both our care and our study and have enough observed what is most like to bring disadvantage to it.

If you desire security for those who in these calamitous times, either wilfully or weakly, have transgressed those bounds which were prescribed and have invaded each other's rights, we have left to you to provide for their security and indemnity, and in such a way as you shall think just and reasonable; and by a just computation of what men have done and suffered, as near as is possible, to take care that all men be satisfied. . . . If there be a crying sin,[1] for which the nation may be involved in the infamy that attends it, we cannot doubt but that you will be as solicitous to redeem and vindicate the nation from that guilt and infamy as we can be.

If you desire that reverence and obedience may be paid to the fundamental laws of the land, and that justice may be equally and impartially administered to all men, it is that which we desire to be sworn to ourself, and that all persons in power and authority should do so too.

In a word, there is nothing that you can propose that may make the kingdom happy, which we will not contend with you to compass; and upon this confidence and assurance, we have thought fit to send you this Declaration, that you may, as much as is possible at this distance, see our heart, which when God shall bring us nearer together (as we hope He will do shortly) will appear to you very agreeable to what we have professed. And we hope that we have made that right Christian use of our affliction, and that the observation and experience we have had in other countries hath been such as that we, and we hope all our subjects, shall be the better for what we have seen and suffered.

We shall add no more but our prayers to Almighty God that He will so bless your counsels and direct your endeavours that His glory and worship may be provided for, and the peace, honour and happiness of the nation may be established upon those foundations which can best support it. And so we bid you farewell.

That done, Charles settled down to deal with the flood of applications, epistolary and personal, which now poured in on him from England—for forgiveness, restitution and reward.

In the midst of this not unwelcome press of business he passionately repudiated the usual insinuations which his rivals were making against his friend and Chancellor, Hyde, and found time to write a line to his sister in Paris.

[1] His father's execution.

88

XXII. To Sir Alan Apsley

Breda, April 19/29, 1660.

I have received yours of the 6th of March, and 'tis not to be wondered at, that at the same time that I have so many enemies (though I hope now the number of them decreases daily), those that are faithful to me should have some. And 'tis from some of those who are not much my friends that the report comes that the Chancellor[1] should have lost my favour. The truth of it is, I look upon the spreaders of that lie as more my enemies than his, for he will always be found an honest man, and I should deserve the name of a very unjust master if I should reward him so ill that hath served me so faithfully. Therefore I do conjure you to let as many as you can of my friends know the falsehood and malice of that report, and I shall take it as a service.

XXIII. To the Princess Henriette-Anne
' Pour ma chère, chère sœur '

April 19/29, 1660.

I wrote to you last week and thought to send the letter in Janton's packet, but she had closed hers so that I was obliged to give my letter to Mason. I have yours of the 23rd in which I find so many marks of friendship that I knew not how to find words with which to express my joy. In return I assure you that I love you as much as is possible and that neither absence nor any other thing can ever cause me to depart in the slightest manner from that friendship which I have promised you. And have no fear that those about me will have advantage over you, for, believe me, the friendship I have for you cannot be shared.

I have sent to Sourceau[2] to make me some clothes for the summer, and I have given him orders to bring you some ribbon so that you may choose the trimming and the feathers. I thank you for the song you have sent me. I do not know if it is pretty, for Janton does not know it yet. If you knew how often we

---

[1] Since 1658 Hyde had been titular Lord Chancellor as well as Chancellor of the Exchequer.
[2] Claude Sourceau, the great Parisian tailor, whom after the Restoration Charles coaxed to London.

talk of you and wish you here you would say we are longing to
see you, and do me the justice to believe that I am entirely yours.

C.

On May 1 (old style), after a brief preliminary adjourn-
ment, Charles's letters to the Speakers of the new Parliament
were officially read to the two Houses, the members standing
bare-headed and reverent. Thereafter they invited him to
return and take the government upon his shoulders. Nor was
there a single condition imposed. There was nothing now left
to do but to bring home the King to England. To Monk
personally, and then to him and Montagu jointly as the Com-
manders of the Fleet, Charles wrote of his impatience to come.

XXIV. To General Monk

Breda, May 10/20, 1660.

General Monk, I was the last week dispatching Bernard
Grenville with my answer to yours of the 20th of last month,
when in the instant as he was departing, I received the good news
of what was done on May-day upon the reception of my letters
and declaration in the two Houses.   I have since received yours
of the 5th by Sir Thomas Clarges,[1] with the address the officers
of the Army made to you, upon which I shall not enlarge till
the return of the same messenger.   I have likewise another from
you of the same date, upon all which, besides the great miracles
which God Almighty hath wrought upon the hearts of the
nation, I must acknowledge your extraordinary affection to me
and your very discreet conduct of this great work, in which you
have had to do with persons of such different humours and contrary affections, which you have wonderfully composed.   And
yet you cannot but expect that there are many persons still contriving the same mischiefs against me and you, and who must
be rather suppressed by your authority and power than won and
reconciled by your indulgences.   And it may be a little severity
towards some would sooner reduce the rest than anything you
can else do.

You may be most confident, and I do again renew my
promise to you, for the performance of which you may engage

[1] Monk's brother-in-law.

your life, that I will make good whatever you have found necessary to promise to those of your Army who have and shall
adhere to you to make your business the more easy. And I am
most confident if I were with you, I should in a much shorter
time satisfy them and put them into a full security than will
be done by those formal ways which I hear some men endeavour
to go about, and in which many obstructions will be found
which I could easily remove and prevent. And if any course
be taken in which a just discontent remains with any and justice
itself be wounded, the foundation is not well laid for a lasting
security. I am confident I shall prevent all inconveniences of
this kind when I am with you, which I must conjure you to
hasten by all your interest. . . .

. . . I expect within a few days the arrival of the Commissioners from the Parliament, and for their better reception and
accommodation, this town being already too full, I resolve to
accept the State's invitation and to go on Monday or Tuesday
next to the Hague as the nearest and most commodious place
from whence I may embark, for which you will easily believe I
have longing enough, that I may see you and let the world see
the sense I have of the great service you have done.

*On May 14 (old style) the English Fleet under Montagu
sighted the Dutch coast, and on the following day the King himself arrived at the Hague. Here for a few days longer he
remained, while storms delayed his embarkation and all the
world came to pay court to the rising sun. Hence he wrote
again to Monk asking him to meet him at Dover.*

xxv. To General Monk

May, 1660.

I need say little to you, since I have informed Dr. Thomas
Clarges of my purpose, and he will tell you with what difficulty
I get one quarter of an hour to myself. I have thought the best
I can of the place where I should disembark . . . and have
resolved, God willing, to land at Dover and to stay some days
at Canterbury to put things into as good order as I can. I
resolve, if it please God, to embark on Monday or Tuesday at

the furthest. . . . But you can hardly imagine the impatience I have to see you, for, till then, I shall take no resolution of moment. I pray bring Mrs. Monk with you and believe me to be, very heartily, Your friend CHARLES R.

On May 23 Charles embarked for England. On the 25th he landed at Dover, writing next day from Canterbury to tell his sister of the amazing reception he had had.

XXVI. TO THE PRINCESS HENRIETTE-ANNE

May 26, 1660.

I was so plagued with business at the Hague that I could not write to you before my departure. But I left instructions with my sister[1] to send you a little present from me which I hope you will soon receive. I arrived yesterday at Dover, where I found Monk with a great number of the nobility, who almost overwhelmed me with friendship and joy at my return. My head is so prodigiously dazed by the acclamation of the people and by quantities of business that I know not whether I am writing sense or no, therefore you will pardon me if I do not tell you any more, only that I am entirely yours.   c.

On May 29 Charles entered his capital. After a delirious reception, he stood in his own palace of Whitehall, within a stone's throw of the place of his father's execution, and replied to the addresses of the Lords and Commons.

XXVII. SPEECH IN REPLY TO THE EARL OF MANCHESTER'S ADDRESS OF WELCOME IN THE NAME OF THE HOUSE OF LORDS

Whitehall, May 29, 1660.

MY LORDS,

I am so disordered by my journey, and with the noise still sounding in my ears (which I confess was pleasing to me, because it expressed the affections of my people), as I am unfit at the present to make such a reply as I desire. Yet thus much I shall say unto you, that I take no greater satisfaction to myself

---

[1] Mary of Orange, who had seen him embark.

in this my change, than that I find my heart really set to endeavour by all means for the restoring of this nation to their freedom and happiness; and I hope, by the advice of my Parliament, to effect it. Of this also you may be confident, that, next to the honour of God, from whom principally I shall ever owe this Restoration to my Crown, I shall study the welfare of my people, and shall not only be a true Defender of the Faith, but a just assertor of the laws and liberties of my subjects.

CHAPTER V

THE RESTORATION SETTLEMENT

Restored at the age of thirty, after long hardships, to his throne and native kingdom, Charles, who had hitherto had to write many letters, henceforward, with the exception of those to his beloved sister, wrote few.   The necessary letters of state were drafted and written by his Ministers and their clerks, and merely signed by him: the real business of government was carried out in the Council Chamber and in the great Committees of State over which the King presided.   Hyde, still the King's right-hand man and Chancellor now of a real kingdom, has preserved for us among his papers some of the scribbled notes that passed between him and his master in the early days of the Restoration, when the tangled affairs of three kingdoms were being unravelled at the Council Table—on the demands of ruined Cavaliers for restitution in estates long since in the hands of bona fide purchasers, or for compensation from an empty Exchequer; on rumours of restless fanatics plotting new rebellions; on the solicitation of men of all parties for posts and petitions of every kind; on the affairs of Scotland and Ireland as well as those of England.

1.COUNCIL NOTES BETWEEN CHARLES AND LORD CHANCELLOR HYDE

June ? 1660.

Chan.   I think it is but just to give my Lord Worcester[1] such papers as may manifest his debt.   I tell them the trunk is in your custody, because I will not suffer my Lord Worcester to look into it, therein being many papers he should not have, which were signed by your father; but what concerns his account of moneys disbursed by him for your father, he ought to have, and I shall deliver them to him, if you please, as soon as I can

[1] Edward Somerset, second Marquess of Worcester (1601-67), had expended vast sums during the Civil Wars on behalf of Charles I. He was not popular with Clarendon, for after some years of exile and imprisonment he had made his peace with the usurpers; moreover, he was a Roman Catholic and a projector of such wild and bombastic propositions as perpetual motion, flying machines and coaches driven by steam. At the Restoration he recovered most of his estates, though not relief from his debts, for payment of which he perpetually bombarded the Government. The £40,000 referred to had been promised in land by Charles I in return for money lent.

get time to peruse them.   And then you may consider of the forty thousand pounds.

King. Let my Lord Worcester have his accounts and papers to that purpose, which I doubt not but will bring forth a new cheat.

Chan. As troublesome as you take him to be, he is an angel in comparison of his wife, and his brother John, who torment me every day to get them forty thousand pounds upon this warrant from my Lord Worcester which you have read.

.   .   .   .

King. I think you have heard of one Swinton,[1] a Scotsman, as great a villain as lives; he be here in town and undoubtedly doing all the mischief he can.   Why he should not be paid up I cannot tell. . . .

Chan. The last time I walked with you upon the leads, I told you of this man and of his intrigues, and then you resolved to lay him by the heels.

I pray resolve that the Secret Committee may attend you to-morrow in the afternoon at my chamber; there are many things of great moment to be thought of.

King. I will not fail to meet to-morrow as you desire and I think it will be necessary to resolve either then or before who I shall send Deputy into Ireland.[2]

I believe you have seen a scurvy pamphlet of queries published.[3]   Why should not this Board think of some way of suppressing such scandalous papers, and that the publishers may be severely punished.

.   .   .   .

---

[1] " Lord Swinton (i.e. John Swinton, Laird of that ilk in Berwickshire), a Scotchman, one of Montrose's judges, was sent yesterday to the Gatehouse."—*News Letter*, July 21, 1660.

[2] At the Restoration, Monk (who was soon afterwards raised to the peerage as Duke of Albemarle) was made Lord Lieutenant of Ireland, but as his presence could not be spared in England, the post had to be fulfilled by deputy until Ormonde succeeded him in November, 1661.

[3] Probably the *Queries* referred to in a news letter of June 30, 1660: " Some unhappy wit, amongst other queries scattered in a paper in the Privy Chamber, made one whether it were not fit His Majesty should pass an Act of Indemnity for his enemies and of Oblivion for his friends."

King. What do you think of my Lord Berkeley's[1] being Deputy of Ireland, if we can find no better?

Chan. Do you think you shall be rid of him by it? For that is all the good of it.

King. The truth of it is, the being rid of him doth incline me something to it; but when you have thought round, you will hardly find a fitter person.

.   .   .   .

Chan. Is not my lord Viscount Hereford Lord Lieutenant for Herefordshire?

King. No: for I find, by most of the gentlemen of that county, that he is not at all beloved; and, besides, I think the man herb John[2]. . . .

.   .   .   .

King. I have been talking with the Scots lords about the business of that kingdom and they find it most necessary that a secretary be named as I must do it to-morrow or next day.[3]

Chan. I know not what to say to it, but I am sure you have so many things to think of that I wonder you can sleep.

.   .   .   .

Chan. I pray be pleased to give an audience to my Lord Broghill,[4] who will say many things to you of moment, and I

---

[1] John, first Baron Berkeley of Stratton, an able and restless intriguer, in high favour with the Duke of York but not with Clarendon, who hated him and described him in his *History* as vain, tactless, and ignorant of human nature. Clarendon carried his point, and on July 25th Lord Robartes, an old Parliamentarian, was appointed Lord Deputy of Ireland, Berkeley having for the moment to content himself with a post on the Navy Board, where he became a colleague of Samuel Pepys. But in 1661 he was made Lord President of Connaught, and in 1670 Lord Lieutenant of Ireland.

[2] The phrase 'herb John', i.e. St. John's Wort, a herb of small power, was used to describe anyone ineffective.

[3] On August 7, 1660, Charles appointed as Secretary of State for Scotland, John Maitland, second Earl of Lauderdale, formerly a leading Covenanter. Since 1647 he had devotedly espoused the royal cause.

[4] Roger Boyle, Baron Broghill (1621-79), the Irish statesman, soldier and dramatist, who had started his career as a Royalist, taken service under Cromwell in Ireland and become one of his chief supporters, and had subsequently anticipated the Restoration at the beginning of the year

think with duty enough : if you will give him leave to attend you to-morrow morning at eight of the clock, I will give him notice of it.

King. You give appointments in a morning to others sooner than you take them yourself; but if my Lord Broghill will come at nine he shall be welcome. . . .

The most urgent of all the duties of the new government was to honour the promises given in the Declaration of Breda by persuading Parliament to pass an Act of Indemnity and Oblivion; till this were done, no man, after all the changes and revolutions of the past twenty years, could feel safe. It proved most difficult, for not only were Royalist members and peers anxious to avenge their past sufferings, but the strong Presbyterian bloc in the Convention Parliament proved obstinately vindictive towards their former allies. It was only by the personal influence of the Crown that the Act was passed before the summer session ended, and the list of persons excepted from pardon limited, Charles on more than one occasion having to intervene to secure its passage through the Houses.

II.SPEECH TO THE HOUSE OF LORDS

July 27, 1660.

My Lords : When I came first hither to you, which was within two or three days after I came to Whitehall, I did with as much earnestness as I could, both by myself and the Chancellor, recommend to you and the House of Commons the speedy dispatch of the Act of Indemnity as a necessary foundation of that security we all pray for. I did since, by a particular message to the House of Commons, again press them to hasten that important work; and did likewise, by a Proclamation, publish to all the kingdom that I did with impatience expect that that Act should be presented to me for my assent as the most reasonable and solid foundation of that peace, happiness and security I hope and pray for, to myself and all my dominions. I will not deny it to you, I thought the House of Commons too

by inviting Charles to Ireland. On September 5, 1660, he was created Earl of Orrery, and, as one of the Lord Justices of Ireland, played an important, if not always trusted, part in the settlement of that kingdom.

32270

long about that work; and therefore, now it is come up to you, I would not have you guilty of the same delay.

I thank God I have the same intentions and resolutions now I am here with you which I had at Breda; and I believe that I owe my being here to God's blessing upon the intentions and resolutions I then expressed to have. . . .

My Lords, if you do not join with me in extinguishing this fear which keeps the hearts of men awake and apprehensive of safety and security, you keep me from performing my promise, which if I had not made, I am persuaded neither I nor you had been now here. I pray, let us not deceive those who brought or permitted us to come together. I knew well there were some men who could neither forgive themselves, or be forgiven by us; and I thank you for your justice towards those, the immediate murderers of my father. And, I will deal truly with you, I never thought of excepting any other.

I pray think well upon what I have offered, and the benefit you and I have received from that offer; and encourage and oblige all other persons by not excluding them from the benefit of this Act. This mercy and indulgence is the best way to bring them to a true repentance and to make them more severe to themselves, when they find we are not so to them. It will make them good subjects to me and good friends and neighbours to you and we have then all our end, and you shall find this the securest expedient to prevent future mischief. Therefore I do earnestly desire and conjure you to depart from all particular animosities and revenge, or memory of past provocations; and that you will pass this Act, without other exceptions than of those who were immediately guilty of that murder of my father. . . .

Even more vital to Charles personally was the question of revenue. At the time of his accession the national Exchequer was not only empty but saddled with a debt of three million pounds, while the great standing Fleet and Army of the Commonwealth continued to swallow what was for those days an appalling monthly sum. As Charles had given his word to Monk that disbandment should be accompanied by the payment of every man's arrears, it was vital to induce Parliament to make

H

101

immediate provision for such expenditure. A Poll Tax, estimated to bring in over £200,000 was voted, but Charles was still without any regular revenue for meeting the normal expenditure of his government, a fact of which he was forced to remind Parliament when giving his consent to the Act of Indemnity.

III.Speech to Parliament

August 29, 1660.

My Lords and Gentlemen of the House of Commons: I have been here sometimes before with you, but never with more willingness than I am at this time: and there be few men in the kingdom who have longed more impatiently to have these Bills passed than I have done to pass them. And I hope they will be the foundation of much security and happiness to us all.

I do very willingly pardon all that is pardoned by this Act of Indemnity, to that time which is mentioned in the Bill; nay, I will tell you, that from that time to this day, I will not use great severity, except in such cases where the malice is notorious and the public peace exceedingly concerned. But for the time to come, the same discretion and conscience, which disposed me to the clemency I have expressed . . . will oblige me to all rigour and severity, how contrary soever it be to my nature, towards those who shall not now acquiesce but continue to manifest their sedition and dislike of the government, either in action or words. . . . Never King valued himself more upon the affections of his people than I do; nor do I know a better way to make myself sure of your affections than by being just and kind to you all; and whilst I am so, I pray let the world see that I am possessed of your affections. For your Poll Bill, I do thank you as much as if the money were to come into my own coffers; and wish with all my heart that it may amount to as great a sum as you reckon upon. If the work be well and orderly done to which it is designed, I am sure I shall be the richer by it in the end; and, upon my word, if I had wherewithal, I would myself help you, so much I desire the business done. I pray very earnestly, as fast as money comes in, discharge that great burden of the Navy and disband the Army as fast as you can; and, till you can disband the rest, make a provision for their support. I do conjure you, as you love me, let me not hear the noise of Free-Quarter, which will be imputed to my want of care and government, how innocent soever I am; and therefore be sure you prevent it.

I am so confident of your affections, that I will not move you in anything that immediately relates to myself; and yet I must tell you, I am not richer, that is, I have not so much money in my purse, as when I came to you. The truth is, I have lived principally ever since upon what I brought with me, which was indeed your money, for you sent it to me, and I thank you for it. The weekly expense of the Navy eats up all you have given me by the Bill of Tonnage and Poundage. Nor have I been able to give my brothers one shilling since I came into England, nor to keep any table in my house but what I eat myself. And that which troubles me most is to see many of you come to me to Whitehall and to think that you must go somewhere else to seek your dinner. . . .

Parliament dutifully, though with some delay, made good the omission by voting the King supplies, which it was reckoned would provide an annual revenue of £1,200,000, but as the melancholy financial history of the next twelve years was to show, the estimate was wildly optimistic and left the government with an annual deficit of about £400,000.

Amid all this press of business Charles contrived to find time for the varied personal interests which he had acquired during his exile and which, though they included, were far from confined to courtship of the other sex. A scribbled note to Hyde gives a glimpse of his passion for regular physical exercise; another, of his delight when his sister, Henriette-Anne, visited England with her mother towards the end of 1660.

IV. TO LORD CHANCELLOR HYDE

October 5, 1660, 8 in the morning.

I am going to take my usual physic at tennis. I send you here the letters which my Lord Aubigny desires me to write, look them over, and if there be no exceptions to them return them by twelve o'clock, for I would willingly dispatch them this afternoon.

v. Council Notes between Charles and Lord Chancellor Hyde

November or December, 1660.

King. I would willingly make a visit to my sister at Tunbridge for a night or two at farthest, when do you think I can best spare that time?

Chan. I know no reason why you may not for such a time, (two nights) go the next week, about Wednesday, or Thursday, and return time enough for the adjournment; which yet ought to be the week following.

I suppose you will go with a light train?

King. I intend to take nothing but my night bag.

Chan. Yes, you will not go without forty or fifty horse!

King. I count that part of my night bag.

Until the King was married the Restoration settlement could not be assured of permanency; after the death of the Duke of Gloucester from smallpox, at Christmas, the whole future of the English monarchy depended on the lives of Charles and his surviving brother, the Duke of York. During the last months of 1660 and the first of 1661, negotiations were going forward to find the King a bride. Both France and Spain, the leading rivals for European power, were anxious to provide one, and presented what Charles described as ' a whole litany of princesses.' As no bride untainted by Catholicism proved suitable—for his subjects were naturally anxious that he should choose a Protestant—the choice of Charles and his advisers gradually turned towards Catherine of Braganza, the Infanta of Portugal, a little country possessed of great colonial possessions but struggling at home for its very existence against Spain, and therefore able and willing to pay heavily for an English alliance. Before the end of 1660 Charles and Hyde were in correspondence with the Queen Regent of Portugal.

vi. To Lord Chancellor Hyde

November or December, 1660.

I send you here my letter that is for the Queen of Portugal; 'tis the worst Spanish that ever was writ, and if it were possible it ought to have been mended. But now that cannot be, look

it over and see if I have written it right, and send it me back
again with the super and subscription.

*Before the marriage terms could be settled, Charles had
made further progress in the task of settling his disorganized
kingdoms. On December 24 he was able to dissolve the Convention Parliament, its work of restoration and pardon accom-
plished, promising at the same time to call a new and legal
Parliament as soon as possible.*

VII.Speech to both Houses on dissolving the Convention Parliament

December 24, 1660.

My Lords and Gentlemen : I will not entertain you with a long
discourse; the sum of all I have to say to you being but to give
you thanks. And I assure you I find it a very difficult work to
satisfy myself in my own expressions of those thanks. Perfunc-
tory thanks, ordinary thanks for ordinary civilities, are easily
given. But when the heart is as full as mine is, it is a labour
to thank you. You have taken great pains to oblige me; and
therefore it cannot be easy for me to express the sense I have of it.

I will enlarge no further upon this occasion than to tell you,
that when God brought me hither, I brought with me an extraordinary affection and esteem for Parliaments. I need not tell
you how much it is improved by your carriage towards me.
You have out-done all the good and obliging acts of your
predecessors towards the Crown; and therefore you cannot but
believe my heart is exceedingly enlarged with the acknowledgement.

Many former Parliaments have had particular denominations
from what they have done. They have been styled learned and
unlearned, and sometimes have had worse epithets; I pray let us
all resolve that this be for ever called ' The Healing and Blessed
Parliament.'

As I thank you, though not enough, for what you have done,
so I have not the least doubt by the blessing of God but when
I shall call the next Parliament, which I shall do as soon as
reasonably you can expect or desire, I shall receive your thanks

for what I have done since I parted with you : for, I deal truly with you, I shall not more propose any one rule to myself in my actions and my councils than this, ' What is a Parliament like to think of this action or this council? ' and it shall be want of understanding in me, if it will not bear that test.

I shall conclude with this, which I cannot say too often, nor you too often where you go, that, next to the miraculous blessing of God Almighty, and indeed as an immediate effect of that blessing, I do impute the good disposition and security we are all in, to the happy Act of Indemnity and Oblivion. That is the principal corner-stone which supports this excellent building, that creates kindness in us to each other; and confidence is our joint and common security. You may be sure I will not only observe it religiously and inviolably myself, but also exact the observation of it from others. And if any person should ever have the boldness to attempt to persuade me to the contrary, he will find such an acceptation from me as he would have who should persuade me to burn Magna Charta, cancel all the old laws, and to erect a new government after my own invention and appetite.

There are many other particulars, which I will not trust my own memory with; but will require the Chancellor[1] to say the rest to you.

Meanwhile the affairs of Scotland and Ireland had still to be settled. Scotland, where the troubles that led to the Civil War had begun and where the unmonarchial ideals of Presbyterianism still prevailed, was an object of perpetual suspicion to the new Government: Charles himself could never quite forgive the Scots for what he had suffered at their hands in 1650. As watchdogs two old Scots Covenanters, long turned Royalist, were appointed to the virtual control of the northern kingdom,— General Middleton, now created Earl of Middleton and Lord High Commissioner to the Scottish Parliament, who quickly proved that a gallant soldier may make a debauched and incompetent administrator, and John Maitland, second Earl of Lauderdale, the new Secretary of the Council, about whose ability, whatever might be thought of his moral character, there was never any doubt.

---

[1] But the Chancellor's hand is very plain in this speech.

VIII.INSTRUCTIONS TO JOHN, EARL OF MIDDLETON, AS COMMISSIONER
TO THE PARLIAMENT OF SCOTLAND

Countersigned by Lauderdale

November 29, 1660.

. . . You shall endeavour that our ancient royal prerogative be asserted, and the just liberties of our people settled as they enjoyed them under our royal ancestors according to law.

And for that purpose you shall endeavour that, seeing it is our undoubted right . . . to call and dissolve Parliaments and Conventions of the Estates of our kingdom, the holding of the Convention of Estates 1643 be declared against, because it did meet and sit without our dearest father's indiction and authority. As also that the Parliament 1649 be declared null.

And because in other Parliaments, which met by his authority, divers Acts have passed during the late unhappy differences which entrenched upon our prerogative, you shall endeavour that such Acts . . . be rescinded. . . .

And because it is our resolution to settle that our kingdom in a firm and lasting unity and peace, you shall give our royal assent to such an Act of Oblivion as shall be drawn up by our Parliament for securing of our subjects there, with such exceptions as our Parliament shall make; which act, together with the exceptions and the reasons of them, you shall first transmit to us before it be past or anything executed against the excepted persons.

You shall endeavour the encouraging of trade and manufactories in that our kingdom, and plantations in our dominions in America or elsewhere.

You shall endeavour the relief of those who have been eminent sufferers for us and our authority during the late usurpations, and particularly that those whose estates were confiscated by the usurpers be not burdened with their annual rents during the time their estates were forfeited and out of their possession. . . .

IX. TO THE EARL OF MIDDLETON
(Draft in Lauderdale's hand)

Whitehall, March 22, 1660/1.

I have given you a full answer to your letter. Yet one thing I must add, and it shall be to yourself. I am sorry to hear from so many hands that a strange course is taken there with many of those who were appointed to be cited to the Parliament. Private bargains I hear are driven, and money received from too many who are represented to have been abominable compliers. I shall be glad that this be not so, for although I should have been apt enough to have pardoned such as had been offered as the fittest objects of mercy, and although I was willing to leave those things very much to the Parliament, yet I did ever understand that the sole power of pardoning resides in me and that fines and forfeitures are wholly at my disposal. You shall therefore privately inform yourself if any such strange way be taken and let it be stopped. For I am clearly of opinion that pardoning and publishing is to be carried above board, and that no private bargains are to be driven to make sale of my grace and mercy. Let me, I pray you, have an account of this.

Ireland proved even more difficult to settle, for here three different parties were struggling for possession of the land—the Catholic Irish, the English Protestants who had supported the King in the Civil Wars, and the later Protestant settlers who had been planted there by the Commonwealth. To act with justice in meeting their irreconcilable claims needed all the tact of Charles and his advisers.

X. COUNCIL NOTES BETWEEN CHARLES AND LORD CHANCELLOR CLARENDON[1]

1661.

King. When will it be fit to call in the Irish as they desired last night?

Chan. Whenever you have a mind to spoil the business; really all will come to nothing if you call them in.

---

[1] Hyde was created Earl of Clarendon at the Coronation, in April 1661.

King. I cannot imagine, with any justice, how I can refuse to hear them since they desire it.

Chan. Have you not heard them? If you do call them, the other side must be called too, and then we are in till morning. If you are tender hearted on their behalf I pray leave them to the House of Commons, and their work is done. They are mad and do not understand their own interest. Sir Nicholas Plunkett is desperate and would make all others so too.

King. For my part, rebel for rebel, I had rather trust a Papist rebel than a Presbyterian one. . . .

.   .   .   .

King. The Irish make a complaint, methinks with reason, that my Lord Anglesey[1] should be both party and judge.

Chan. He ought not to be, nor can when you are by.

King. I mean in the committee for Irish affairs where he may impose unreasonable things upon the rest, who are not so much concerned as he is.

Chan. My Lord Privy Seal[2] will watch him, but I think when you have taken your resolutions in the main, that committee will not be able to do much.

King. But methinks 'tis an ugly thing for me to make a party judge.

.   .   .   .

King. Will not you be here to-morrow at Council about the business of Ireland? It will be likewise necessary for you to meet me at the General's on Friday, before Council, about the business of Portugal.

Chan. I shall attend you in both places, if I am able, the con-

---

[1] Arthur Annesley (1614-86), an Anglo-Irish landowner of Presbyterian leanings who had been rewarded for his part in the Restoration by being made Vice-Treasurer of Ireland and Earl of Anglesey. With Lord Robartes, Lord Holles, the Marquis of Dorchester and the two Secretaries of State, he was one of the Committee of the Privy Council responsible for Irish affairs.

[2] John, Lord Robartes (see above), who besides being Lord Deputy of Ireland, held the English office of Lord Privy Seal.

trary whereof I do not suspect. You have a world of other business too, which must be settled at my Lord Treasurer's.

King. When can we meet there?

Chan. I am afraid not till Sunday. Will you put us to deliver our opinions in this matter this night? It will take much time. My Lord Dorchester must be very long, and my Lord Anglesey as long; since I presume they will differ both from their learning they last published in this place.

King. If those two learned persons could be sent to supper, we might dispatch it now; but by my Lord of Dorchester's face, I fear his speech will be long, which will be better for a collation than a supper.

On May 8, 1661, a few weeks after his coronation, Charles greeted his new Parliament. In the strong reaction towards Royalism the elections had produced an aggressively Cavalier House of Commons, which threatened in its zeal for revenge and compensation to undo the work of its more moderate predecessor. Charles welcomed the members with the news that he had completed a marriage treaty with Portugal, but realizing the strength of their partisan feeling, felt it wise to warn them that the personal honour of his Government would be at stake if they did not confirm the Act of Indemnity.

XI. SPEECH TO BOTH HOUSES AT THE FIRST SESSION OF THE SECOND PARLIAMENT

May 8, 1661.

My Lords and Gentlemen of the House of Commons: I will not spend the time in telling you why I called you hither; I am sure I am very glad to see you here. I do value myself much upon keeping my word, upon making good whatsoever I promise to my subjects: and I well remember, when I was last in this place, I promised that I would call a Parliament as soon as could be reasonably expected or desired. And truly, considering the season of the year, and all that has been done since we parted, you could not reasonably expect to meet sooner than now we do. . . .

I think there are not many of you who are not particularly known to me; there are few of whom I have not heard so much good that I am as sure as I can be of anything that is to come that you will all concur with me, and that I shall concur with you, in all things which may advance the peace, plenty, and prosperity of the nation. I shall be exceedingly deceived else.

My Lords and Gentlemen: You will find what method I think best for your proceeding, by two Bills I have caused to be prepared for you; which are for confirmation of all that was enacted at our last meeting. And above all, I must repeat what I said when I was last here: 'That, next to the miraculous blessing of God Almighty, and indeed, as an immediate effect of that blessing, I do impute the good disposition and security we are all in to the happy Act of Indemnity and Oblivion. That is the principal corner-stone which supports this excellent building, that creates kindness in us to each other; and confidence is our joint and common security.'

I am sure I am still of the same opinion, and more if it be possible of that opinion, than I was, by the experience I have of the benefit of it, and from the unreasonableness of what some men say against it, though I assure you not in my hearing. In God's name, provide full remedies for any future mischiefs; be as severe as you will against new offenders, especially if they be so upon old principles, and pull up those principles by the roots. But I shall never think of him as a wise man, who would endeavour to undermine or shake that foundation of our public peace by infringing that Act in the least degree; or that he can be my friend, or wish me well, who would persuade me ever to consent to the breach of a promise I so solemnly made when I was abroad. . . .

I will not conclude without telling you some news that I think will be very acceptable to you; and therefore I should think myself unkind and ill-natured if I should not impart it to you. I have been often put in mind by my friends that it was high time to marry; and I have thought so myself ever since I came into England. But there appeared difficulties enough in the choice, though many overtures have been made to me: and if I should never marry till I could make such a choice against which

III

there could be no foresight of any inconvenience that may ensue, you would live to see me an old bachelor, which I think you do not desire to do. I can now tell you, not only that I am resolved to marry, but whom I resolve to marry, if God please . . . and, trust me, with full consideration of the good of my subjects in general, as of myself : it is with the daughter of Portugal.

When I had as well as I could weighed all that occurred to me, the first resolution I took was to state the whole overtures which had been made to me, and in truth all that had been said against it, to my Privy Council; without hearing whose advice I never did, nor ever will, resolve anything of public importance. And I tell you with great satisfaction and comfort to myself that after many hours debate in a full council (for I think there was not above one absent) . . . my Lords, without one dissenting voice (yet there were very few sat silent), advised me with all imaginable cheerfulness to this marriage. Which I looked upon as very wonderful, and even as some instance of the approbation of God Himself; and so took my own resolution and concluded all with the ambassador of Portugal, who is departing with the whole Treaty signed, which you will find to contain many great advantages to the kingdom. And I make all the haste I can to fetch you a Queen hither, who, I doubt not, will bring great blessings with her to me and you. I will add no more, but refer the rest to the Chancellor.

Charles's fears were justified, for the new House of Commons was soon at work discussing a Bill for executing nineteen more Regicides.

XII. COUNCIL NOTES BETWEEN CHARLES AND LORD CHANCELLOR CLARENDON

July, 1661.

Chan. What is to be wished should be done in the Bill that is now ordered to be brought in for the execution of those ill men who are condemned? Would it not be better that the Bill should sleep in the Houses, and not be brought to you? Shall I speak of it to the Board?

King. I must confess that I am weary of hanging except upon new offences.

Chan. After this business is settled, shall I move it here, that we may take care that it comes not to you?

King. By all means, for you know that I cannot pardon them.

In deference to the royal wishes the Bill was ultimately allowed to drop, and the distasteful leniency of the previous year was confirmed in a new Act of Oblivion, to which Charles gave his consent on July 8th.

In his speech he thanked the Houses both for this and for a Bill for collecting free gifts to bring up the already inadequate revenue to the promised £1,200,000.

XIII. SPEECH TO PARLIAMENT ON PASSING THE ACT OF OBLIVION

July 8, 1661.

My Lords and Gentlemen: It is a good time since I heard of your passing this Bill for money; and I am sure you would have presented it to me sooner if you had thought I had desired it. But the truth is, though I have need enough of it, I had no mind to receive it from you till I might at the same time give my assent to this other very good Bill that accompanies it, for which I longed very impatiently. . . .

I am confident you all believe that my well-being is of some use and benefit to you; and I am sure your well-being, and being well pleased, is the greatest comfort and blessing I can receive in this world. I hope you will be ready within few days to dispatch those other Public Bills which are still depending before you, that I may come hither and pass all together, and then adjourn till winter. . . . The last Parliament, by God's blessing, laid the foundation of the happiness we all enjoy; and therefore I thought it but justice to the memory of it to send you Bills for the confirmation of what was enacted then; and I cannot doubt but you will dispatch what remains of that kind with all convenient speed; and that you will think that what was then thought necessary or fit for the public peace to be enacted ought not to be shaken now, or any good man less secure of what he possesses, than he was when you came together. . . .

My Lords and Gentlemen : Let it be in no man's power to charge me or you with breach of our word or promise, which can never be a good ingredient to our future security. Let us look forward, and not backward; and never think of what is past, except men put us in mind of it by repeating faults we had forgot; and then let us remember no more than what concerns those very persons. God hath wrought a wonderful miracle in settling us as he hath done. I pray let us do all we can to get the reputation at home and abroad of being well settled. We have enemies and enviers enough, who labour to have it thought otherwise; and if we would indeed have our enemies fear us, and our neighbours love and respect us, and fear us enough to love us, let us take all the ways we can, that, as the world cannot but take notice of your extraordinary affection to me and of the comfort I take in that affection, so that it may likewise take notice of your affection to and confidence in each other; which will disappoint all designs against the public peace and fully establish our joint security.

Charles's personal correspondence that summer was of a matrimonial turn. In June he was negotiating a match between his twelve-year-old son, James ' Crofts ', later to be made Duke of Monmouth, and the infant heiress of the great Scottish House of Buccleuch. In July he was writing with full formality to his own bride at Lisbon and to her mother.

xiv. To Lady Margaret Leslie, Countess of Wemyss

Whitehall, June 14, 1661.

Madam, I have received your letter of the 28th of May by William Fleming, and am very sensible of the affection which you show to me in the offer you make concerning the Countess of Buccleuch, which I do accept most willingly, and the rather for the relation she hath to you. I will in a short time send more particularly to you about settling that whole affair, which I look upon now as my own interest. In the meanwhile I must thank you again for it, and be most assured that I am, Madame, Your very affectionate friend, CHARLES R.

XV. TO CATHERINE OF BRAGANZA

London, July 2, 1661.

My Lady and Wife : Already, at my request, the good Count da Ponte has set off for Lisbon. For me the signing of the marriage has been great happiness, and there is about to be dispatched at this time after him one of my servants,[1] charged with what would appear necessary, whereby may be declared, on my part, the inexpressible joy of this felicitous conclusion, which, when received, will hasten the coming of Your Majesty.

I am going to make a short progress into some of my provinces . . . seeking in vain tranquillity in my restlessness, hoping to see the beloved person of Your Majesty in these kingdoms, already your own, and that with the same anxiety with which, after my long banishment, I desired to see myself within them. . . . The presence of your Serenity is only wanting to unite us, under the protection of God, in the health and content I desire. . . .

The very faithful husband of Your Majesty, whose hand he kisses. CHARLES REX.

At the end of July Charles adjourned the Houses, referring in his speech to their ecclesiastic measures, which included an Act restoring the Bishops to their seats in the House of Lords.

XVI. SPEECH AT THE ADJOURNMENT OF PARLIAMENT

July 30, 1661.

My Lords and Gentlemen : I perceive, by the thin appearance of the members of both Houses this day, that it is high time to adjourn. In truth, the season of the year as well as your particular affairs require it; and therefore I do willingly consent to it.

I thank you for the many good Bills you have presented me with this day, of which, I hope, the benefit will redound to the

---

[1] Sir. Richard Fanshawe was appointed ambassador to Portugal on August 10th and reached Lisbon on the 14th September. He was charged not only with polite messages, but with the supervision of the execution of the onerous terms imposed on Portugal for the privilege of an English alliance—half a million in cash, Tangier and Bombay, and free trade with Brazil and the East Indies.

whole kingdom. I thank you for the care you have taken for the safety of my person, which, trust me, is the more valuable to me for the consequence I think it is of to you. And, upon my conscience, there is nobody wishes ill to me but they who would quickly revenge themselves of you if they could. I thank you for the care you have taken of yourselves, of your own safety and honour, in the Act against tumults and disorders upon pretence of petitions, to which licence we owe much of the calamities we have undergone. But I thank you with all my heart, indeed as much as I can do for anything, for the repeal of that Act which excluded the Bishops from sitting in Parliament. It was an unhappy Act, in an unhappy time, passed with many unhappy circumstances and attended with miserable events; and therefore I do again thank you for repealing it. You have thereby restored Parliaments to their primitive institutions. And I hope, my Lords and Gentlemen, you will in a short time restore them to the primitive order and gravity of debates and determinations which the licence of the late distempered times had so much corrupted; which is the only way to restore Parliaments to their primitive veneration with the people, which I heartily wish they should always have.

My Lords and Gentlemen : You are now going to your several countries, where you cannot but be very welcome for the services you have performed here. I do very earnestly recommend the good government and peace of your countries to your care and your counsel, and your vigilancy. There are distempered spirits enough, which lie in wait to do mischief, by laying reproaches upon the Court, upon the Government; reproaches upon me and reproaches upon you. Your wisdoms and reputation and authority will, I doubt not, weigh down their light credit; and the old and new good laws will, I hope, prevent any mischief they intend. However, you have done very well (and I do very heartily thank you for it) in declaring my sole right over the Militia, the questioning of which was the fountain from which all our bitter waters flowed. I pray make haste to put the whole kingdom into such posture that evil men, who will not be converted, may yet choose to be quiet, because they find that they shall not be able to do the harm they desire to do.

I know you have begun many Bills in both Houses which cannot be finished till your meeting again. And, that they may be finished then, I forbear to make a sessions now, but am contented that you adjourn till the 20th of November, when I hope, by God's blessing, we shall come happily together again. . . .

To the business of the Crown and its entourage, an adjournment of Parliament in the seventeenth century meant no more than it does to-day to the permanent Civil Service: the ordinary administration of governing continued, though with less interruption. For the King personally, the core of such business lay in the multitudinous work of the Privy Council, over which he presided, and its various committees—for Naval Affairs, Intelligence, and Foreign Affairs. The following are notes to the Lord Chancellor.

XVII. To the Lord Chancellor

July 29, 1661.

The Swedish resident will come to me after dinner to know what he shall say to their ambassador at Breda. He will ask me two questions, one concerning the money which they were put in hopes of, and the other how far I am engaged with France that his master may govern himself accordingly. And because we may agree in one song, let me know as soon as you can what you have said to him upon these two points, for I suppose he has been with you already.

XVIII

Whitehall, September 15, 1661, 11 at night.

He must be a harder hearted man than I that can refuse you a few days in a place you are so well pleased with as I perceive you are with Cornbury.[1] The truth is, till we hear from Portugal there can be little resolved upon with the French ambassador, and 'tis good reason I should give you now a little time to play after the passing of so many ill hours as you have done of all sorts in my service.

My Lord Aubigny knows nothing of our intrigue with the

---

[1] Charles had granted the great forest estate of Cornbury to Clarendon in reward for his services.

Superintendent, and by his discourse I am confident the ambassador tells him nothing of it. At my first discourse with the ambassador I told him what sums of money you had been offered by the Superintendent, which undoubtedly he hath acquainted his master with by this time. But for fear he should forget it I will clear you again in that matter to him to-morrow when (he) comes to me.[1]

Have a care of the game about Cornbury that I may have good sport next year when I come hither.

XIX

October 2, 1661, 10 in the morning.

The French ambassador was with me last night and gave me the enclosed paper. He desires to be dispatched with all speed and that he may speak with you this afternoon. Let me know the time and place, that I may advertise him this morning. I find him much discontented, the particulars whereof you shall know when I see you.

XX

October 11, 1661, 11 in the morning.

As soon as I returned last night I sent for Harry Progers and examined him whether ever he had received any money from the Spanish ambassador, but he swore he never had. And by his looks, which were very little concerned, though I asked him the question very short and quick, I dare swear he told me truth.

I received the enclosed this morning from Monsieur L'Estrades, by which you will see the confirmation of what my Lord St. Albans[2] writ to me, though with greater sweetness towards us than he apprehended. I think it were necessary for me to answer to it, which if you think convenient send Dick Bellings[3] to me in the evening and we will make one.

[1] Bastide de la Croix, agent to Fouquet, the French Superintendent of the Finances, who was negotiating an Anglo-French understanding on the basis of a joint protection of Portugal against Spain, had just injured Clarendon's upright feelings by privately offering him £10,000.

[2] Now English ambassador at Paris.

[3] Richard Bellings, a Catholic and an Irishman, much employed by Charles and Clarendon on secret diplomatic missions.

XXI

November 8, 1661, Friday night.

My brother[1] tells me that there are two ships now at Portsmouth expecting a wind for the Straits, who may land any messenger at Lisbon. They shall have order to stay until further order, therefore let the dispatch be hastened all you can. And I think a letter from me to my wife will be necessary. You may send for H. Bennet to prepare it and give him instructions for the contents of it.

On November 20, at the re-opening of Parliament, the King again stressed the inadequacy of the national revenue, and begged that some provision should be made to meet the debts incurred by himself and his predecessors before the Restoration, which the Convention Parliament had promised but failed to pay. The French ambassador, describing the scene, refers to the King's excellent delivery, but complained that he frequently glanced at his notes. 'I was informed,' he adds, ' that this was the custom in England, the reason being that the King may not expose himself to the laughter of the people by stopping short through loss of memory. Preachers in the pulpit do the same.'

XXII.SPEECH AT THE MEETING OF PARLIAMENT

November 20, 1661.

My Lords and Gentlemen of the House of Commons : I know the visit I make you this day is not necessary. . . . Yet, if there were no more in it, it would not be strange that I come to see, what you and I have so long desired to see, the Lords Spiritual and Temporal and the Commons of England met together to consult for the peace and safety of Church and State, by which Parliaments are restored to their primitive lustre and integrity. I do heartily congratulate with you for this day.

But, my Lords and Gentlemen, as my coming hither at this time is somewhat extraordinary; so the truth is the occasion of my coming is more extraordinary. It is to say something to you on my own behalf, to ask somewhat of you for myself; which is more than I have done of you, or of those who met here before

---

[1] The Duke of York was Lord High Admiral.

you, since my coming into England. I needed not have done it then; and, upon my conscience, I need not do it now. They did, and you do, upon all occasions, express so great an affection and care of all that concerns me, that I may very well refer both the matter and manner of your doing anything for me to your own wisdoms and kindness. And indeed, if I did think that what I am to say to you now did alone or did most concern myself; if the uneasy condition I am in, if the straits and necessities I am to struggle with, did not manifestly relate to the public peace and safety more than to my own particular otherwise than as I am concerned in the public, I should not give you this trouble this day. I can bear my necessities which merely relate to myself with patience enough.

Mr. Speaker, and you gentlemen of the House of Commons, I do not now importune you to make more haste in settling the constant revenue of the Crown, than is agreeable to the method you propose to yourselves; to desire you seriously to consider the insupportable weight that lies upon it; the obligations it lies under to provide for the interest, honour and security of the nation in another proportion than in any former times it hath been obliged to. But I come to put you in mind of the crying debts which do every day call upon me; of some necessary provisions which are to be made without delay for the very safety of the kingdom; of the great sum of money that should be ready to discharge the several fleets when they come home; and for the necessary preparations that are to be made for the setting out new fleets to sea against the spring, that revenue being already anticipated upon as important services which should be assigned to those preparations.

These are the pressing occasions which I am forced to recommend to you with all possible earnestness, and to conjure you to provide for as speedily as is possible, and in such a manner as may give us security at home and some reputation abroad. I make this discourse to you with some confidence, because I am very willing and desirous that you should thoroughly examine whether these necessities I mention be real or imaginary, or whether they are fallen upon us by my fault, my own ill managery, or excesses, and provide for them accordingly. I am very willing that you make a full inspection into my revenue, as well the disbursements as receipts; and if you find it hath been ill-managed by any corruption in the officers I trust, or by my own unthriftiness, I shall take the information and advice you shall give me very kindly. I say, if you find it; for I would not have you believe any loose discourses, how confidently soever urged, of giving away four score thousand pounds in a morning, and many other extravagances of that kind. I have much more reason to be sorry that I have not to reward those who have ever faithfully served the King my father and myself than ashamed of any bounty I have exercised towards any man. . . .

Since her visit to England in the previous year Charles had continued to correspond with his sister, Henriette-Anne. She was now 'Madame' of France, the wife of Monsieur, Duke of Orleans, brother and heir-presumptive to the French King. Charles wrote to her about her health, which was tragically delicate, and of other intimate things, but also about affairs of State; when Louis tried to evade the customary salute to the English flag in the narrow seas—a point of honour on which Charles was always adamant—he used her as his unofficial ambassador.

XXIII. To Madame

Whitehall, December 16, 1661.

For my Dearest Sister.

I have been in very much pain for your indisposition, not so much that I thought it dangerous, but for fear that you should miscarry. I hope now you are out of that fear too, and for God's sake, my dearest sister, have a care of yourself, and believe that I am more concerned in your health than I am in my own, which I hope you do me the justice to be confident of, since you know how much I love you.

Crofts hath given me a full account of all you charged him with, with all which I am very well pleased, and in particular with the desire you have to see me at Dunkirk the next summer, which you may easily believe is a very welcome proposition to me; between this and then, we will adjust that voyage. I am sure I shall be very impatient till I have the happiness to see *ma chère Minette* again.

I am very glad to find that the King of France does still continue his confidence and kindness to you, which I am so sensible of, that if I had no other reason to ground my kindness to him but that, he may be most assured of my friendship as long as I live. And pray upon all occasions assure of this.

I do not write to you in French, because my head is now dosed with business, and 'tis troublesome to write anything but English. And I do intend to write to you very often in English that you may not quite forget it. c.

XXIV. To Madame

Whitehall, December 23, 1661.

I received yours of the 27th so late this night, and the post being ready to go, that I have only time to tell you that I extremely wonder at that which you write to me of. For certainly never any ships refused to strike their pavilion when they met any ships belonging to the Crown of England. This is a right so well known, and never disputed by any king before, that, if I should have it questioned now, I must conclude it to be a *querelle d'Allman*. I hope what you say to me is only your fears, for I will never believe that anybody who desires my friendship will expect that which was never so much as thought of before. Therefore all I shall say to you is, that my ships must do their duties, let what will happen of it! And I should be very unworthy if I quit a right and go lower than ever any of my predecessors did. Which is all I have to say, only that I am very glad to find you are so well recovered, and be assured, my dearest sister, that I am entirely yours. c.

Early in the new year Charles was again forced to appeal to the Commons for some permanent settlement of the national revenue, whose inadequacy to meet necessary and current expenditure was assuming alarming dimensions. They were, however, more interested in debating a Bill for Uniformity in Public Prayer to deprive all incumbents who would not accept the Anglican Prayer Book of their livings, and were far from pleased when the King tried to moderate this proceeding, which (though not displeasing to the majority of Englishmen who, after the experiences of the past generation, were content to dwell peaceably in the Anglican fold) struck at the religious union which the Declaration of Breda had essayed, and ultimately produced the gravest schism in the national life.

XXV. SPEECH TO THE COMMONS IN THE BANQUETING HOUSE
CONCERNING HIS NECESSITIES

March 1, 1661/2.

Mr. Speaker, and Gentlemen of the House of Commons. . . .

I do speak my heart to you when I tell you that I do believe that, from the first institution of Parliaments to this hour, there was never a House of Commons fuller of affection and duty to their King than you are to me; never any that was more desirous and solicitous to gratify their King than you are to oblige me; never a House of Commons in which there were fewer persons without a full measure of zeal for the honour and welfare of the King and country than there are in this. . . . In a word, I know most of your faces and names, and can never hope to find better men in your places.

You will wonder now, after I have willingly made this just acknowledgement to you, that I should lament, and even complain, that I, and you, and the kingdom, are yet without that present . . . advantage which we might reasonably promise ourselves from such a harmony of affections . . . to advance the public service and to provide for the peace and security of the kingdom; that you do not expedite those good counsels which are necessary for both. I know not how it comes to pass, but for these many weeks past, ever since your last adjournment, private and particular business have almost thrust the consideration of the public out of doors. And, in truth, I do not know that you are nearer settling my revenue than you were at Christmas. I am sure I have communicated my condition to you without reserve; what I have coming in, and what my necessary disbursements are : and I am exceedingly deceived if whatsoever you give me be any otherwise given to me than to be issued out for your own use and benefit. Trust me it shall be so; and, if you consider it well, you will find that you are the richer by what you give; since it is all to be laid out that you may enjoy the rest in peace and security.

Gentlemen, I need not put you in mind of the miserable effects which have attended the wants and necessities of the Crown. I need not tell you that there is a Republican party still in the kingdom, which have the courage to promise themselves another revolution : and, methinks, I should as little need to tell you that the only way, with God's blessing, to disappoint their hopes . . . is to let them see that you have so provided for the Crown that it hath wherewithal to support itself. . . . Therefore I do conjure you, by all the professions of affection you have made to me, by all the kindness I know you have for me, after all your deliberations, betake yourselves to some speedy resolutions; and settle such a real and substantial revenue upon me as may hold some proportion with the necessary expenses I am at. . . .

Gentlemen, I hear you are very zealous for the Church, and very solicitous and even jealous that there is not expedition enough used in that affair. I thank you for it, since, I presume, it proceeds from a good root of piety and devotion. But I must tell you I have the worst luck in the world, if, after all the reproaches of being a Papist, whilst I was abroad, I am suspected of being a Presbyterian now I am come home. I know you will not take it unkindly if I tell you that I am as zealous for the Church of England as any of you can be . . . that I am as much in love with the Book of Common Prayer as you can wish, and have prejudice enough to those that do not love it; who, I hope, in time will be better informed and change their minds. And you may be confident, I do as much desire to see a uniformity settled as any amongst you. . . . I have transmitted the Book of Common Prayer, with those alterations and additions which have been presented to me by the Convocation, to the House of Peers, with my approbation, that the Act of Uniformity may relate to it : so that I presume it will be shortly dispatched there. And when we have done all we can, the well settling that affair will require great prudence and discretion and the absence of all passion and precipitation.

I will conclude with putting you in mind that the season of the year, the conveniences of your being in the country, in many respects for the good and welfare of it (for you will find much tares have been sowed there, in your absence), the arrival of my wife, who I expect some time this month, and the necessity of my own being out of town to meet her, and to stay sometime before she comes hither, makes it very necessary that the Parliament be adjourned before Easter, to meet again in the winter. . . . The mention of my wife's arrival puts me in mind to desire you to put that compliment upon her, that her entrance into the town may be with more decency than the ways will now suffer it to be : and, to that purpose, I pray you would quickly pass such laws as are before you, in order to the mending those ways; and that she may not find Whitehall surrounded with water. . . .

The chief business of the spring of 1662 was the King's marriage. There were some formal difficulties to be settled about the ceremony, as the bride, being a Catholic, had need to be married by the rites of the Catholic Church as well as the Anglican; after long disuse Hampton Court Palace had to be got ready for the honeymoon, and the lady herself brought over from her native country by a British Fleet.

XXVI. COUNCIL NOTES BETWEEN CHARLES AND CLARENDON

April ? 1662.

King. I think we have not yet thought of the manner of my marriage. It will be necessary we meet about it.

Chan. It is so long since it was thought of, that it may be forgotten, but you did think of every part of it before the ambassador went : you must have a Bishop with you, and he must marry you before you go to bed, and she is prepared to submit to it, as a civil obligation, for the legitimation of her children.

King. That which you say was quite all out of my mind. I hope she hath consulted with the Jesuits, who are best able to vote an ecclesiastical obligation into a civil one.

Chan. It was the ground of the pressing you presently to style her your wife, and that she be reputed as married before she come thence. After she comes hither, she will do that that is neces-

sary for herself and children. You cannot be married by a
Roman priest, therefore she must by a Bishop of yours.

*On May 14 Catherine, very sick from her voyage, landed at
Portsmouth, and on the evening of the 19th the King, delayed
till the last moment by ceaseless business in Council Chamber
and Parliament, drove hastily out of London to receive her.*

XXVII. COUNCIL NOTE TO CLARENDON

May, 1662.

I shall have one conveniency in it too, that if I should fall
asleep too soon when I come to Portsmouth, I may lay the fault
upon my long journey.

XXVIII. TO CLARENDON

Portsmouth, May 21, 1662. 8 in the morning.

I arrived here yesterday about two in the afternoon, and as
soon as I had shifted myself, I went to my wife's chamber, who
I found in bed, by reason of a little cough, and some inclination to a fever, which was caused, *as we physicians say,* by having
certain things stopped at sea which ought to have carried away
those humours. But now all is in their due course, and I believe
she will find herself very well in the morning as soon as she
wakes.

It was happy for the honour of the nation that I was not put
to the consummation of the marriage last night; for I was so
sleepy by having slept but two hours in my journey as I was afraid
that matters would have gone very sleepily. I can now only
give you an account of what I have seen a-bed; which, in short,
is, her face is not so exact as to be called a beauty, though her
eyes are excellent good, and not anything in her face that in the
least degree can shock one. On the contrary, she has as much
agreeableness in her looks altogether, as ever I saw : and if I have
any skill in physiognomy, which I think I have, she must be as
good a woman as ever was born. Her conversation, as much as
I can perceive, is very good; for she has wit enough and a most
agreeable voice. You would much wonder to see how well we

are acquainted already. In a word, I think myself very happy; but am confident our two humours will agree very well together. I have not time to say any more. My Lord Lieutenant will give you an account of the rest.

XXIX. To Madame

May 23, 1662.

My Lord St. Albans will give you so full a description of my wife as I shall not go about to do it, only I must tell you I think myself very happy. I was married the day before yesterday, but the fortune that follows our family is fallen upon me, *car Monr. Le Cardinal m'a fermé la porte au nez,* and though I am not so furious as Monsieur was, but am content to let those pass over before I go to bed with my wife, yet I hope I shall entertain her at least better the first night than he did you. . . .

XXX. To the Queen of Portugal

Portsmouth, May 23, 1662.

Being now freed from dread of the sea and enjoying in this springtime the company of my dearest wife, I am the happiest man in the world and the most enamoured, seeing close at hand the loveliness of her person and her virtues, not only those which Your Majesty mentioned in your letter—simplicity, gentleness and prudence—but many others also. These things oblige me to think of the interests and procure the tranquillity of her beloved country, as will be seen by my deeds and by the orders and powers which I give to my ambassador, whom, on arriving at Hampton Court, I shall dispatch to that of Portugal. And I wish to say of my wife that I cannot sufficiently either look at her or talk to her. May the good God preserve her to me and grant Your Majesty long years of life, in which to be a comfort to us both.

XXXI. To the Lord Chancellor

Portsmouth, May 25, 1662.

My brother will tell you of all that passes here, which I hope will be to your satisfaction. I am sure it is so much to mine, that I cannot easily tell you how happy I think myself; and I must be the worst man living (which I hope I am not) if I be not a good husband. I am confident never two humours were better fitted together than ours are. We cannot stir from hence till Tuesday, by reason that there is not carts to be had to-morrow to transport all our guarda infantas, without which there is no stirring; so as you are not to expect me till Thursday night at Hampton Court.

The royal marriage was followed by a State trial. For the past year Parliament had been petitioning the King to try Sir Henry Vane, the stormy petrel of English republicanism, who, though spared as to his life, had been one of the twenty persons other than Regicides exempted from full pardon by the Convention. On June 2, 1662, he was arraigned in the Court of King's Bench on a charge of high treason for compassing the death of King Charles I and subverting the ancient forms of government. He boldly based his defence on the argument that any action ordered by a section of Parliament, however illegally constituted, could not be questioned in a Court of Law. This proved over much for Charles's patience, who wrote to Clarendon that he thought him too dangerous a man to live. Vane was found guilty by the jury on June 6, and on June 11 sentenced to be hanged, drawn and quartered, the usual barbarous punishment for high treason, subsequently mitigated by the King to decapitation.

XXXII. To the Lord Chancellor

June 7, 1662.

The relation that has been made to me of Sir H. Vane's carriage yesterday in the Hall is the occasion of this letter, which, if I am rightly informed, was so insolent as to justify all he had done, acknowledging no supreme power in England but a Parliament, and many things to that purpose. You have had a true account of all, and, if he has given new occasion to be hanged, certainly he is too dangerous a man to let live, if we can honestly put him out of the way. Think of this and give me some account of it to-morrow and till when I have no more to say to you.

Charles had soon afterwards to write to Clarendon on a more personal matter. His bride was not long in discovering that her husband's marriage had been preceded by other and more informal unions, the partner of one of which, Barbara Palmer (whose titular husband Charles had created Earl of Castlemaine), was insistent that he should honour an old promise to make her a Lady of the Queen's Bedchamber. Charles, who never found it easy to resist a woman, found himself subjected to the irreconcilable demands of two angry and distressed women, both of whom reinforced their entreaties by tears. In the end he took the side of an injured and more beautiful mistress against a more injured and less beautiful queen. When Clarendon, always a great stickler for propriety, encouraged the Queen to resist, he was quickly made aware of the King's feelings.

XXXIII. To Lord Chancellor Clarendon

July or August, 1662.

I forgot, when you were here last, to desire you to give Broderick good counsel, not to meddle any more with what concerns my Lady Castlemaine, and to let him have a care how he is the author of any scandalous reports. For if I find him guilty of any such thing, I will make him repent it to the last moment of his life. And now I am entered on this matter, I think it necessary to give you a little good counsel in it, lest you may think that, by making a further stir in the business, you may divert me from my resolution, which all the world shall never do. And I wish I may be unhappy in this world and the world to come if I fail in the least degree of what I have resolved, which is, of making my Lady Castlemaine of my wife's bed-chamber. And whosoever I find use any endeavour to hinder this resolution of mine (except it be only to myself), I will be his enemy to the last moment of my life.

You know how true a friend I have been to you. If you will oblige me eternally, make this business as easy as you can, of what opinion soever you are of, for I am resolved to go through with this matter, let what will come on it; which again I solemnly swear before Almighty God. Therefore, if you desire to have the continuance of my friendship, meddle no more with this business, except it be to beat down all false and scandalous reports, and to facilitate what I am sure my honour is so much concerned in.   And whosoever I find to be my Lady Castlemaine's enemy in this matter, I do promise, upon my word, to be his enemy as long as I live.   You may show this letter to my Lord Lieutenant; and if you both have a mind to oblige me, carry yourselves like friends to me in this matter.

Charles showed himself in a more amiable light that autumn in a letter to his sister describing the welcome he had given his mother on her return from France to England.

XXXIV. To Madame

Whitehall, September 8, 1662.

I am so ashamed for the *faute* I have committed against you that I have nothing to say for myself, but ingeniously confess it, which I hope in some degree will obtain my pardon, assuring you for the time to come I will repair any past failings.   And I hope you do not impute it in the least degree [to] want of kindness, for I assure you there is nothing I love so well as my dearest Minette, and if ever I fail you in the least, say I am unworthy of having such a sister as you!

The Queen has told you, I hope, that she is not displeased with her being here.   I am sure I have done all that lies in my power to let her see the duty and kindness I have for her.   The truth is, never any children had so good a mother as we have, and you and I shall never have any dispute but only who loves her best, and in that I will never yield to you. . . .

The Chevalier de Gramont[1] begins his journey to-morrow, or next day; by him I will write more at large to you.   I am doing all I can to get him a rich wife here.   You may think this is a jest, but he is in very good earnest, and I believe he will tell you that he is not displeased with his usage here, and with the way of living.   And so farewell, my dearest Minette, for this time.

---

[1] Philibert, Comte de Gramont, the hero of the famous *Memoirs* written by his brother-in-law, Anthony Hamilton.

*The Restoration Settlement may be said to have been com-
pleted with the liquidation of one last republican liability,
Dunkirk, which had been conquered from the Spaniards in
1657. The place was costing £130,000 a year to garrison and
maintain, which was beyond the slender means of the English
Government. Accordingly, in October 1662 it was sold to
France for five million livres, the preliminary negotiations being
conducted in the utmost secrecy.*

XXXV. COUNCIL NOTES BETWEEN CHARLES AND CLARENDON

August (?), 1662.

King. The Secretary has a letter from my Lord Rutherford,[1]
which takes notice of the rumour of parting with Dunkirk, and
desires to know the truth of it. What answer is to be given?

Chan. That the Secretary neither knows nor believes any such
thing; but I would be glad to speak with you upon this argument, that it may be resolved how far to communicate it at
the next Council, which is Friday. How much of it have you
imparted to the Queen, or my Lord St. Albans?—which
D'Estrades desires to know, that he may behave himself
accordingly.

King. Dick Bellings told me of this yesterday. My Lord
St. Albans did only pump Monsieur D'Estrades; and he need
not take any notice of anything yet.

Chan. If you had leisure this afternoon, why should you not
appoint your brother, my Lord Treasurer, and the General to
attend you at four or five of the clock at Worcester House, that
we might there agree of the whole method of carrying on this
affair.

.   .   .   .

October 17 (?), 1662.

King. Am I not to break this business of Dunkirk?

Chan. Yes: and first declare that you have somewhat of
importance to propose, and therefore that you will have a close
Council, and that the clerk withdraw: then state it as you
resolved.

[1] Governor of Dunkirk, afterwards Earl of Teviot.

King. I think the first opening of the matter must be upon Monsieur D'Estrades's desire of having the place.

Chan. No: but upon several representations my Lord Treasurer hath made to you: of your expenses, how far they exceed your receipts. That you have spent some time in the consideration how to improve the one and to lessen the other. That you find the expense of Dunkirk to be £130,000 a year. You find, if it were fit to part with it, you could not only take off that expense, but do believe you might get a good sum of money. Ask the advice of the Board in an affair of this moment.

CHAPTER VI

THE FIRST APPROACH TO FRANCE AND THE SECOND DUTCH WAR

The bulk of Charles's personal correspondence after the Restoration was addressed to his sister, the Duchess of Orleans, the one being to whom he appears ever to have completely given his heart. Though often confined to family matters (the Stuarts were famed for the strength of their family attachments), this correspondence became of increasing political importance with Charles's growing confidence in his sister's diplomatic tact and ability. Louis XIV was essentially a ' personal ' monarch, and in foreign affairs at least Charles did his best to emulate him, and the relationships between England and France were coming to be the crucial factor in European politics.

I. To Madame
[*Translation*]

October 26, 1662.

I avail myself of that liberty which you have accorded me to assure you of the continuation of those sentiments which you approve and of my design to employ all the most suitable means to ensure the success of our desires. To which end I consider nothing of greater value than the intimate friendship between the King my brother and myself, and I assure you that this consideration has strongly influenced me to make this last treaty to forge a very close correspondence between us, in which I am strongly persuaded of your intervention. And if it pleases you to propose to him that we may communicate our thoughts to each other in our own hands by this private channel I shall be very glad, knowing how much this mutual confidence will contribute towards maintaining our friendship. . . .

II. To Madame

London, November 4, 1662.

. . . The chief business of this letter shall be to tell you that I am now settling a certain fund for the payment of what I owe you,[1] which I assure you had not been so long undone but that my condition has been such hitherto, as there was no possibility of doing it till now.   And I promise you it has given me very much trouble and shame that I could not perform what I so much desire, and to one I love so well as you.   By my next you shall have a more certain account, and I doubt not but to your satisfaction.

You will have heard before now of the Alarum we have had of the risings here of the Anabaptists.   But our spies have played their parts so well amongst them, as we have taken many of them, who will be hanged very speedily,[2] so as I believe for this time, their designs are broken.   This is all I shall say to you at this time, but be assured that I will always have as much care of all your interests, as of his who is entirely yours.   c.

III.COUNCIL NOTES BETWEEN CHARLES AND LORD CHANCELLOR CLARENDON

November, 1662.

Chan.   You know you do now every day expect the Muscovite ambassadors,[3] who bring with them several valuable toys as a present to you.   Now there goes no extraordinary wit, to make this discovery, and to beg this present before it comes.

I pray remember the entertaining these ambassadors will be chargeable to you, and therefore if this suit be made to you, as sure it will be, I pray say you are engaged, and so keep it to yourself, that what is to be sold may discharge the expenses.   I hope you have [not] given it away already.

King.   You need not have given me this caution, for I love to keep myself warm with the furs and for the other part of the present will be as necessary for other things. . . .

---

[1] Probably the residue of her dowry, which Charles was having diffi-culty in paying.

[2] Four ringleaders were executed on Tower Hill on December 22nd.

[3] The Russian ambassadors arrived on November 27, 1662, and Pepys a month later recorded, ' I saw all the presents, being rich furs, hawks, carpets, cloths of tissue, and sea-horse teeth.'

IV. TO MADAME

Whitehall, December 4, 1662.

You may easily believe that any request which comes from Bablon[1] will be quickly dispatched by me. I am striving all I can, to take away the difficulties which obstruct this desire of hers, which in truth are very great, all those things being farmed; and 'tis not hard to imagine that people on this side the water love their profit as well as they do everywhere else. I have sent to inquire farther into it, and within five or six days will give you an account, for I am very unwilling not to grant Bablon's desires, especially when they come recommended by you. . . .

V. TO MADAME

Whitehall, February 9, 1662/3.

Mr. Montagu[2] is arrived here, and I wonder Monsieur would let him stay with you so long, for he is undoubtedly in love with you. But I ought not to complain, having given me a very fine sword and belt, which I do not believe was out of pure liberality, but because I am your brother. He tells me that you pass your time very well there.

We had a design to have had a masquerade here, and had made no ill design in the general for it, but we were not able to go through with it, not having one man here that could make a tolerable entry. I have been persuading the queen to follow Queen Mother of France's example and go in masquerade before the carnival be done; I believe it were worth seeing my Lord St. Albans[3] in such an occasion. My wife hath given a good introduction to such a business, for the other day she made my Lord Aubigny[4] and two other of her chaplains dance country dances in her bed chamber.

---

[1] Elizabeth-Angélique de Montmorency-Bouteville, Duchesse de Châtillon, with whom, fourteen years before, Charles had had a boyish love affair.
[2] Ralph Montagu, afterwards Duke of Montagu, who had just returned from his first diplomatic mission to France.
[3] Lord St. Albans was very fat.
[4] Ludovic Stuart, Seigneur d'Aubigny, Grand Almoner to Queen Catherine.

I am just now called for to go to the play, so as I can say no more at present but that I am entirely yours.   c.

VI. To Madame

[Translation from the French]

London, February 16, 1662/3.

The great desire I have not to leave any shadow of doubt in the mind of the King my brother in regard to the perfect friendship established between us has persuaded me to send him this gentleman, Mr. Trevor,[1] especially to satisfy him about my reasons regarding the demand made by his ambassador, Monsieur de Comminges,[2] concerning his audience.   I have also charged him to impart them to you, being equally desirous that you should remain persuaded of my desire to satisfy the King my brother in everything so far as the welfare of my kingdom allows. The difficulty in question concerns the preservation of a regulation which is very necessary for the peace and the security of the City of London.[3]   I entreat you to be assured of this and to contribute towards making my intentions well understood in this occasion, for I desire nothing more strongly than to preserve the perfect friendship of the King my brother. . . .

VII. To Madame

Whitehall, February 16, 1662/3.

I send this bearer, Sir John Trevor, to the King my brother about a business which, though it may seem at first to be of a very slight nature, I assure you it may prove of dangerous consequence to me.   He will inform you of the particulars, and

---

[1] Sir John Trevor (1626-72), son of an old Parliamentarian who had himself held office under the Commonwealth, and was several times employed by Charles in negotiations with France.

[2] Gaston Jean-Baptiste, Comte de Comminges, the new French ambassador in London.

[3] After an embroglio of the previous year between the retainers of the French and Spanish embassies in the London streets, Charles, to avoid similar disputes, had issued a decree forbidding the coaches of the ' Corps Diplomatique ' from taking part in the processions customary at the entries of new ambassadors. Louis, having in the meantime obtained an admission of French precedence from the Spanish Court, now wanted the decree withdrawn.

then you will see that it cannot be of any consequence to France, only may be of a very ill one to me.

The Parliament is to meet again after to-morrow, which gives me so much business to prepare all things for that purpose, as I hope you will excuse me if this letter be a little short. I have sent Monsieur Van der Does *à la foyre de St. Germain* to buy little things to play for here. I had not time to write to you by him, as he desired, and I think you know him so well, as it will be sufficient to introduce him into your presence when he comes, and so my dearest sister farewell for this time.

When Parliament re-assembled on February 18, 1663, Charles had an important matter to explain. On December 26, in Clarendon's absence through illness, he had made, by a Declaration to Tender Consciences, his first attempt to modify the rigid religious settlement forced on him by the Anglican Parliament. The Declaration had proclaimed that, until a Bill could be laid before Parliament for this purpose, the King would out of his prerogative dispense with the execution of the penal laws against all religious dissentients who were prepared to live peaceably.

VIII. SPEECH TO PARLIAMENT

February 18, 1662/3.

My Lords and Gentlemen : I am very glad to meet you here again, having thought the time long since we parted, and often wished you had been together, to help me in some occasions which have fallen out. I need not repeat them unto you; you have all had the noise of them in your several countries, and (God be thanked!) they were but noise without any worse effects.

To cure the distempers and compose the differing minds that are yet among us, I set forth my Declaration of the 26th of December, in which you may see I am willing to set bounds to the hopes of some, and to the fears of others; of which when you shall have examined well the grounds, I doubt not but I shall have your concurrence therein. The truth is, I am in my nature an enemy to all severity for Religion and Conscience, how mistaken soever it be, when it extends to capital and sanguinary

139

punishments, which I am told were begun in Popish times: Therefore, when I say this, I hope I shall not need to warn any here not to infer from thence that I mean to favour Popery. I must confess to you there are many of that profession who, having served my father and myself very well, may fairly hope for some part in that indulgence I would willingly afford to others who dissent from us. But let me explain myself, lest some mistake me herein, as I hear they did in my Declaration. I am far from meaning by this a toleration or qualifying them thereby to hold any offices or places of trust in the government; nay, further, I desire some laws may be made to hinder the growth and progress of their doctrine.

I hope you have all so good an opinion of my zeal for the Protestant religion, as I need not tell you, I will not yield to any therein, nor to the bishops themselves, nor in my liking the uniformity of it as it is now established; which, being the standard of our Religion, must be kept pure and uncorrupted, free from all other mixtures. And yet, if the Dissenters will demean themselves peaceably and modestly under the government, I could heartily wish I had such a power of indulgence, to use upon occasions, as might not needlessly force them out of the kingdom, or, staying here, give them cause to conspire against the peace of it.

My Lords and Gentlemen, it would look like flattery in me to tell you to what degree I am confident of your wisdom and affection in all things that relate to the greatness and prosperity of the kingdom. If you consider well what is best for us all, I dare say we shall not disagree. I have no more to say to you at present, but once again to bid you heartily welcome.

The Commons lost no time in disillusioning the King as to their attitude towards his Declaration of Indulgence. Toleration to Presbyterian and Independent dissenters was bad enough; extended to Catholics it was intolerable. Within a month, Charles, with the best grace he could muster, was forced to yield. But the correspondence with Madame, and through her with the Catholic and untrammelled and absolute monarch of France, continued.

IX. To Madame

Whitehall, March 5, 1662/3.

I writ to you yesterday by de Chapelles, who will tell you what a cruel cold I have got, which is now so general a disease here, after the breaking of the frost, that nobody escapes it. And though my cold be yet so ill as it might very well excuse my writing, I thought it necessary to let you know that the Queen, my mother, finds an absolute ease of the headache which she had all night, by being let blood this afternoon, and she finds so great benefit by it as I hope her cold will in two or three days be gone, especially if the weather continues so fair and warm as it is to-day. Excuse me that I say no more at this time, for really this little holding down my head makes it ache. . . .

X

Whitehall, April 20, 1663.

You must not by this post expect a long letter from me, this being James's[1] marriage day. And I am going to sup with them, where we intend to dance and see them a-bed together, but the ceremony shall stop there, for they are both too young to lie all night together.

The letters from France are not yet come, which keeps me in pain to know how Queen-mother[2] does. I hope James Hamilton will be on his way home before this comes to your hands.

I send you here the title of a little book of devotion in Spanish, which my wife desires to have. By the directions you will see where 'tis to be had, and pray send two of them by the first conveniency. My dearest sister, I am entirely yours.   c.

XI

Whitehall, April 27, 1663.

Hamilton came last night to town, and was so weary with his journey as he was not able to render me a full account of all

---

[1] James, Charles's eldest bastard by Lucy Walter, had been created Duke of Monmouth, and was married at the age of fourteen to the twelve-year-old heiress of the House of Buccleuch.

[2] Anne of Austria, who was dangerously ill.

141

that you commanded him.   Yet he hath said so much to me, in general, of the continuance of your kindness to me and the obligations I owe you, that I cannot tell how to express my acknowledgements for it.   I hope you believe I love you as much as 'tis possible.   I am sure I would venture all I have in the world to serve you, and have nothing so near my heart as how I may find occasions to express that tender passion I have for my dearest Minette. . . .

XII

Whitehall, May 11, 1663.

If I do not write to you so often as I would, it is not my *faute,* for most of my time is taken up with the business of the Parliament, in getting them to do what is best for us all, and keeping them from doing what they ought not to do.   And though I find by Hamilton, that there is great endeavours used in France to persuade all men there that this Parliament does mean me no good, yet you will see before they part that they will show their affections to me by helping me in my revenue.

I hope you have, before this, fully satisfied the King, my brother, of the sincerity of my desire to make a strict alliance with him, but I must deal freely with you in telling you that I do not think that his ambassador here, Monsieur de Comminges, is very forward in the business.   I cannot tell the reasons which makes him so, but he finds upon all occasions so many difficulties, as I cannot choose but conclude that we shall not be able to advance much in that matter with him.   Therefore I am hastening away my Lord Holles with all possible speed to let the King, my brother, see that there shall nothing rest, on my part, to the finishing that entire friendship I so much desire.   My wife sends for me just now to dance so I must end, and can only add that I am entirely yours.   c.

Once again in the summer of 1663 Charles, who had recalled his Declaration of Indulgence to please them, was forced to appeal to his faithful Commons for some adequate settlement of the revenue.

XIII.SPEECH TO THE HOUSE OF COMMONS

June 12, 1663.

Mr. Speaker, and you gentlemen of the House of Commons; I have sent for you this day to communicate with you, as good friends ought to do, when they discover the least jealousy growing which may lessen their confidence in each other. It is a freedom very necessary to be used between me and you : and you may all remember that when there was lately a little jealousy amongst you, upon somewhat I had said or done, I made all the haste I could to give you satisfaction; for which you all returned me your hearty thanks, and were, I think, satisfied.

Gentlemen, it is in no man's power, no, not in your own power, to make me suspect, or in the least degree imagine it possible that your affection or kindness is lessened or diminished towards me. I know very well that the people did never in any age use that vigilance and circumspection in the election of persons of known and tried affections to the Crown, of your good principles and unquestionable inclinations to the peace of the Church and the State, for their representatives in Parliament as they did when they chose you. You are the very same men who at your first coming together gave such signal testimonies of your affection and friendship to my person of your zeal for the honour and dignity of the Crown and liberal support of the Government. . . . You are the same men who, at your first meeting, by a wonderful and cheerful harmony and concurrence in whatsoever I could wish, gave me reputation abroad and security at home, made our neighbours solicitous for our friendship, and set a just value upon it. . . . And is it possible that the same persons can continue the same together without the same affection for me? I am sure it is impossible.

And yet, I must tell you, the reputation I had from your concurrence and tenderness towards me is not at all improved since the beginning of this session; indeed it is much lessened. And I am sure I never stood in more need of that reputation than·at present, to carry me through the many difficulties in which the public is at least concerned as much as myself. Let me and you think never so well of ourselves, if all the world knows or believes that we are poor, that we are in extremity of want, if our friends think we can do them no good or our enemies believe we can do them no harm, our condition is far from being prosperous. You cannot take it amiss (you shall use as much freedom with me) that I tell you there hath not appeared that warmth in you of late in the consideration of my revenue, as I expected. . . .

It hath been said to myself that it is usual for the Parliament to give the Crown extraordinary supplies upon emergent occasions, but not to improve the constant revenue of the Crown. I wish, and so do you, that nothing had lately been done in and by Parliaments but what is usual : but if ill Parliaments contrive the ruin and disinherison of the Crown, God forbid but good Parliaments should repay it, how unusual soever it is. If you yourselves had not in an extraordinary manner improved my revenue, the Government could not have been supported; and if it be not yet improved to the proportion you have designed, I cannot doubt but you will proceed in it with your old alacrity.

I am very well contented that you proceed in your inspection; I know it will be to my advantage, and that you will neither find my receipts so great, nor my expenses so exorbitant, as you imagine. And for an evidence of the last, I will give you an account of the issues of the twelve hundred thousand pounds you so liberally gave me : one penny whereof was not disposed but upon full deliberation with myself, and by my own order, and I think you will all say for the public service. But, gentlemen, this inquisition cannot be finished in the short time we can now conveniently stay together : and yet, if you do not provide before we part for the better paying and collecting what you have already given me, you can hardly presume what it will amount to. . . .

Believe me, gentlemen, the most disaffected subjects in England are not more unwilling to pay any tax or imposition you lay upon them than I am to receive it. God knows, I do not long more for any blessing in this world than that I may live to call a Parliament and not ask or receive any money from them; I will do all I can to see that happy day. I know the vast burdens the kingdom hath borne these last twenty years and more; that it is exceedingly impoverished : but, alas! what will that which is left do them good, if the Government cannot be supported; if I am not able to defray the charge that is necessary for their peace and security? I must deal plainly with you (and I do but discharge my conscience in that plainness), if you do not, besides the improving my revenue in the manner I have recommended to you, give me some present supply of money to enable me to struggle with those difficulties I am pressed with, I shall have a very melancholic summer. . . .

The Commons were more inclined to institute inquiries into public extravagance than to make the provision which could alone ensure a sound financial administration, but they voted the King four not very generous subsidies. In thanking them Charles promised to retrench the expenses of his Court, and orders, though not very effective ones, were duly issued for reducing salaries, pensions and tables.

XIV. SPEECH TO PARLIAMENT

July 27, 1663.

My Lords and Gentlemen : I thank you for the present you have made me this day; and I hope your countries will thank you when you come home for having done it. I am not conscious of having brought the straits and necessities I am in upon myself, by any improvidence or ill husbandry of my own : I know the contrary; and, I assure you, I would not have desired or received the supply you have now given me, if it were not absolutely necessary for your peace and quiet as well as mine. And, I must tell you, it will do me very little good, if I do not improve it by very good husbandry of my own, and by retrenching those very expenses which in many respects may be thought necessary enough. But you shall see, I will much rather impose upon myself than upon my subjects; and if all men will follow my example in retrenching their expenses, which (it may be) they may do with much more convenience than I can do mine, the kingdom will in a very short time gain what you have given me this day. . . .

. . . I shall not need to desire you to use all diligence in levying and collecting the subsidies you have given me; and heartily wish the distributions may be made with all equality and justice, and without any animosity or faction, or remembering anything that hath been done in the late ill times, which, you know, we are all obliged to forget as well as to forgive. And indeed, till we have done so, we can never be in perfect peace; and therefore I can never put you too much in mind of it.

I think it necessary to make this a session, that so the current of justice may run the two next terms without any obstruction by privilege of Parliament; and therefore I shall prorogue you till the 16th day of March, when I doubt not, by God's blessing, we shall meet again to our joint satisfaction, and that you shall have cause to thank me for what I do in the interval.

xv. To the Board of Greencloth
[Countersigned by Sir H. Bennet]

August 25, 1663.

Finding ourself necessitated to retrench all expenses as possibly we can, we have thought fit, for the better example to the rest, to begin with those of our household. Our will and pleasure therefore is, and we do hereby declare that from Michaelmas Day next following the date hereof there be a total suspension of all Diets, Chambermesses, Bouche of Court, Wages, Boardwages, Allowances of any kind whatsoever to any of our household servants, which we will and command you to signify in our name to all concerned therein. And to take care that no further provision be made from that time for our household, but so much as shall be necessary for the furnishing ten dishes a meal for our own and our dearest Consort the Queen's diet, six dishes a meal for the diet of our entirely beloved Cousin Prince Rupert, and seven dishes for the diet of the Maids of Honour, and for the providing of our household with fitting proportion of fire and candles, both above and below stairs. . . .

In the autumn of 1663 Charles made a royal progress into the west of England. A letter from Bath to Clarendon, resting at his pleasaunce at Cornbury, shows the King in holiday mood.

XVI. To Lord Chancellor Clarendon

Bath, September 8, 1663.

I did not think it necessary to answer yours till I could give
you certain information of the time my wife would stay here,
which I could not do till this day, it being the first time she has
made use of the bath. We intend then, God willing, to leave
this place on Monday next come sennight, and a' Tuesday to
be at Oxford, where we will dine with you at Cornbury the day
we come to Oxford, which I think sufficient trouble for you.
It would have been impossible for us to have lain there with
half the women we have, for you know the baggage and
baggages of an army is the troublesomest part of it. But when I
am at Oxford, I may from thence go thither and to Woodstock
as I please and make a train accordingly.

It is impossible for me to go to Worcester this time, for my
train is so absolutely nothing that I have no conveniency at all to
perform such a journey without robbing my wife of hers, so as
I must not think of that voyage till next year. I have directed
Sir Rob: Moray to write in to Scotland about my Lady Brent-
ford's business and you need not doubt but she will have full
satisfaction. My wife is very well pleased with the bath and
finds herself in very good temper after it, and I hope the effects
will be as she desires, and so God keep you.

*The holiday was followed by a dangerous illness of the
Queen's, during which Charles showed great tenderness for the
woman whom in other ways he had so much wronged. His
letters to his sister that autumn have several references to her
convalescence.*

XVII. To Madame

Whitehall, November 2, 1663.

I could not write more to you by Monsieur Catheux,[1] having
then the colic, which troubled me very much, but I thank God
'tis now perfectly over. And pray make my excuse to the King

[1] One of Louis's Gentlemen-in-Ordinary whom he had sent over to
inquire after Catherine.

of France and Monsieur, that I write to them in another hand, for, seriously, I was not able to make use of my own. . . .

. . . You will have heard of the unlucky accident that befell the French ambassador[1] at my Lord Mayor's feast. I was very much troubled at it. My Lord Mayor has been since with him to give him all imaginable satisfaction, and I hope he is now fully persuaded that it was a mere misfortune, without any further intent, though I must tell you that the ambassador is a man very hardly to be pleased, and loves to raise difficulties even in the easiest matters.

My wife is now out of all danger, though very weak, and it was a very strange fever, for she talked idly four or five days after the fever had left her. But now that is likewise past, and [she] desires me to make her compliments to you and Monsieur, which she will do herself as soon as she gets strength. And so, my dearest sister, I will trouble you no more at this time, but beg of you to love him who is entirely yours. c.

XVIII

Whitehall, November 20, 1663.

I shall say little to you by this bearer, le Chevalier de Clermont, because I will dispatch Monsieur d'Araquien in a day or two, only by way of advance, I thank you and Monsieur for the great part you take in the recovery of my wife. She mends very slowly, and continues still so weak as she cannot yet stand upon her legs, which is the reason that she does not thank you herself, but she does constantly desire me to do it both to you and Monsieur. And so, my dearest sister, farewell for this time.

XIX

December 10, 1663.

I have received yours, in which you take notice of the receipt of mine by the Marquis d'Araquien, and you shall see that I will be very punctual in writing to you every week. I am now

---

[1] The unpopular Comminges had arrived late at the Lord Mayor's Banquet on October 30th, and been offended because the company, who had begun dinner, had not risen to receive him.

dispatching the judges into Yorkshire, to try those rogues that had the late plot,[1] and I believe a good many of them will be hanged. And, to prevent all further mischief of that kind, I am in deliberation of raising two regiments of horse more, of 500 men apiece, the one to lie in the north, and the other in the west, which will, I doubt not, for the future, prevent all plotting.

My wife is now so well, as in a few days she will thank you herself for the concernment you had for her in her sickness. Yesterday, we had a little ball in the privy chamber, where she looked on, and, though we had many of our good faces absent, yet, I assure you, the assembly would not have been disliked for beauty, even at Paris itself, for we have a great many young women come up since you were here who are very handsome.

Pray send me some images, to put in prayer books. They are for my wife, who can get none here. I assure you it will be a great present to her, and she will look upon them often, for she is not only content to say the great office in the breviary every day, but likewise that of our Lady too, and this is besides going to chapel, where she makes use of none of these. I am just now going to see a new play, so I shall say no more. . . .

During the winter of 1663/4 Charles was still cultivating those closer relations with France that were for long to be the central, though secret, aim of his foreign policy. In this he relied increasingly on his sister, being little aided either by Comminges, the French ambassador, whom he distrusted, or by his official representative in Paris, the Presbyterian Lord Holles, who was anything but friendly to France and precipitated a crisis that December by an aggressive insistence on the right of his coach to take precedence over French Princes of the Blood. Charles supported his ambassador's pretensions so far as they affected the honour of England, but, as the following letters show, did his best through Madame to smooth the ruffled feelings of the French Court.

---

[1] The Farnley Wood rising in Yorkshire, one of the numerous minor plots of old republican soldiers and religious fanatics which constantly alarmed the Government during the early years of the Restoration.

xx. To Madame

December 28, 1663.

I did not write to you the last post, it being Christmas Eve, and I was preparing myself for my devotions, but I bade J.H.[1] make my excuse to you. Since which time, I have seen both your letter to the Queen, and my Lord Holles's to the secretary, concerning the pretension of the Princes of the Blood about my Lord Holles's entry. And truly I thought that I had found out a very fair expedient to avoid all dispute, in proposing that there might have been no entry at all, but that he might have gone directly to his audience, which, considering all former precedents, who are clearly on our side, ought not to be refused on the side of France. For I find, by the records of Sir Thomas Edmonds, my Lord Scudamore and the Earl of Leicester, who were all three ambassadors in France, the two latter being now alive, that it was clearly decided on their side. 'Tis true, that when the Princes of the Blood saw they could not get their point, they forbore sending their coaches, and I hope when the King my brother sees that it has been always the custom, that he will not insist to bring in a new method, which is so contrary to right and reason. I wonder very much that the Prince of Condé should say, that even I yielded the precedency to the King of Spain, and I thank you for holding up our right so handsomely as you did, for I assure you I am so far from that, that I will not yield it to any King whatsoever. . . .

. . . There is nobody desires more to have a strict friendship with the King of France than I do, but I will never buy it upon dishonourable terms. And I thank God my condition is not so ill but that I can stand upon my own legs, and believe that my friendship is as valuable to my neighbours as theirs is to me.

I have reason to believe that the French ambassador here is no great friend to this place, otherwise there had been much more advanced in the strict alliance with France than there is. I am certain his informations thither are not at all to our advantage, and now and then very far from the truth. I say this, that you may know that I have the same good inclination for a true

[1] James Hamilton.

150

friendship with the King there I ever had, and that it is not my
fault if it do not succeed, according to my inclinations and desire.
I think this letter is of a sufficient length, therefore I will conclude
with assuring you that I am entirely yours.   c.

XXI

January 4, 1663/4.

I have sent this post the extracts of the letters to my Lord
Holles, by which you will see how much reason I have to stand
upon the right my father had, touching the precedency of my
ambassador's coach before those of the Princes of the Blood there.
I do assure you I would not insist upon it, if I had not clearly the
right on my side, for there is nobody that hates disputes so much
as I do, and will never create new ones, especially with one whose
friendship I desire so much as that of the King of France.   But
on the other side, where I have reason, and when I am to yield
in a point by which I must go less than my predecessors have
done, I must confess that concerns me so much, as no friendship
shall make me consent unto. . . .

My wife thanks you for the care you have in sending her
les images.   We are both going to supper to my Lady Castlemaine's, so I have no time to add anything to this letter, but that
I am yours entirely.   c.

XXII

Whitehall, January 18, 1663/4.

I am very glad that I received yours of the 19th before that
which the Comte de Gramont[1] brought.   You see that I have
reason to insist upon a matter which is so clearly my right, and
whensoever I tell you anything which afterwards proves not to
be so, I must be very concerned myself, for I will never deceive
you.   But I will say no more on this subject, being confident
that the examples I sent will put an end to all dispute, and then
my Lord Holles will enter upon his negotiation, and proceed
with greater frankness and ingenuity than your ambassador does

---

[1] The hero of the *Memoirs*, who had just married the beautiful
Elizabeth Hamilton.

151

here, by which you will perceive that the delay has not lain on this side. And I cannot choose but tell you, between you and me, that this ambassador is good for nothing but to give malicious and wrong intelligence. . . .

My Lord Fitzhardinge[1] has acquainted me with your letter concerning Monsieur de Turennes' niece.[2] I think you believe that the relation she has to him would make me very glad to serve her upon any occasion, but I am afraid I shall not be able to do her the service I could wish, for I find the passion Love is very much out of fashion in this country, and that a handsome face without money has but few gallants upon the score of marriage.

My wife thanks you very kindly for the images you sent her; they are very fine ones, and she never saw such before. I have not had yet time to talk with the Comte de Gramont; he is so taken up with his wife, as I have scarce seen him these two days that he has been here. But that fury continues not long, and I believe he will be as reasonable in that point as most men are, and then I will give you a further account of our conversation. . . .

XXIII

Whitehall, 'Last of February,' 1663/4.

I was in great pain to hear of the fall you had, lest it might have done you prejudice, in the condition you are in,[3] but I was as glad to find by your letter that it had done you no harm. We have the same disease of Sermons that you complain of there, but I hope you have the same convenience that the rest of the family has, of sleeping out most of the time, which is a great ease to those who are bound to hear them.

I have little to trouble you with this post, only to tell you that I am now very busy every day in preparing business for the Parliament that meets a fortnight hence. Mr. Montagu has had the sciatique, but is now pretty well. I thank you for the care

[1] Charles Berkeley, Lord Fitzhardinge, Keeper of the Privy Purse, and one of Charles's closest friends.
[2] Charles was right: the young lady, Mademoiselle de Duvez, died a spinster.
[3] She was with child, and had twisted her ankle during a Court masque.

you have taken of the snuff; at the same time pray send me some wax to seal letters that has gold in it, the same you sealed your letters with before you were in mourning, for there is none to be got in this town. . . .

XXIV

Whitehall, March 17, 1663/4.

I did not write to you the last post, because I had so much business in order to the Parliament as I had no time.   This day I received a letter from my Lord Holles, in which he gives me an account of his audience, which I am very well satisfied with and his whole treatment there.   And pray let the King my brother know how well I am pleased with it, and that upon all occasions I will strive, if it be possible, to outdo him in kindness and friendship. He tells me, likewise, how much I am beholding to you in all his business, which I assure you I am very sensible of, and though it can add nothing to that entire kindness I had for you before, yet it gives me great joy and satisfaction to see the continuance of your kindness upon all occasions, which I will strive to deserve by all the endeavours of my life, as the thing in the world I value most.

The Queen showed me your letter about the operation done upon Mademoiselle Montausier, and by her smile, I believe she had no more guess at the meaning than you had at the writing of the letter.   I am confident that this will be the only operation of that kind that will be done in our age, for, as I have heard, most husbands had rather make use of a needle and thread than of a knife.   It may be you will understand this no more than what you writ in your own letter, but I do not doubt you will very easily get it to be explained without going to the Sorbonne.   Therefore I need add no more, but that I am entirely yours.   c.

Parliament reassembled on March 16, 1664.   Charles, in greeting the members, referred to the rising in the North of the previous year and to the continued inadequacy of his revenue. He also spoke of the attempts which were being made to dis-

credit the Cavalier Parliament by references to the old Triennial
Act, passed by the Long Parliament in 1641 to prevent long
intervals between successive Parliaments, and which ill-disposed
persons (the Opposition as we should say to-day) were now
maintaining meant that no Parliament could continue for more
than three years. The first business of the new session was
therefore to repeal the Act.

XXV. SPEECH TO PARLIAMENT

March 16, 1663/4.

My Lords and Gentlemen : You see, God be thanked, you
have met together again at the time appointed. And I do assure
you, I have been so far from ever intending it should have been
otherwise, that I do not know one person who ever wished it
should be otherwise. Think, therefore, I pray, what good meaning those men could have, who, from the time of the prorogation
to the day of your meeting, have continually whispered, and
industriously infused into the minds of the people, that the
Parliament should meet no more; that it should be presently dissolved; or so continued by prorogation, that they should be kept
without a Parliament. I pray, watch these whisperers all you
can, as men who use their utmost endeavours to sow jealousies
between you and me. And I do promise you, they shall not
prevail with me; and I do promise myself, they shall not prevail
with you. . . .

You may judge by the late treason in the North, for which
so many men have been executed, how active the spirits of many
of our old enemies still are, notwithstanding all our mercy. I
do assure you, we are not yet at the bottom of that business.
This much appears manifestly, that this conspiracy was but a
branch of that which I discovered as well as I could to you about
two years since, and had been then executed nearer-hand, if I had
not, by God's goodness, come to the knowledge of some of the
principal contrivers, and so secured them from doing the mischief
they intended. And if I had not, by the like providence, had
timely notice of the very hour and several places of their rendez-
vous in the North, and provided for them accordingly, by sending
some of my own troops, as well as by drawing the trained bands

together, their conjunction would have been in greater numbers than had been convenient. . . .

. . . I cannot omit, upon this occasion, to tell you, that these desperate men in their counsels (as appears by several examinations) have not been all of one mind in the ways of carrying on their wicked resolutions. Some would still insist upon the authority of the Long Parliament, of which, they say, they have members enough willing to meet; others have fancied to themselves, by some computation of their own upon some clause in the Triennial Bill, that this present Parliament was at an end some months since; and that, for want of new writs, they may assemble themselves and choose members of Parliament; and that is the best expedient to bring themselves together for their other purposes.

For the Long Parliament, you and I can do no more than we have done, to inform and compose the minds of all men. Let them proceed upon their peril. But methinks there is nothing done to disabuse them in respect of the Triennial Bill. I confess to you, my Lords and Gentlemen, I have often myself read over that Bill; and though there is no colour for the fancy of the determination of this Parliament, yet I will not deny to you that I have always expected that you would, and even wondered that you have not considered the wonderful clauses in that Bill, which passed in a time very uncareful for the dignity of the Crown, or the security of the people. I pray, Mr. Speaker, and you gentlemen of the House of Commons, give that Triennial Bill once a reading in your House; and then, in God's name, do what you think fit for me, and yourselves and the whole kingdom.

I need not tell you how much I love Parliaments. Never King was so much beholden to Parliaments as I have been; nor do I think the Crown can ever be happy without frequent Parliaments. But, assure yourselves, if I should think otherwise, I would never suffer a Parliament to come together by the means prescribed by that Bill. . . .

. . . I will conclude with desiring and conjuring you, my Lords and Gentlemen, to keep a very good correspondence together, that it may not be in the power of any seditious or factious spirits to make you jealous of me, till you see me pretend one thing and do another, which I am sure you never have yet done. Trust me, it shall be in nobody's power to make me jealous of you.

I pray contrive any good short Bills which may improve the industry of the nation. And since the season of the year will invite us all shortly to take the country air, I desire you would be ready for a session within two months or thereabouts; and we will meet next earlier in the year. And so God bless your councils.

XXVI. TO MADAME

Whitehall, March 24, 1663/4.

The Parliament has sat ever since Monday last, and if they continue as they have begun, which I hope they will, I shall have great reason to be very pleased with them. . . .

The House of Commons are now upon breaking that wild act of the Triennial Bill, which was made at the beginning of our troubles, and have this day voted it, so that now it wants nothing but putting it into form. The truth is, both Houses are in so good humour, as I do not doubt but to end this session very well.

By the letters I have received from my Lord Holles, he has, by this time, demanded commissioners to treat with him, and I hope that treaty will go on to all our satisfactions; I am sure there shall be nothing wanting, on my part, to bring it to a good conclusion.

My Lord Holles[1] writes such letters of you, as I am afraid he is in love with you, and they say his wife begins already to be jealous of you. You must excuse me, as long as the Parliament sits, if I miss now and then a post, for I have so much business as I am very often quite tired. . . .

---

[1] This was a good joke. Old Denzil Holles had been one of the Five Members whom Charles I had tried to arrest twenty-two years before, and was a particularly rigid Presbyterian.

XXVII. TO MADAME

Whitehall, March 28, 1664.

You may be sure that I would not have missed so many posts, but that I have been overlaid with business. . . .

The Bill passed this [day] in the House of Commons for the repeal of the Triennial Bill, and all things goes on in both Houses as I can wish. I am too much Madame de Châtillon's servant to tell her that I am glad that she is married into Germany.[1] If she knew the country, that's to say the way of living there, and the people, so well as I do, she would suffer very much in France before she would change countries. But this is now past, and I shall desire you to assure her that, upon any occasion that lies within my power, I shall ever be ready to serve Bablon.

I thank you for the wax to seal letters you sent me by de Chapelles. I desire to know whether it be the fashion in France for the women to make use of such a large size of wax, as the red piece you sent me. Our women here find the size a little extravagant, yet I believe when they shall know that 'tis the fashion there, they will be willing enough to submit to it. . . .

XXVIII. SPEECH TO PARLIAMENT UPON REPEALING THE TRIENNIAL ACT

April 5, 1664.

My Lords and Gentlemen : You will easily believe that I have come very willing to give my assent to this Bill. I do thank you very heartily for your so unanimous concurrence in it, and for desiring me speedily to finish it. And if I understand anything that concerns the peace and security of the kingdom, and the welfare of my subjects (all which I study more than my prerogative, and indeed I consider my prerogative only in order to preserving the other), every good Englishman will thank you for it. For the Act you have repealed could only serve to discredit Parliaments, and to make the Crown jealous of Parliaments, and Parliaments of the Crown, and persuade neighbour princes that England was not governed under a monarch. It could never have been the occasion of frequent Parliaments. I

---

[1] She had married the Duke of Mecklenburg-Schwerin.

do promise you, I will not be one hour the less without one for this Act of repeal, nor am I sure will you be the less kind to me in Parliament. . . .

XXIX. To Madame

Whitehall, May 19, 1664.

I have been all this afternoon playing the good husband, having been abroad with my wife, and 'tis now past twelve o'clock, and I am very sleepy. . . .

. . . I hope you will pardon me for having missed writing to you so many posts, but the truth is, I had very much business at the end of the Parliament, which hindered me. And I hope you will think my pains not ill employed, when I shall tell you that never any Parliament went away better pleased than this did. And I am sure that I have all the reason in the world to be well satisfied with them, and when they meet again, which will be in November, I make no doubt but that they will do all for me that I can wish. And so good night, for I am fast asleep.

In the spring of 1664 King and Parliament turned their attention from domestic to external affairs. On April 22 both Houses, after receiving a report from a Parliamentary Committee of Trade on the long accumulated injuries suffered by English traders at the hands of their Dutch rivals, had passed a resolution ' that the wrongs, dishonours and indignities done to His Majesty by the subjects of the United Provinces . . . are the greatest obstructions of . . . foreign trade,' and begged the King to obtain redress. The correspondence with Madame took a new turn. Her services had become of vital importance, for the Dutch in resisting the English claims depended on the support of their ally, France, and Charles looked to his sister to persuade Louis to substitute an English for a Dutch alliance.

XXX. To Madame

June 2, 1664.

This bearer has been so long resolving to leave this place, that I did not believe he would go, till I see now his boots are on, and he has taken his leave of me. And he gives me but a moment to write this letter, for 'tis not a quarter of an hour since he was losing his money at tennis, and he should have been gone two hours ago. I am afraid he comes very light to you, for though his wife has her load, I fear his purse is as empty, having lost very near five thousand pounds within these three months. . . .

Sir George Downing is come out of Holland, and I shall now be very busy upon that matter. The States keep a great bragging and noise, but I believe, when it comes to it, they will look twice before they leap. I never saw so great an appetite to a war as is, in both this town and country, especially in the Parliament men, who, I am confident, would pawn their estates to maintain a war. But all this shall not govern me, for I will look merely [to] what is just and best for the honour and good of England, and will be very steady in what I resolve, and if I be forced to a war, I shall be ready with as good ships and men as ever was seen, and leave the success to God.

I am just now going to dine at Somerset House with the Queen, and 'tis twelve o'clock, so as I can say no more. . . .

XXXI

June 20, 1664.

This bearer, Mr. Walters, being one of my servants, and having asked me leave to go into France to see the country, I would not let him kiss your hands without a letter.

I see you are as hot upon setting up an East India Company at Paris as we are here upon our Guinea trade. We are now sending eight ships thither, to the value of £50,000, and I have given them a convoy of a man-of-war, lest the Dutch in those parts might do them some harm in revenge for our taking the fort of Cape Verde,[1] which will be of great use to our trade. . . .

I hope it is but in a compliment to me, when you say my niece is so like me, for I never thought my face was even so much as intended for a beauty. I wish, with all my heart, I could see

---

[1] The English Royal Africa Company had recently struck at their Dutch rivals by employing Sir Robert Holmes and three battleships to capture Cape Verde. When the Dutch ambassador demanded restoration, Charles, pressing his subjects' own grievances against the Dutch, replied airily—" And pray what is Cape Verde?—a stinking place."

her, for at this distance I love her.   You may guess, therefore, if I were upon the place, what I should do!

I am very sorry that my Lord Holles continues those kind of humours; I have renewed, by every post, my directions upon it, and have commanded him to proceed in his business and not to insist upon trifles.   I am newly returned from seeing some of my ships, which lie in the Hope, ready to go to sea, and the wind has made my head ache so much as I can write no longer. Therefore I can say no more but that I am yours.   c.

In the midst of his negotiations with the Dutch, Charles found time to gratify his old Governor, Lord Newcastle, with a Dukedom.

XXXII. To the Marquis of Newcastle

June 7, 1664.

I have received yours by your son and am resolved to grant your request.   Send me therefore word what title you desire to have, or whether you will choose to keep your old and leave the rest to me.   I do not tell you I will dispatch it to-morrow; you must leave the time to me, to accommodate it to some other ends of mine; but the differing it shall not be long, nor with any circumstance that shall trouble you.   I am glad you enjoy your health, for I love you very well. . . .

XXXIII. To Madame

Whitehall, June 27, 1664.

The last letter I writ to you, I had so great a pain in my head as I could not make an end of my letter.   I did intend to have told you then of the Holland ambassador's being arrived here; he had two private audiences before his public one.   If his masters be but as apprehensive of a war with us as he in his discourse seems to be, I may expect to have very good conditions from them, and I have reason to believe by the letter they writ to me, their fears are no less at home.   For, after taking great pains to assure me of the great affection they have for me, they desire by all means that I will not let my ships, which I am preparing, go out to sea, lest, by the indiscretion of some of the captains, the quarrel might be begun.   And they promise me that they will not send out more men-of-war but such as are of absolute necessity to look to the East India fleet and fishermen, and they desire me that I would likewise give it under my hand that those ships which I set out may not fight with theirs.

You may guess, by such a simple proposition, whether these people are not afraid!   I have made no other answer to all this, but that I do intend, very speedily, to dispatch Sir George Downing to Holland, and by him they shall have a return of all this. . . .

I do not doubt but your weather there is as hot as ours here; nobody can stir anywhere but by water, it is so very hot and dusty.   I am just now called away by very good company to sup upon the water, so I can say no more but I am entirely yours.

C.

XXXIV

Whitehall, July 14, 1664.

My fever[1] had so newly left me, and my head was so giddy, as I could not write to you on Monday last, to tell you the extreme joy I have at your being safely brought to bed of a son.   I assure nothing could be more welcome to me, knowing the satisfaction it must be to you, and all your concerns shall ever be next my heart.   I thank God I am now perfectly quit of my fever, though my strength is not fully come to me again, for I was twice let blood, and in eight days ate nothing but water-gruel, and had a great sweat, that lasted me almost two days and two nights. You may easily believe that all this will make me a little weak!

I am now sending Sir George Downing into Holland to make my demands there.   They have never yet given me any satisfaction for all the injuries their subjects have done mine, only given good words and nothing else, which now will not be sufficient, for I will have full satisfaction, one way or other. We have six East India ships arrived here this week, which bring us news of a great loss the Hollanders have received there, three

---

[1] At the beginning of July Charles had been laid low with a feverish cold, caught while returning from a visit down the river to the Fleet.

of their ships, which trade to Japan, being cast away, whereof two richly laden, and besides this, they had sent twenty-four sail upon some design in China, who are all blocked up in a river in that country so as they cannot escape. This will cool the courage of the East India Company at Amsterdam, who are yet very impertinent.

I am just now come from seeing a new ill play, and it is almost midnight, which is a fair hour for a sick man to think of going to bed, and so, good night.

XXXV

Whitehall, July 22, 1664.

The Queen showed me yesterday your long letter, in which I perceive you have been very ill-used, but I am very glad to find that the King is so kind and just to you. I did not think it possible that some persons could have had so ill a part in that matter, as I see they have had by your letter. I shall have by this a better opinion of my devotion for the time to come, for I am of those bigots who think that malice is a much greater sin than a poor frailty of nature. . . .

I will say no more to you at present, because I shall write more at large to you by J. Hamilton, only again I must give you joy for your son. c.

XXXVI

August 23, 1664.

I told you in my two last that I would write to you more at large upon the subject of your two letters by the Comte de Gramont and James Hamilton. The truth is, I am sorry to see you believe that the fault is on our side, that the alliance with France is not further advanced. 'Tis true there has been very unlucky accidents which have fallen out, that have retarded it, as the dispute with the Princes of the Blood at my ambassador's entry, and, since that, others of the like nature. But if the ambassadors on both sides have had the misfortune to render themselves unacceptable where they negotiate, why must it be thought their masters' fault? For I assure you, if I had made that the rule, I must have long since concluded that France had very little inclination to advance in the treaty.   But you shall see now that my Lord Holles will go on very roundly in the matter, so as there shall be no neglect on our part, and when the general treaty is concluded, it will be then the proper time to enter upon the particular one, of that kindness and friendship which I have always desired there should be between the King, my brother, and myself.

But, now that I am upon this matter, I must deal freely with you, and tell you that nothing can hinder this good alliance and friendship which I speak of, but the King, my brother's, giving the Hollanders some countenance in the dispute there is between us.   For I assure you, they brag very much already of his friendship, and it may be they would not be so insolent as they are, if they had not some such hopes.

My Lord Holles will give you a true state of that business, wherein you will find how much the Hollanders are in the wrong. I mean the two Companies of the East and West India, against whom my complaints are, and the States hitherto have given them more countenance and assistance than they ought to have done.   I must confess I would be very glad to know what I may expect from France, in case the Hollanders should refuse me all sort of reason and justice, for upon that, I must take my measures accordingly.

I am very glad that the King, my brother, is so kind to you. There can be nobody so fit to make a good correspondent and friendship between us as yourself.   I take the occasion of this safe messenger to tell you this because I would not have this business pass through other hands than yours.   And I would be very willing to have your opinion and counsel how I shall proceed in this matter.   I do not doubt but you will have that care of me that I ought to expect from your kindness, and as you are an Exeter woman.   And if you are not fully informed of all things as you complain of in your letters, it is your own fault, for I have been a very exact correspondent and have constantly answered all your letters.   And I have directed my Lord Holles to give a full account of our dispute with Holland, if you will have the patience to hear it.

I shall sum up all, in telling you that I desire very much to have a strict friendship with France, but I expect to find my account in it, as 'tis as reasonable that they should find theirs. And so I shall make an end of this long letter, by assuring you that I am entirely yours. c.

XXXVII

Whitehall, September 19, 1664.

I am very glad to find you are satisfied with my long letter. I do assure you I will ever behave myself so in all that concerns a good intelligence with France as you shall be satisfied with me. But when I have said this I expect the same forwardness on their side, and that I may find the effects of those good words you mention. If the King my brother desires to have a strict friendship with me there is nobody so proper to make it as yourself. And I am sure I will put all my interest into your hands, and then you shall be the judge who desires most the good alliance.

I received just now my letters out of Holland by which I find they make all the haste they can to get out their fleet for Guinea, and I am using all diligence to put Prince Rupert in a condition to follow them in case they go. And as they have always hitherto made the first step in their preparations for war, so I am resolved they shall now send first, that all the world may see I do not desire to begin with them, and that if there comes any mischief by it, they have drawn it upon their own heads. The truth is they have no great need to provoke this nation, for except myself I believe there is scarce an Englishman that does not desire passionately a war with them.

I do expect with impatience to hear something from you upon the subject of my long letter that I may know what I may depend upon. I am confident the conjuncture will be such before it be long wherein I may be useful to France. And I tell you freely I had much rather make my friendships where you are, and with those I know, than with others, but it will be impossible for this nation to be idle when they see their neighbours busy, and I cannot deny to you it agrees with my humour likewise. I write thus freely to you that you may know the truth, for I assure you I consider your interest in it, and so my dearest sister good night for 'tis late. c.

XXXVIII

Whitehall, October 3, 1664.

I have received yours of the 7th from Vincennes but just this moment as the post is going away and therefore can say nothing to you now, the paper in your letter referring to a treaty[1] which I never saw, it being made when I was Prince of Wales, and at a great distance from the King my father. I shall immediately look out for that treaty, but for fear I shall not be able to find a copy of it here, it being made in a disorderly time, pray get a copy of it and send it immediately hither, so that there may be no time lost. In the meantime I shall only add that I am very glad to see the King my brother so ready to make a good friendship with me, and pray assure him that nothing can be more welcome to me than a strict friendship between us. I have no more time left me only to assure you that I am entirely yours. c.

XXXIX

Whitehall, October 17, 1664.

I have deferred this long to answer yours, that I might as well do it, to your satisfaction as my own, for being very well satisfied with the King, my brother's, expressions of kindness, I was very willing to find that the method proposed by him would with most expedition have brought us to the end we both desire. I do in the first place desire you to use your interest and credit to remove all jealousies of any change in me, or that I am less warm in my inclinations towards a firm friendship with France, than I have professed to be. Those apprehensions will in the end be found to be without ground, and if I were naturally inclined to suspicion I have more cause to believe the change may be there. I do assure you, there is nothing more in my wish and endeavour than that this present treaty may be finished, that we

---

[1] A project for an Anglo-French treaty discussed in 1644.

may the better and the sooner and with less noise think of a more strict and useful friendship.

I called for the treaty of 1610 (which, in the confusion the late time hath cast all our papers, could not be presently found), and have perused it myself and by myself, and find the whole so unapplicable to this conjuncture, and that in truth scarce any article of it hath ever been observed on either side, and that the whole traffic and commerce (which is quite another thing from what it was then) is referred to former treaties, the copies where-of are lost, or cannot yet be found, that much more time must inevitably be spent in making that treaty intelligible and practical than will serve to finish this, which, in my opinion, having been so lately, can take up very little time before it be again concluded. And if my Lord Holles (who upon my credit is very well affected to this work in hand, and heartily desires a very fast friendship between us, though in matters relating to himself he may possibly be formal and punctual enough) hath made any unseasonable addition to what he proposed at first, the King may reject it, what I desire being no more than that the Dutch may not enjoy any privileges in France, which shall be denied to my subjects, which is a preference I am sure the King will never give to them.

In a word, it is in the King, my brother's, power to have what kind of correspondence, or what kind of friendship he will with me, and if I do understand his or my own interest and designs, a very fast friendship is good and necessary for us both. And it cannot but be a manifestation to him of the sincerity of my intentions, that I engage you to undertake for it, which I would not do, if they were otherwise. I have written my heart to you, which I will not undertake to do so in French, but you may have this translated, and so, my dearest sister, I am yours.

C.

Since the writing of this, I have received yours of the 21st, with a copy of the treaty of 1610, the same I mention to have read here, with the *procès-verbal* of the ceremonies passed at my Lord Goring's swearing this, and all other treaties then subsisting between France and us, which, as I have said, cannot come home to the present case now before us. This makes me still remain in the conclusion that we must lay for a foundation the project my Lord Holles hath now given in, and add to it other private articles of mutual defence and succour as may be easily agreed upon between us. And this will not be a work of much time, if our minds be according to our professions, and so I am yours.

C.

Pray let Le Nôtre[1] go on with the model, and only tell him this addition, that I can bring water to the top of the hill, so that he may add much to the beauty of the descent by a cascade of water.

XL

Whitehall, October 23, 1664.

I hope you will be well satisfied with the last letter I writ to you, for in it I said nothing but what came from my heart, and as I then told you, I do now again, that if I did not intend what I write I would not address it to you. The Comte de Gramont will give you this, and he will tell you how kind I am to you. I pray be kind to him, and to his wife, for my sake, and if at any time there be an occasion to send hither one of his talent, there is nobody will be more welcome to me than him. I will say no more to you now, because this letter will be long upon the way, only again recommend them both to your protection. . . .

XLI

Whitehall, October 24, 1664.

I writ to you yesterday, by the Comte de Gramont, but I believe this letter will come sooner to your hands, for he goes by the way of Dieppe with his wife and family, and now that I have named her, I cannot choose but again desire you to be kind to her, for besides the merit her family has on both sides, she is as good a creature as ever lived. I believe she will pass for a handsome woman in France, though she has not yet, since her lying in, recovered that good shape she had before, and I am afraid never will. . . .

[1] The great landscape gardener.

Poor O'Neill[1] died this afternoon of an ulcer in his guts. He was as honest a man as ever lived. I am sure I have lost a very good servant by it. I have nothing to say more to you, upon our public business, till I have an answer from you, of my last letter by the post; only that I expect with impatiency to know your minds there, and then you shall find me as forward to a strict friendship with the King, my brother, as you can wish.

You will have heard of our taking of New Amsterdam,[2] which lies just by New England. 'Tis a place of great importance to trade, and a very good town. It did belong to England heretofore, but the Dutch by degrees drove our people out of it and built a very good town, but we have got the better of it, and 'tis now called New York. . . .

In October the Fleet was ordered to sea under Prince Rupert, the King himself taking the closest personal interest in all the arrangements for equipping the ships, and at the beginning of November orders were given to the Duke of York, the Lord High Admiral, to hoist his flag at Portsmouth.

XLII. To Prince Rupert

October 27, 1664

As soon as Will Legge showed me your letter of the accident in your head, I immediately sent Choquen to you in so much haste as I had not time to write by him; but now I conjure you, if you have any kindness for me, have a care of your health, and do not neglect yourself, for which I am so much concerned.

I am very glad to hear your ships sail so well. I was yesterday to see the new ship at Woolwich launched,[3] and I think when you see her (which I hope you will do very quickly under Sir J. Lawson[4]) you will say she is the finest ship

---

[1] Daniel O'Neill, the Postmaster-General, a faithful servant of long standing, who had married Mary of Orange's lady-in-waiting, Lady Stanhope, in the old days of exile.

[2] Rechristened New York after the King's brother. It had surrendered to the Duke of York's agent, Governor Nicholls of Massachusetts, on August 29, 1664.

[3] The *Royal Catherine*. There is a very amusing account of the launching from the pen of De Comminges, the French ambassador, who became very sea-sick, and another from that of Pepys.

[4] The Vice-Admiral.

that has yet been built. The *Charles, James, Henry,* and some others, are already in the Hope, and men begin to come in reasonably fast. But to make the more speed, yesterday in council I ordered there should be an embargo of all things till the fleet were manned. There are one thousand men ready to come out of Scotland and the North, which I hope this N.W. wind will quickly bring. I write to you without ceremony, and pray do the like to me, for we are too good friends to use any. I must again beg you to have a care of your health. . . .

XLIII. To the Duke of York

November ? 1664.

Reflecting upon the many injuries and wrongs done to our subjects as well in as out of Europe by our neighbours of the United Provinces . . . we have caused to be made ready a Fleet, whereon at your instant desire we are consented that you embark yourself. . . . And for your further instruction, we have thought fit to direct, authorize and empower you that uniting, ordering and conducting our said Fleet, as shall seem best to your wisdom, you in the first place (if you find yourself in a condition to do it) endeavour to stop and hinder the Fleet or Fleets of the United Provinces of what quality soever from passing our Channel; and in case any of them shall attempt to pass, that you endeavour to seize them. And if they shall resist you, that you fight, burn, smoke and destroy them. And next that you order all Captains and Commanders of any ships in our service to seize and detain all ships and vessels whatsoever belonging to the States or subjects of the United Provinces; which ships and vessels they shall cause to be brought into some of our ports, there to be reserved without embezzling the goods, or injury to the persons, till we shall order the further disposal of them. And so praying to God to preserve you, and to give you good success herein, we bid you most heartily farewell.

On November 24 Charles appealed to Parliament for money to prosecute a naval war, should the Dutch, whose actions were becoming increasingly hostile, refuse his terms. Two and a half millions were enthusiastically voted, a sum which seemed vast at

*the time but which subsequent events were to prove altogether
inadequate for maintaining the largest fleet the country had ever
set out.*

XLIV. TO MADAME

Whitehall, November 21, 1664.

The Parliament being to meet on Thursday next, gives me
so much business to put all things in a good way at their first
coming together, as I have only time to tell you that C. Berkeley
arrived here late last night; so as yet I have not had full time to
receive an account of the success of his negotiation.   I shall only
tell you now the great satisfaction I receive in the obliging
reception he had from the King, my brother, which I am sure
I will return with all imaginable kindness, and I hope there will
not be many steps more before the entire friendship be made
between us.

Pray tell Monsieur I am as sensible of his friendship and
kindness as I ought to be, but that I have not now time to tell
it him in writing till the next post.   For yourself, I am too much
obliged to you to say anything of it in so short a letter, nor
indeed can I ever deserve it from you.   You have my heart,
and I cannot give you more.

XLV. SPEECH TO PARLIAMENT

November 24, 1664.

My Lords and Gentlemen : When we parted last in this place,
I told you that I did not think we should meet here again till
November. . . . But I must now tell you, that if I could have
suspected . . . that our neighbours would have dealt so un-
neighbourly with me, and have forced me to make such
preparations as they have done for my defence at so vast an
expense . . . I should not have prevented your coming together
then.   Yet truly I have reason even to be glad that it hath been
deferred thus long.   You have had leisure to attend your own
conveniences in the country and the public service there; and I
have been able to let our neighbours see that I can defend myself
and my subjects against their insolence upon the stock of my

own credit and reputation; and that, when I find it necessary for the good of my people, I can set out a fleet to sea which will not decline meeting with all their naval power, even before the Parliament comes together. . . .

I will not deny to you, I have done more than I thought I could have done; which I impute to the credit your vote gave me, and to the opinion all men have, that I did what you wished I should do. By borrowing very liberally from myself out of my own stores, and by the kind and cheerful assistance the city of London hath given me, I have a fleet now at sea worthy of the English nation, and (to say no more) not inferior to any that hath been set out in any age, and which . . . to discharge to-morrow, and replenish all my stores, I am persuaded, would cost me little less than £800,000.

What hath passed between me and the Dutch, and by what degrees, accidents, and provocations, I have been necessitated to the preparation and expense I have made, you shall be told when I have done. I shall only tell you, that if I had proceeded more slowly, I should have exposed my own honour and the honour of the nation, and should have seemed not confident of your affections, and the assurance you gave me to stand by me in this occasion. That which I am now very earnestly to desire, and indeed expect from you, is, that you will use all possible expedition in your resolutions; lest that, by unnecessary formalities, the world should think that I have not your full con-currence in what is done, and that you are not forward enough in the support of it; which I am sure you will be, and that, in raising the supplies, you take such sure order that when the expense is obvious and certain, the supplies be as real and sub-stantial, not imaginary as the last subsidies were, which you all well enough understand.

Master Speaker, and you gentlemen of the House of Com-mons: I know not whether it be worth my pains to endeavour to remove a vile jealousy, which some ill men scatter abroad, and which I am sure will never sink into the breast of any man who is worthy to sit upon your benches, that, when you have given me a noble and proportionable supply for the support of a war, I may be induced by some evil counsellors

. . . to make a sudden peace and get all that money for my own private occasions. I am sure you all think it an unworthy jealousy, and not to deserve an answer.

I would not be thought to have so brutish an inclination as to love war for war-sake. God knows, I desire no blessing in this world so much as that I may live to see a firm peace between all Christian princes and states : but let me tell you . . . that when I am compelled to enter into a war for the protection, honour, and benefit of my subjects, I will (God willing) not make a peace but upon the obtaining and securing those ends for which the war is entered into; and when that can be done, no good man will be sorry for the determination of it. To conclude : my Lords and Gentlemen, I conjure you all, in your several stations, to use all possible expedition, that our friends and enemies may see that I am possessed of your hearts, and that we move with one soul. And I am sure you will not deceive my expectation.

Despite his preparations Charles still hoped that the Dutch would yield to his terms when they realized war must otherwise follow, and had every confidence that Louis would prefer his friendship to an unprofitable alliance with Holland. To this end the correspondence with Madame continued, although the Channel was blazing with fights between English cruisers and home-coming Dutch merchantmen and every shipbuilding yard in Holland was hard at work.

XLVI. To Madame

Whitehall, December 15, 1664.

I wish very much that the treaty of commerce were finished, that then we might enter into that of the strict alliance which I am very impatient of, for I assure you my own inclination carries me to it, and I am confident we shall find both our accounts in it. And I believe my friendship to France is and will be more considerable than that of the Hollanders in many respects, and you may have it, if you will.

The House of Commons hath this day settled the several rates upon the counties for the raising of the five-and-twenty hundred thousand pounds, and there is a Bill preparing for that purpose, so as that matter is as good as done. Since my last to you, we have taken many more Dutch ships; the truth is, hardly any escapes us that pass through the Channel. I believe we have taken already above fourscore, and every day there comes in more. They brag very much that they will eat us up in the spring, and so they did some two months ago, but as yet we are all alive. By the letters from Paris, I perceive that the blazing star[1] hath been seen there likewise. I hope it will have the same effect here as that in Germany had, and then we shall beat our neighbour Turks, as well as they beat theirs. . . .

XLVII. TO MADAME

Whitehall, December 26, 1664.

. . . I send you here a printed paper, which will clearly inform you of the state of the quarrel between me and Holland, by which you will see that they are the aggressors and the breakers of the peace, and not we. I pray read it with care that you may be fully instructed, for I do not doubt but Van Beuninghen[2] will use all sorts of arts to make us seem the aggressors, and I would be glad that you might be able to answer anything that may be objected in that matter.

We have seen here the Comet, but the weather has been so cloudy, as I never saw it but once. It was very low and had a tail that stood upwards; it is now above twelve days since I saw it. But upon Christmas Eve and the night before, there was another seen very much higher than the former. I saw it both nights and it looks much lesser than the first, but none of the astronomers can tell whether it be a new one or the old one grown less and got up higher, but all conclude it to be no ordinary star. Pray inquire of the skilful men, and let me know whether it has been seen at Paris. This new one was seen here, the 23rd and 24th of this month, old style, and had a little tail which stood north-east. I have no more to trouble you with, but that I am yours. c.

---

[1] The famous comet which was seen universally that Christmas.
[2] The Dutch ambassador at the French Court.

XLVIII

Whitehall, January 5, 1664/5.

I have little to say to you at this time, expecting that the Treaty of Commerce will be finished, that then we might enter upon the strict alliance. I perceive that Van Beuninghen does use all possible arts and tricks to make me appear the aggressor, but if you have read over the printed paper I sent you, you will clearly find the contrary, and that 'tis the Dutch hath begun with us, which now plainly appears by what de Ruyter hath done in Guinea. And I am sure there is nothing in the King of France's treaty that obliges him to second them, if they be the attackers, so that except he has a mind to help them, he is in no ways obliged to it by treaty. For, by the Treaty, he is only to defend them in case they be attacked, and they are now the attackers, so that we only defend ourselves.

I say this to you, because the ambassador here came to me by order from his master, and said many things to me, from him, upon the subject of Holland, a little too pressing, and not in the style Charles Berkeley was spoken to in that matter when he was there. And I cannot choose but observe that Monsieur de Comminges is much more eloquent when there is anything to be said that looks not so kind towards me, than when there is any kindness to be expressed.

I wish with all my heart that there were a good occasion for Charles Berkeley to make another voyage to you, for my inclinations are to give my friendship to France. But if that cannot be had, I am not so inconsiderable but that I can make very considerable friendships elsewhere. The truth of it is I am pressed at this time very much, and am offered very advantageous conditions, but I prefer the friendship with France in the first place, in case I can have it. And I assure you one of the great reasons why I do so, is because you are there. I write all this only to yourself, though you may make what use of it you please, so as you do not use my name, for I would not be thought to seek anybody's friendship who is not ready to meet me half-way.

The weather is so cold as I can hardly hold a pen in my

hand, which you may perceive by my scribbling, and I am afraid you will hardly read this letter. . . .

XLIX

Whitehall, January 12, 1664/5.

. . . Monsieur de Comminges was with me again yesterday, to press me concerning the business of Holland. And I told him I would not fail to give the King, my brother, the true state of that matter, and that my ambassador there had already given Monsieur de Lionne those papers, which would clearly make it appear that the Dutch were the aggressors, which now is evident by what de Ruyter hath done in Guinea, who had his orders to take our ships before we had so much as the least stop of any of their ships. And you may tell the King, my brother, that I will let him know what my pretensions are, that Van Beuninghen may not have the least pretence to say that I desire war for war's sake, for I know that he does use all sorts of arts to make me the aggressor, and does not stick to affirm matters of fact which are not true, and which will be proved to be so. I am sure, if I can have what is just and reasonable, I shall not desire the effusion of blood, nor wish to run the hazard of a war, though I may say that, reasonably speaking, the advantage lies on our side for many reasons which are visible enough.

The Dutch ambassador did yesterday in discourse with me say that de Ruyter had orders from the States to go for Guinea, which he never acknowledged before, and I believe it came out before he thought of it. I have put Holmes into the Tower for his taking of Cape Verde without orders, and I am certain they can have no pretence that we have done anything like an act of hostility but that, and that was done by a private captain without authority, and there was a particular article in the treaty in case of such accidents, which the Dutch have absolutely broken, by sending de Ruyter thither, and providing another fleet which was to have followed if they durst have come out. In fine, I do not doubt, but to make it evident to the King, my brother, that he is in no way obliged to favour them, they being the attackers, and if there be any kindness to be shown, I hope I may reasonably expect it before those who used France so unworthily in the treaty at Munster.   You may make what use you think fit of this letter to the King, my brother, and I will as soon as I can let him know what in justice I expect from the Dutch. . . .

L

Whitehall, January 19, 1664/5.

I have received yours of the 20th and you have reason to wonder that you have been so long without hearing from me, but I have had nothing to say.   And it has been so cold here, as it did not invite one to write. . . . I shall not say much to you now, because Ruvigny[1] will be dispatched in two or three days, and by him you shall hear at large from me.

Only I cannot choose but observe to you now, that I see that Monsieur Comminges does me all good offices there, by foretelling my intentions in as ill a sense as he uses to do.   My Lord Holles writes something to me about my giving commissions to the City of Bremen, which the King, my brother, says he will be satisfied in before he goes on with our treaty, which is so great a dream to me as I know not from whence this fancy proceeds except it be from Monsieur de Comminges, who, I am confident, you will find in the end hath done me as many ill offices as it hath lain in his power to do.   And I do wonder that after all the advances I made by C. Berkeley, I should find the treaty go on slower than it did, my Lord Holles having received not yet an answer to his last paper, which is now almost two months ago.   After all this, when Ruvigny returns, you shall find my mind not changed, but that I will be as sincere in that matter as I promised you to be, and if there be anything altered in my condition, since we first talked of this matter, it is for the better.   And so good night for 'tis late.   c.

LI

Whitehall, January 22, 1664/5.

In my last, I told you that I would not enlarge myself upon the matters between me and the King, my brother, till the

___

[1] Henri de Massué, Marquis de Ruvigny, who had been sent to England by Louis to explain the nature of his commitments to Holland.

return of Ruvigny, to whom I have now fully opened my mind in all particulars, which I would not do to Monsieur de Comminges, because I am most confident, by all the observations I can make, he does not desire there should be a good correspondence between us. And if the advances I now make have not the success I wish, I must conclude there is no inclination to have a friendship with me. I shall not enlarge myself upon the particulars because Ruvigny will do it better by word of mouth, to whom I refer you.

Since the loss of my two ships at Gibraltar, I have had some good fortune to recompense it, for Captain Allen, with but seven of my ships, hath met hard by Cadiz the Dutch Smyrna fleet of thirty ships, has taken three of them and sunk two. And if the weather had not been very bad, they would not have escaped so well. I do not yet know of what value the ships are which are taken, but they write from Holland that that which is sunk was worth one hundred thousand pounds; and if their Admiral had not been so very near the Port, he had been sunk likewise, for he got in with seven foot water in hold. They behaved themselves very poorly, for they had four men-of-war to convoy them and many of their merchants had thirty guns apiece, which might have made good resistance if their hearts had not failed them, and two of our seven had but twenty-four guns apiece.

I will not trouble you more at this time, only expect a return from Ruvigny with impatience. I am entirely yours. c.

LII

Whitehall, February 9, 1664/5.

I must, in the first place, ask your pardon for having missed so many posts. The truth of it is, what between business and the little masquerades we have had, and besides the little business I had to write, with the help of the cold weather, I did not think it worth your trouble and my own to freeze my fingers for nothing, having said all to Ruvigny that was upon my heart. I am very glad to find by yours that you are so well satisfied with what he brings. It lies wholly on your part now to answer the advances I have made, and if all be not as you wish, the fault is not on my side.

I was this morning at the Parliament house, to pass the Bill for the five-and-twenty hundred thousand pounds, and the commissioners are going into their several countries, for the raising of it according to the Act. We are using all possible diligence in the setting out the fleet for the spring. My Lord Sandwich set sail two days since, with eighteen good ships, to seek out a squadron of the Dutch fleet, which we hear was seen upon the north coast of England. And if he has the good fortune to meet with them, I hope he will give a good account of them.

I am very glad to hear that your indisposition of health is turned into a great belly. I hope you will have better luck with it than the Duchess[1] here had, who was brought to bed, Monday last, of a girl. One part I shall wish you to have, which is that you may have as easy a labour, for she dispatched her business in little more than an hour. I am afraid your shape is not so advantageously made for that convenience as hers is; however, a boy will recompense two grunts more, and so good night, for fear I fall into natural philosophy before I think of it. . . .

LIII

Whitehall, February 27, 1664/5.

I am sorry that my Lord Holles has asked justice upon a point of honour[2] that I should never have thought of. You know the old saying in England, the more a T— is stirred, the more it stinks, and I do not care a T— for anything a Dutchman says of me. And so I think you have enough upon this cleanly subject, which nothing but a stinking Dutchman could have been the cause of. But pray thank the King, my brother, and desire him not to take any kind of notice of it, for such idle discourses are not worth his anger or mine. I have been all this day at Hampton Court, and it is so long since I have been on horseback, as with this small day's journey I am weary enough to beg your pardon if I say no more now. . . .

---

[1] The Duchess of York. This daughter was in later years to become Queen Anne.

[2] A Dutchman's foul-mouthed insult in a Bordeaux street.

LIV

Whitehall, March 26, 1665.

There is no such thing as that news you heard of Guinea.[1] At first it looked like truth, for a seaman, pretending to be a Swede, came to me, and made a very particular relation of it, and afterwards took his oath of it before the Admiralty. But upon some contradictions he gave himself in examining, we found him to be a Dutchman, who thought by this invention to get some money, but at last he was found out, and has been whipped through Cheapside for his perjury.

I could wish that what you write to me, concerning the treatment of some French seamen by ours, were as false. I have received a memorial this day about it from the French ambassador, and have given orders that, if it be found to be true, it be severely punished. I do assure you I am extremely troubled at it, there shall (be) very severe justice done. I am going to Portsmouth to-morrow, for four or five days, for the ordering of some things there, and have no more time left me now, only to assure you that I am entirely yours. c.

War was declared officially between England and the United Provinces before the spring. Negotiations between England and France, however, still continued, a special French Embassy—the célèbre Ambassade Extraordinaire—reaching London in April to try and compose the differences between the two nations. But the rival fleets, after the winter storms, were once more at sea. By the end of May a fleet action was imminent.

LV. TO MADAME

Whitehall, May 29, 1665.

By the time this letter comes to your hands, I believe Monsieur d'Humières[2] will be with you, and I pray be kind to him upon my score, for I take him to be very much my friend, and as

[1] An example of Charles's sense of justice. The usual rumours of atrocities started by both combatants at the beginning of a war were being circulated, and false tales of horrible cruelties done to Englishmen by the Dutch in Guinea had reached London.

[2] The Maréchal d'Humières, who had just visited England.

worthy a man as I do know. He will inform you how all things are here. And I do not give him this commendation upon an ordinary score of civility, but upon the confidence of his being as good a friend where he applies himself as ever lived, which, in this age, is no little virtue, there being so few persons in the world worth a friendship. And I will answer for him that he will not make me ashamed of the good opinion I have of him. He expresses to me, upon all occasions, how much he is your servant, for which you may easily believe I do not love him the less, and I am confident you cannot find a man in all France worthier of your good opinion and trust than himself.

The ambassadors have given me this day propositions in writing from the Hollanders, in order to the composing of the differences now between us. I have not yet had time to consider them and to make answer to them, but I hope in a few days my brother will meet with their fleet and make them much more reasonable than they are at present. I have had no letters from my brother this day, but I believe he will be ready to set sail in two or three days, and then I believe a battle will follow very quickly.

I have here sent you some lessons for the guitar, which I hope will please you; the Comte de Gramont did carry over with him others, which it may be you have. And as Francesco[1] makes any more that pleases me, I will send them to you. I have no more to say at present but that I am entirely yours.   c.

On June 2 the English fleet defeated the Dutch off Lowestoft in a gigantic encounter of over two hundred ships, and had the Duke of York been active to follow it up, it might well have been decisive. Among the dead was Charles's dearest friend, Charles Berkeley, Earl of Falmouth.

LVI. TO MADAME

Whitehall, June 6, 1665.

I thank God we have now the certain news of a very considerable victory over the Dutch. You will see most of the particulars by the relation my Lord Holles will show you,

---

[1] Francesco Corbetta, the Italian guitarist.

though I have had as great a loss as 'tis possible in a good friend, poor C. Berkeley. It troubles me so much as I hope you will excuse the shortness of this letter, having received the news of it but two hours ago.

This great success does not at all change my inclinations towards France, which you may assure the King, my brother, from me, and that it shall be his fault if we be not very good friends. There is one come from Dunkirk who says that there were bonfires made on Sunday last for the great victory the Dutch had over the English. Methinks Monsieur de Monpezat[1] might have had a little patience, and then it may (be) his rejoicing might have been on our side. Pray let me know what the meaning of this can be. My head does so ache as I can only add that I am entirely yours. c.

Being anxious for dynastic reasons that the heir to the throne should not be exposed to the danger of a second engagement, the command of the victorious Fleet was now entrusted to the Earl of Sandwich, who during the action had greatly distinguished himself as Admiral of the Blue. He sailed in July with the object of intercepting the Dutch East India Fleet as it passed down the North Sea—an attempt that ended in an unsuccessful endeavour to capture it as it lay in the neutral harbour of Bergen.

LVII. To the Earl of Sandwich

June 9, 1665.

My Lord Sandwich, though you have already done me very eminent service, yet the great part you have had in this happy victory, which it hath pleased God to send us, adds very much to the former obligations I have to you. I send this bearer, my Lord Hawly, on purpose to let you know more particularly my sense of it, and will say no more myself till I see you, that I may take you in my arms and give you other testimonies how truly I am your affectionate friend. c.r.

---

[1] The French Governor of Dunkirk.

LVIII. To the Earl of Sandwich

July 6, 1665.

I have little to say to [you] in order to the business of the Fleet, my brother having sent you all the directions necessary. And I am sure I need not be in pain for the good conduct of the Fleet now 'tis in your hands. The chief business of this letter is to recommend this bearer, my Lord Rochester,[1] to your care, who desires to go a volunteer with you, so I have nothing more to say to you at this time, only to wish you good success, and to assure you of my constant friendship and kindness.

Meanwhile the plague having broken out in London, the Court removed to Hampton Court and thence to Salisbury. The French plenipotentiaries were still in England, but it was plain by now that both their efforts to effect a peace, and Charles's to detach France from her alliance with Holland were doomed to failure.

LIX. To Madame

Hampton Court, July 13, 1665.

My going with the Queen[2] as far as the mouth of the river, the business I met with there about the Fleet, my hasty return hither, and the daily trouble I have had with neighbours' collations and the Irish Bill,[3] is the reason you have not heard from me in answer to so many letters, and to congratulate your health after such a misfortune to your child.[4] But now at last I have set myself down to give you a full answer to your letter of the 5th, which indeed requires it, and I should be wanting to the care and concernment I have for you, if I should not clearly let you know my mind in the negotiation now depending here with France, that you may govern yourself accordingly.

You remember very well the several and pressing advances I

---

[1] The poet and libertine, son to Charles's old friend and benefactor, Harry Wilmot.

[2] The Queen Mother, who was now returning to France for the last time.

[3] A Bill then under discussion in Parliament to prohibit the importation of Irish cattle to England.

[4] A still-born daughter.

made by you, the last year, afterwards by Charles Berkeley, and at last by Ruvigny, for the perfecting our treaty and entering into a stricter alliance with France than ever, which were all in appearance so well accepted, that I may truly say I lost many opportunities of strengthening myself with other alliances abroad, to be in a state of embracing that, which, upon the coming of the ambassadors, I looked would have been completed.   Instead of which, all I have heard from them (after I had accepted their mediation) hath been overtures towards an agreement with Holland, but upon propositions which they who made them to me could not but undervalue, and declaring themselves tied by a treaty to help the Hollanders, which was disowned when the treaty was the first made, and now cannot be produced to be appealed unto.

If this be the true state of the case (as I dare say you will agree it to be) where is my fault?   Would anybody advise me to make any advances towards a peace, after all the expense I have been at to support the war, and such a success in it, upon such weak invitations?   It is most certain they who propose it do not think I ought to agree to it, and standers-by say these ambassadors are kept here only till France can agree with Holland upon what terms they shall help them.   Which, if they do agree, I shall be necessitated to take part with Spain, and to your exception thereunto, let me mind you that, according to the course of the World, those are better friends who see they have need of us than those whose prosperity makes them think we have need of them.   And whatever be my fortune in this, I should run it cheerfully if my concernment for you did not perplex me, who I know will have a hard part to play (as you say), between your brother and brother-in-law.

And yet methinks it is too early to despair of seeing all things well agreed betwixt us, and though that should not happen so quickly, it must be your part to keep yourself still in a state of contributing thereunto, and having a most principal part therein, which will not be a hard task to your discretion and good talent. And be assured the kindness I have for you, will in all occasions make me mindful of what I owe you, and of reserving the obliging parts for you, and leaving the contrary for others if there should be any such. And this would be enough in answer to your long letter, if looking it over again, I did not find you endeavouring to persuade me the King, my brother, is no way guilty towards me of censuring my actions. I do verily believe it and should do so, though I should furnish him occasion for it, that being an action infinitely below the opinion and character I have always figured to myself of him, which may also serve to assure you these reports have never made any impression in me to the prejudice of our friendship. I will conclude this long letter, assuring you the kindness and friendship I have for you is as entire as ever, and that no alteration or change in my affairs shall make any in that.

LX. To Madame

Salisbury, August 5, 1665.

I hope you will pardon my long silence, which I should not have been guilty of if I had stayed long enough in one place to have written to you since my coming from Hampton Court. But I have been at Portsmouth about the fortifications there, and went thence to the Isle of Wight, which place I had never seen before, in order to the putting that island in a good posture.

I hope the French ambassadors are well satisfied with the answer I gave them upon what they proposed concerning the business with Holland. I have not had time to desire you to return my thanks to the King of France for the kind expressions he made me by G. Porter, and I assure you it shall be his fault if ever there be the least dispute between us. I have been hunting all this day, and am so sleepy as I hope you will pardon the shortness of this, but you shall now hear constantly from me.

LXI. To Madame

Salisbury, September 9, 1665.

I find by yours of the 11th of September that you are very much alarmed with the retreat of the fleet to Sole Bay.[1] But when you shall know that the fleet had no other business there

---

[1] Where Sandwich's fleet had returned to revictual after its unsuccessful attempt on Bergen.

but to take in some drink, and to join with twenty fresh ships (whereof the *Sovereine* is one), and stayed but seven days there, it will in some degree satisfy those able seamen at Paris, who judge so suddenly of our want of conduct in naval matters. And in all news *il faut attendre le boiteux*. I am confident my Lord Sandwich is some days before this between the Dutch fleet and home, with a better fleet than that which beat them last time. And, if God will permit it, I do not doubt to send you a good account and conclusion of this summer's campaign.

I have been troubled these few days past with a colic, but I thank God I am now perfectly well again. It has been almost a general disease in this place. I am going to make a little turn into Dorsetshire for eight or nine days to pass away the time till I go to Oxford, believing that this place was the cause of my indisposition.

I am very glad that Queen Mother is so well of her breast. Pray make my compliments to her upon it. I do confess myself very faulty in my failing so many weeks. I will repair my fault for the time to come, but the truth is I have been somewhat indisposed ever since my being here, and consequently out of humour. But I beg of you to be assured that what failings soever I may have, nothing can ever change me in the least degree of that friendship and kindness I have for you. . . .

Charles's hopes were proved right, for a few days later, while staying at Lord Ashley's house in Dorset, he was able to send Madame news of the capture of two great East India ships and six or seven lesser ones, full of treasure.

LXII. To Madame

St. Giles, September 11, 1665.

For my Dearest Sister.

You will see by the list here enclosed that my Lord Sandwich did not lose much time in Sole Bay, and I hope these prizes we have taken will be accompanied with more considerable ones, though these are very rich and of great loss to the Dutch. My Lord Sandwich writes me word that he is in very great hopes to meet with the rest of the fleet who are dispersed by foul weather, and his fleet entirely together and you may easily believe in very good heart by this happy success. We lost a small frigate in this encounter called the *Hector* of twenty-four guns, and one Captain hurt.

I could not sleep till I gave you part of this good news, though I am weary by being a-hunting all this afternoon, and the first time I have used this exercise since my indisposition. So I hope you will excuse me if I end here, hoping that I shall send you more good news of this kind very speedily. . . .

LXIII. TO THE EARL OF SANDWICH

St. Giles, September 16, 1665.

I could not give you my thanks for the first good news of the 5th because I knew not whither to send them to you. Now my Lord Rochester hath brought me also yours of the 12th: with a second success upon the Dutch for which I thank God first and you next. There was nothing desirable beyond this but the beating the enemy in a body, which it seems they could not present themselves to, having been dispersed by the foul weather. You did very well not to attempt Bankert by tacking so near their coast; the foul weather coming upon you, you might have endangered the fleet.

Though your letter doth not say it, my Lord of Rochester doth, that the whole fleet was coming to the Buoy of the Nore, where I think they will be better than anywhere else, where you must with all possible care and strictness keep your men and officers on board till we hear with certainty what the enemy will do, whether lay up their ships or come out again, if but to make a bravado and do some mischief upon the coast, as they have some new great ships ready for it. At the same time you must take care that the ships be repaired and fitted with all things necessary upon this project. And if upon receipt of this, anything occurs to you worth my knowledge dispatch it away to Oxford where I have appointed my brother to meet me on the 25th of this month, it being not possible to do it sooner, dispersed as we are. And then we will take a final resolution of all kinds relating to the fleet, and dispatch them immediately to you. In the meantime be assured that I am constantly Yours. C.R.

The summer's campaign ended with the capture of some further prizes, somewhat tarnished by a disgraceful scramble for their precious cloths and spices by the English admirals.

Meanwhile the naval administration, faced by overwhelming demands and ever-growing debts, had long ago exhausted the moneys voted for the war by Parliament, to whom Charles explained the melancholy situation when it met again at Oxford on October 9.

LXIV.SPEECH TO PARLIAMENT

October 9, 1665.

My Lords and Gentlemen : I am confident you all believe that if it had not been absolutely necessary to consult with you, I would not have called you together at this time, when the contagion hath so spread itself over so many parts of the kingdom. I take it for a good omen to see so good an appearance this day; and I doubt not every day will add to your number. And I give you all my thanks for your compliance so far with my desires.

The truth is, as I entered upon this war by your advice and encouragement, so I do desire that you may, as frequently as is possible, receive information of the conduct and effects of it; and that I may have the continuance of your cheerful supply for the carrying it on. I will not deny to you that it hath proved more chargeable than I could imagine it would have been. The addition they still make to their fleets beyond their first purpose made it unavoidably necessary for me to make proportionable preparations, which God hath hitherto blessed with success in all encounters. . . .

. . . This expense will not suffer you to wonder that the great supply which you gave me for this war in so bountiful a proportion is upon the matter already spent, so that I must not only expect an assistance from you to carry on this war, but such an assistance as may enable me to defend myself and you against a more powerful neighbour, if he shall prefer the friendship of the Dutch before mine.

I told you, when I entered upon this war, that I had not such a brutal appetite as to make war for war-sake. I am still of the same mind. I have been ready to receive any propositions that France hath thought fit to offer to that end; but hitherto nothing hath been offered worthy of my acceptance; nor is the Dutch less insolent; though I know no advantage they have, but the continuance of the contagion. God Almighty, I hope, will shortly deprive them of that encouragement. . . .

Though Parliament voted a further aid its members were more concerned in debating a Cattle Bill against the Irish and a Five Mile Act against Nonconformist preachers than in ending the financial constipation which was crippling the conduct of the war. In addition, the effects of the Plague on the trade of the nation had seriously diminished the standing revenue.

To make matters worse, the French ambassadors departed, leaving the outbreak of war between England and France inevitable.

lxv. To Madame

Hampton Court, January 29, 1665/6.

I did intend to have answered last week yours and Monsieur's letters, upon the subject of doing good offices between me and France, but that I found, by the letter the Queen writ me of a later date, that mediations of that kind were not seasonable at this time, France being resolved to declare for Holland. So that I only write now to Monsieur a letter of condolence upon the death of Queen Mother, which I assure you, gave me an equal share in the loss.

I have been two days in this place, and do intend for to go to Whitehall this week, for to dispatch all my preparations against the spring, which are already in very good forwardness. We had some kind of an alarm, that the troops which Monsieur de Turenne went to review were intended to make us a visit here, but we shall be very ready to bid them welcome, either by sea or land.

I have left my wife at Oxford, but hope that in a fortnight or three weeks to send for her to London, where already the Plague is in effect nothing. But our women are afraid of the name of Plague, so that they must have a little time to fancy all clear.

I cannot tell what kind of correspondence we must keep with letters, now that France declares war with us; you must direct me in it, and I shall observe what you judge convenient for you. But nothing can make me lessen in the least degree of that kindness I always have had for you, which I assure you is so rooted in my heart, as it will continue to the last moment of my life.

The official declaration of war between the two countries followed on February 19, and the correspondence between Charles and Madame was accordingly interrupted. But as neither party to the quarrel had any real hostility towards the other, talk of peace remained in the air and occasionally provided a chance for an interchange of letters between brother and sister.

LXVI. TO MADAME

Whitehall, May 2, 1666.

There are few occasions could be unwelcome to me when they give you a pretence to make me happy with a letter from you. I do assure you that, if there were no other reason but this constraint which is upon our commerce of letters, I should use all my endeavours to have a good intelligence between me and France, but I do fear very much that the desire to peace is not wished for there as it is on my part. For else my Lord Holles would not have been stopped so long to so little purpose, there being less proposed at the conference than I refused last year, which certainly does not show any great inclination to an agreement, but rather to amuse me. And certainly they must think me in a very ill condition to accept of such propositions as were offered to my Lord Holles, in which I believe they will find themselves mistaken. However, I shall always be very ready to hearken to peace, as a good Christian ought to do, which is all I can do to advance it, for I have long since had so ill luck with the advances I made to that end, as I can now only wish for peace and leave the rest to God.

I am going to-morrow to see the Fleet, which will be ready very speedily, and I do assure you 'tis much better in all respects than it was the last year.   And the great want the Hollanders have of seamen we are in no danger of, for we have more and better seamen than we had the last year.

I will be very careful of the choice of your horses.   My Lord Crofts has promised me two, which he assures me will fit you, and I will look out for others when I can light upon them, for if I had had any good of my own, you should not have stayed so long.   But the plague of horses has been in my stable, and I shall have much ado to mount myself with so much as jades for this summer's hunting, the scarcity of good ones is so great at this present.

I will say no more, but only to assure you that nothing can alter that passion and tenderness I have for you, and to beg of you that you will continue your kindness to me. . . .

The summer campaign of 1666 was not attended by all the happy results Charles's optimism had anticipated. At the beginning of June, the English Fleet, under Albemarle, suffered heavy loss in a four days' battle against the Dutch and French. And though, despite the almost complete bankruptcy of the naval administration, an English Fleet was again got to sea before the end of July, and even revenged its defeat by a cutting-out expedition on the Dutch coast, the Fire of London at the beginning of September came as a crushing blow to the nation.

Yet out of that disaster in time grew a new city, and it is not the least of the entries to be made on the credit side of Charles's account with the nation that he did everything within his power to ensure that the new London built on the ruins of the old should be no mean city.[1]

---

[1] Mr. Walter Bell, the historian of the Great Fire, gives it as his considered opinion that ' London as it was created after the Fire owed more (always apart from Wren's individual buildings, which glorified it) to King Charles II than to Sir Christopher Wren.   His,' he writes, ' was the active, agitating mind.   His hand was seen everywhere.'

LXVII. PROCLAMATION TO PROHIBIT THE REBUILDING OF HOUSES AFTER THE GREAT FIRE

September 13, 1666.

As no particular man hath sustained any loss or damage by the late terrible and deplorable fire in his fortune or estate in any degree to be compared with the loss and damage we ourself have sustained, so it is not possible for any man to take the same more to heart, and to be more concerned and solicitous for the rebuilding this famous city with as much expedition as is possible.   And since it hath pleased God to lay this heavy judgement upon us all this time as an evidence of His displeasure for our sins, we do comfort ourself with some hope that He will, upon our due humiliation before Him, as a new instance of His signal blessing upon us, give us life, not only to see the foundations laid, but the buildings finished, of a much more beautiful city than is at this time consumed; and that as the seat and situation of it is the most convenient and noble for the advancement of trade of any city in Europe, so that such care will be taken for the re-edification of it, both for use and beauty, and such provision made for the future against the ordinary and casual accidents by fire, as may, as far as human wisdom can provide . . . reasonably secure the same, and make it rather appear to the world as purged with the fire (in how lamentable a manner soever) to a wonderful beauty and comeliness than consumed by it. . . . We have therefore thought fit, most necessary, and agreeable to the great and constant affection we have always had and always shall retain for this our native city, to use this expedition in publishing our thoughts, resolutions and intentions upon this great affair; that though such present rules and directions cannot be formed as must, upon more mature deliberation, be established for the re-edification; yet such inconveniences may and shall be prevented, which may arise by the hasty and unskilful buildings many may purpose to erect for their present conveniences before they can know how the same will suit and consist with the design that shall be made. . . . And if this our seasonable animadversion shall not meet with that prudent submission we expect, but that some obstinate and refractory persons will presume to erect such buildings as they shall think fit, upon pretence that the ground is their own, and that they may do with it what they please, such their obstinacy shall not prevail to the public prejudice : but we do hereby require the Lord Mayor, and the other magistrates of the City of London, in their several limits, to be very watchful in such cases. . . .

. . . The woeful experience in this late heavy visitation hath sufficiently convinced all men of the pernicious consequences which have attended the building with timber, and even with stone itself, and the notable benefit of brick, which in so many places hath resisted and even extinguished the fire : and we do therefore hereby declare our express will and pleasure, that no man whatsoever shall presume to erect any house or building, great or small, but of brick or stone; and if any man shall do the contrary, the next magistrate shall forthwith cause it to be pulled down, and such further course shall be taken for his punishment as he deserves. And we suppose that the notable benefit many men have received from those cellars, which have been well and strongly arched, will persuade most men, who build good houses, to practise that good husbandry by arching all convenient places.

We do declare that Fleet Street, Cheapside, Cornhill, and all other eminent and notorious streets, shall be of such a breadth as may, with God's blessing, prevent the mischief that one side may suffer if the other be on fire; which was the case lately in Cheapside; the precise breadth of which several streets shall be, upon advice with the Lord Mayor and aldermen, shortly published, with many other particular orders and rules, which cannot yet be adjusted. In the meantime we resolve, though all streets cannot be of equal breadth, yet none shall be so narrow as to make the passage uneasy or inconvenient, especially towards the water-side. Nor will we suffer any lanes or alleys to be erected, but where, upon mature deliberation, the same shall be found absolutely necessary; except such places shall be set aside, which shall be designed only for buildings of that kind, and from whence no public mischief may probably arise.

The irreparable damage and loss by the late fire being, next to the hand of God in the terrible wind, to be imputed to the place in which it first broke out, amongst small timber houses standing so close together that as no remedy could be applied from the river for the quenching thereof, to the contiguousness of the buildings hindering and keeping all possible relief from the land-side, we do resolve and declare that there shall be a fair key or wharf on all the river-side; that no house shall be erected within so many feet of the river as shall be within few days declared in the rules formerly mentioned; nor shall there be in those buildings which shall be erected next the river, which we desire may be fair structures, for the ornament of the city, any houses to be inhabited by brewers, or dyers, or sugar-bakers; which trades by their continual smokes contribute very much to the unhealthiness of the adjacent places. But we require the Lord Mayor and aldermen of London, upon a full consideration, and weighing all conveniences and inconveniences that can be foreseen, to propose such a place as may be fit for all those trades which are carried on by smoke to inhabit together, or at least several places for the several quarters of the town for those occupations, and in which they shall find their account in convenience and profit, as well as other places shall receive the benefit in the distance of the neighbourhood; it being our purpose that they who exercise those necessary professions shall be in all respects as well provided for and encouraged as ever they have been, and undergo as little prejudice as may be by being less inconvenient to their neighbours.

These grounds and foundations being laid from the substance whereof we shall not depart . . . we have, in order to the reducing this great and glorious design into practice, directed, and we do hereby direct, that the Lord Mayor and court of aldermen do, with all possible expedition, cause an exact survey to be made and taken of the whole ruins occasioned by the late lamentable fire, to the end that it may appear to whom all the houses and ground did in truth belong, what term the several occupiers were possessed of, and at what rents, and to whom . . . the reversion and inheritance appertained; that so provision may be made that, though every man must not be suffered to erect what buildings and where he pleases, he shall not in any degree be debarred from receiving the reasonable benefit of what ought to accrue to him from such houses or lands; there being nothing less in our thoughts than that any particular person's right and interest should be sacrificed to the public benefit or convenience without such recompense as in justice he ought to receive for the same.

. . . In the meantime, we do heartily recommend it to the charity and magnanimity of all well-disposed persons, and we do heartily pray unto Almighty God that He will infuse it into the hearts of men, speedily to endeavour by degrees to re-edify some of those many churches, which, in this lamentable fire, have been burned down and defaced; that so men may have those public places of God's worship to resort to, to humble themselves together before Him upon His heavy displeasure, and join in their devotion for His future mercy and blessing upon us; and, as soon as we shall be informed of any readiness to begin such a good work, we shall not only give our assistance and direction for the model of it, and freeing it from buildings at too near a distance, but shall encourage it by our own bounty, and all other ways we shall be desired. . . .

Lastly, that we may encourage men by our own example, we will use all the expedition we can to rebuild our custom house in the place where it formerly stood, and enlarge it with the most conveniencies for the merchants that can be devised; and, upon all the other lands which belong unto us, we shall depart with anything of our own right and benefit for the advancement of the public service and beauty of the city; and shall further remit, to all those who shall erect any buildings according to this declaration, all duties arising to us upon the hearth-money for the space of seven years.

Given at our court at Whitehall the 13th day of September, 1666, in the eighteenth year of our reign.

LXVIII. TO THE MAYOR AND COMMON COUNCIL

March 22, 1666/7.

The Acts of the Common Council of the 21st of March inst. concerning rebuilding the City of London, being this day presented to His Majesty, wherein they have declared which shall hereafter be deemed streets and lanes of note and high and principal streets within the said city and the liberties thereof, His Majesty was graciously pleased to approve thereof. And doth likewise well approve of their Order for the making the street from the late Greyhound Tavern in Fleet Street into Cheapside, to be of the breadth of 45 foot, and Fleet Bridge of the same breadth, and their making a new postern on that side of Ludgate they judge most convenient. And His Majesty doth further recommend to the Lord Mayor, Aldermen and Common Council, that the surveyors take care that all new buildings in each street may be carried on without breaks or projectings into the street, and may run in a line as the streets will bear it.

That the front of all the buildings at the ends of any cross street, coming into the High streets, be of the same height and form with the building of the High streets.

That all passages (not 14 foot broad) that abut on the High streets be forthwith staked out to the breadth.

And His Majesty doth further recommend to the Lord Mayor and Court of Aldermen that they endeavour by mediation and advice, in which they shall have all assistance from His Majesty, to procure the consent of all persons concerned, that such places may be enlarged, and such other things done as may contribute to the beauty, ornament and convenience of the city, although they may not seem to have full power and authority to direct and order the same by the strict letter of the Act of Parliament, as the widening Pater Noster Row, where the same can well be done, and doing such other things as His Majesty hath formerly recommended to them.

When Parliament reassembled a fortnight after the Fire, the King spoke of the exhausted state of his Treasury; only by anticipating his revenue at a ruinous rate of interest and relying on the personal credit of Carteret, the Navy Treasury, had it proved possible to refit the Fleet in July.

LXIX. Speech to both Houses

September 21, 1666.

My Lords and Gentlemen : I am very glad to meet so many of you together again; and God be thanked for our meeting together in this place! Little time hath passed since we were almost in despair of having this place left us to meet in; you see the dismal ruins the fire hath made; and nothing but a miracle of God's mercy could have preserved what is left from the same destruction. I need make no excuse to you for dispensing with your attendance in April. I am confident you all thanked me for it. The truth is, I desire to put you to as little trouble as I can; and I can tell you truly, I desire to put you to as little cost as is possible. I wish with all my heart, that I could bear the whole charge of this war myself, and that my subjects should reap the benefit of it to themselves. But we have two very great and powerful enemies, who use all the means they can, fair and foul, to make all the world concur with them; and the war is more chargeable (by that conjunction) than anybody thought it would have been. I need not tell you the success of this summer, in which God hath given us great success, and no question the enemy hath undergone great losses. And if it had pleased God to have withheld His late judgement by fire, we had been in no ill condition.

You have given me very large supplies for the carrying on the war. And yet I must tell you, if I had not, by anticipating my own revenue, raised a very great sum of money, I had not been able to have set out the Fleet this last spring. . . . You will consider what is to be done next, when you are well informed of the expense. And I must leave it to your wisdom to find out the best expedients for the carrying on this war with as little burden to the people as is possible. I shall add no more than to put you in mind that our enemies are very insolent; and if they were able this last year to persuade their miserable people, whom they mislead, that the contagion had so wasted the nation, and impoverished us, that we would not be able to set out any fleet, how will they be exalted with this last impoverishment of this city, and contemn all reasonable conditions of peace! And therefore I cannot doubt but you will provide accordingly.

Still defiant, Parliament voted a further £1,800,000 for the prosecution of the war, but with the whole trade of the kingdom dislocated by pestilence, fire and war, it was long before any money was even allocated, while the existing debts of the Navy were enough to swallow every penny of it.

To the Government at least peace was imperative. Fortunately Louis XIV was also anxious for peace, and in October made tentative approaches through Ruvigny and old Lord St. Albans. The long interrupted correspondence with Madame was accordingly resumed.

LXX. TO MADAME

Whitehall, October 18, 1666.

It seems to me by that which my Lord St. Albans says to me, that this commerce may at present begin again, and continue, even till the next campaign. It was a great displeasure to me to find it forbidden, and by so much the more that as I do not think this to be an eternal war, I should be very glad that you should have part in all the things that may conduce to the ending of it. I was likewise very glad to learn that the King, my brother, makes professions still of having as just a sense in this subject as I have, that is to say, believing it neither good for him, nor for me, and desiring an end of it as much as I do; but allow me to tell you that in this occasion 'tis not enough to speak in general terms, especially after having given so much place to doubt of his intentions. To re-establish the trust, it were very good to speak more particularly. When that shall be you may assure yourself I shall correspond on my side as far as reason ought to guide me. This is all I shall trouble you with at present, only to tell you the joy I have to assure you myself with how much tenderness and kindness I am yours. c.

For the present, however, the war continued. Wild rumours at home, mostly directed against the Papists who were popularly suspected of having burnt the city, financial stringency and a rising of armed Covenanters in Scotland—defeated by General

Dalyell at Rullion Green in November—left the Government little time to attend to its external enemies. It was an unusually short-tempered King who rated his Parliament in January, 1667, for their delay in allocating supplies and complained of its attempt to tack to the Poll Bill a proviso for setting up a committee to examine his accounts.

LXXI. TO GENERAL SIR THOMAS DALYELL

December 5, 1666.

Lieutenant-General Dalyell. Having received a full account of the happy success you have had against the rebels in Scotland, and the great care and diligence you have used in the suppressing of it, I could not but give my hearty thanks for it myself, by letting you know how well I am satisfied with your conduct and zeal in my service, assuring you that you shall always find by the effects the sense I have of those who serve me so well as you have done, and that upon all occasions you shall have reason to believe that I am, Your very loving friend.

I pray tell Will Drummond that I am very sensible of the share he hath had in this victory, which he shall find upon all occasions.

LXXII. SPEECH TO BOTH HOUSES

January 18, 1666/7.

My Lords and Gentlemen : I have now passed your Bills; and I was in good hope to have had other Bills ready to pass too. I cannot forget that within few days after your coming together in September both Houses presented me with their vote and declaration, that they would give me a supply proportionable to my occasions; and the confidence of this made me anticipate that small part of my revenue which was unanticipated for the payment of the seamen. And my credit hath gone farther than I had reason to think it would; but it is now at an end.

This is the first day I have heard of any money towards a supply, being the 18th of January, and what this will amount to, God knows. And what time I have to make such preparations as are necessary to meet three such enemies as I have, you can well enough judge. . . . But, by the grace of God, I will not give over myself and you, but will do what is in my power for the defence of myself and you.

It is high time for you to make good your promise; and it is high time for you to be in the country, as well for the raising of money, as that the Lord-Lieutenants and Deputy-Lieutenants may watch those seditious spirits which are at work to disturb the public peace; and therefore I am resolved to put an end to this session on Monday next come seven night. Before which time, I pray, let all things be made ready that I am to dispatch.

I am not willing to complain you have dealt unkindly with me in a Bill I have now passed, in which you have manifested a greater distrust of me than I have deserved. I do not pretend to be without infirmities: but I have never broken my word with you; and, if I do not flatter myself, the nation never had less cause to complain of grievances, or the least injustice or oppression, than it hath had in these seven years it hath pleased God to restore me to you. I would be used accordingly.

LXXIII.SPEECH TO BOTH HOUSES BEFORE THE PROROGATION

February 8, 1666/7.

My Lords and Gentlemen : I thank you for this other Bill of Supply which you have given me; and I assure you, the money shall be laid out for the ends it is given. I hope we shall live to have Bills of this nature in the old style, with fewer provisos. I looked to have had somewhat offered to me concerning the accompts of the money that hath been already raised since the war; which since you have not done, I will take care (after so much noise) that the same be not stifled, but will issue out my commission in the manner I formerly promised the House of Peers: and the commissioners shall have very much to answer, if they do not discover all matters of fraud and cozenage.

The season of the year is very far spent, in which our enemies have got great advantages over us; but, by the grace of God, I will make all the preparations I can, and as fast as I can. And yet I must tell you, that if any good overtures be made for an honourable peace, I will not reject them; and I believe all sober men will be glad to see it brought to pass.

I shall now prorogue you till towards winter, that you may in your several places intend the peace and security of your several countries, where there are unquiet spirits enough working. And I do pray you, and I do expect it from you, that you will use your utmost endeavours to remove all those false imaginations in the hearts of the people, which the malice of ill men have industriously infused into them of I know not what jealousies and grievances. For I must tell you again, and I am sure I am in the right, that the people had never so little cause to complain of oppression and grievances as they have had since my return to you. If the taxes and impositions are heavy upon them, you will put them in mind that a war with such powerful enemies cannot be maintained without taxes; and I am sure the money raised thereby comes not into my purse. . . .

Meanwhile the peace negotiations were proceeding. The royal cousins of France and England having agreed on the terms which were to be put to Holland, plenipotentiaries were appointed to meet at Breda in the spring. In February the English Government decided, since it was manifestly impossible any longer to obtain credit enough to equip them, to lay up the larger battleships in harbour, and rely for its aims on the peace negotiations, supported by a couple of light commerce-raiding squadrons and the harbour guns.

LXIV. To the Duke of York
[*Countersigned* ' Arlington ']

May 24, 1667.

Most dear brother, we greet you well, etc. Whereas by our order of the 6th February last we did signify our pleasure unto you that for the service of this present summer only our ships of war of the third and other inferior rates should be fitted and put forth to sea, for the reasons therein expressed, since which time the City of London being in a good measure supplied with coals, and much of the trade of our subjects, especially from the Mediterranean, being happily and securely arrived, and we continuing still our intentions of making war by small parties, unless the same shall be happily and honourably ended by the present Treaty at Breda, having thought fit to signify our further pleasure to you, that considering how unnecessary it is for that way of making war to keep in pay all our ships of the third rate (divers of which we are informed are out of repair, so as to require a considerable time for their refitting) you cause an inquiry to be made into such of our ships of the third rate as now are or hereafter shall come into the Port of Portsmouth, which we conceive to be the most fitting port for laying up such of them as shall be discharged, and that you cause such of them as require considerable repairs to be discharged as soon as the condition of our treasure in the hands of our treasurer of our Navy shall enable you to do it, that so all means may be used for the preventing unnecessary charge. Nevertheless least our intentions herein should be mistaken, we think it fit to recommend to your care that such considerable squadrons of our ships be still kept at sea, especially on the western and northern stations, as may serve to distract the forces of the enemy, and disturb their trade, so as that they may not be able by dividing their fleet to block up the said squadrons, or secure their trade. . . .

The Dutch, with a better financial system, preferred bolder measures. In June their fleet entered the Thames, and storming the entrances to the Medway, revenged the injuries done by Admiral Holmes's cutting out expedition of the previous year by capturing the English flagship and burning several other great ships. The humiliation was followed by feverish but unavailing activity on the part of the English Government.

LXXV. To Prince Rupert
[*Countersigned* ' Arlington ']

June 13, 1667.

Most dear Cousin, we greet you well. Whereas we have appointed certain works and batteries to be forthwith raised at or near Woolwich for the better security of the river against the attempts of the enemy in this conjuncture of affairs, we have thought fit hereby to signify our pleasure to you, and we do hereby authorize and require you to transport yourself thither, there to issue out such orders and directions as from time to time you in your discretion shall find fit for the speedy and effectual carrying on and perfecting those works and batteries for the doing all and all manner of things that shall be judged convenient for the safety as well of the Yard at Woolwich, as for the preventing any designs the enemy may have of passing up the river. And we do hereby straightly charge and require all persons of what rank or kind soever employed in that service, to obey and observe your orders and directions in this particular. . . .

LXXVI. To Prince Rupert

[*Countersigned* ' Arlington ']

July 6, 1667.

Most dear Cousin, etc.   Whereas we find it necessary upon the retreat of the enemy out of the river that all immediate care be taken for the putting the river of Chatham in a condition capable to resist any new attempt in case they should adventure to return again into the river, we have thought good hereby to signify our pleasure to you, and accordingly we do hereby sufficiently authorize and require you that forthwith upon receipt hereof you transport yourself to Rochester, Chatham, Sheerness, or other ports upon the river of Medway within our county of Kent, there to issue out such orders and directions as you from time to time in your discretion shall find fit as well for the raising, carrying on, and perfecting, all such works batteries, fortifications as already have, or hereafter shall be found necessary to be made and raised for the strength and security of the river. . . .

But the Dutch were as tired of the war as the English. Before the end of July a peace was signed at Breda, which, though overshadowed by the humiliation of the Medway and falling far short of England's former proud demands, at least secured her New York, New Jersey, New Delaware and the consolidation of her embyro empire in the West. And though for a week or two longer Dutch fleets still hovered around the English coasts, Charles with customary nonchalance was soon writing of other matters—of Prince Rupert's desire to become Constable of Windsor, the public thrashing which the Duke of Buckingham gave Harry Killigrew in the playhouse, and his own anger at the elopement of his wife's favourite Maid of Honour, Frances Stuart, with the Duke of Richmond.

LXXVII.TO PRINCE RUPERT

July 22, 1667.

I deferred writing to you till now, in hope to have given you a good account of the business of Windsor; but as yet nothing more is done in it, though new propositions have been made, of which I shall give you an account when you come to town; assuring you I have done my part in it, and shall continue, in that or anything else, to do my part towards your satisfaction.

For news, here is little but what you know, and I am sure you cannot be ignorant of the difference between my Lord of Buckingham and H. Killigrew; the particulars of which are too long for a letter, otherwise you should have it from me.

Just now I am told, that on Saturday last were seen about sixty sail of ships, small and great, at an anchor to the westward of Portland, which I believe to be de Ruyter's squadron. A privateer come into Cornwall says he met about thirty-eight French men-of-war plying to the eastward of the mouth of the Channel.

LXXVIII.TO MADAME

Whitehall, August 26, 1667.

I do assure you I am very much troubled that I cannot in everything give you that satisfaction I could wish, especially in this business of the Duchess of Richmond,[1] wherein you may think me ill natured. But if you consider how hard a thing 'tis to swallow an injury done by a person I had so much tenderness[2] for, you will in some degree excuse the resentment I use towards her. You know my good nature enough to believe that I could not be so severe, if I had not great provocation, and I assure you her carriage towards me has been as bad as breach

---

[1] Frances Stuart—'la belle Stuart'—for whom Charles had long cherished an affection and who had much offended him by the manner of her marriage with the Duke of Richmond.

[2] In the original in Charles's hand the word 'love' is crossed out and 'tenderness' substituted.

of friendship and faith can make it. Therefore I hope you will pardon me if I cannot so soon forget an injury which went so near my heart.

I will not now answer the letter you writ by your waterman who fell sick upon the way, and so I had the letter but some days since, but will expect a safer way to write than by the post. I believe Ruvigny will be here in two or three days, and the other gentleman whose name I cannot read in your letter. The peace was proclaimed here on Saturday last, and so I will end my letter, and will only add the assurance of my being entirely yours. C.

The nation, however, was still restless and demanded a scapegoat. Universally the choice fell on Clarendon, whose pride, obstinacy and old-fashioned pomposity had temporarily obscured his noble virtues. The mob had already smashed the windows of his palace in Piccadilly, and there was talk of an impeachment. As there seemed no other way of averting revolution, Charles intimated through the old man's son-in-law, the Duke of York, that his retirement was necessary. But Clarendon refused to resign, and he was forced to demand the seals.

LXXIX. To the Marquess of Ormonde

September 15, 1667.

I should have thanked you sooner for your melancholy letter of 26th August, and the good counsel you gave me in it, as my purpose was also to say something to you concerning my taking the seals from the Chancellor, of which you must needs have heard all the passages, since he would not suffer it to be done so privately as I intended it. The truth is, his behaviour and humour was grown so insupportable to myself, and to all the world also, that I could not longer endure it, and it was impossible for me to live with it and do those things with the Parliament that must be done or the government will be lost.

When I have a better opportunity for it, you shall know many particulars that have inclined me to this revolution, which already seems to be well liked in the world and to have given a real and visible amendment to my affairs. This is an argument too big for a letter, so I will add but this word to it, to assure you that your former friendship to the Chancellor shall not do you any prejudice with me, and that I have not in the least degree diminished that value and kindness I ever had for you, which I thought fit to say to you upon this occasion, because it is very possible malicious people may suggest the contrary to you.

When Charles greeted Parliament in October, he addressed them with frankness and gave them leave to call whoever they chose to account. Clarendon, too proud of a good conscience, instead of discreetly retiring till the anger of his foes was spent, waited boldly to justify himself: then when it was too late and his enemies in Parliament were about to impeach him he fled the kingdom precipitately. It was the end of his attempt to restore England to the old pre-Civil War constitution which she had outgrown. A new era was now to begin.

LXXX. TO MADAME

Whitehall, November 30, 1667.

If you look upon our condition here, as it is reported by common fame, I do confess you have reason to have those apprehensions you mention in your letter by this bearer. The truth is, the ill conduct of my Lord Clarendon in my affairs has forced me to permit many inquiries to be made, which otherwise I would not have suffered the Parliament to have done, though I must tell you that in themselves they are but inconvenient appearances rather than real mischiefs.

There can be nothing advanced in the Parliament for my advantage till this matter of my Lord Clarendon be over, but after that I shall be able to take my measures so with them, as you will see the good effects of it. I am sure I will not part with any of my power, nor do I believe that they will desire any unreasonable thing. I have written at large to the Queen, in the particular of my Lord Clarendon, which I could not do but by a safe way, and I doubt not that you will in that matter, and many others, have informations very far from the truth. I will add no more, only thank you for your kindness in being so free with me, which I pray continue upon all occasions, and be assured that I am entirely yours. C.

CHAPTER VII

THE SECRET TREATY OF DOVER

The new orientation which English policy was to take after Clarendon's departure was not at first perceptible. For the moment England seemed to be inclining violently towards her old foe, Holland. A succession of French victories in the Spanish Netherlands had disturbed the balance of power, and Charles, who always dreaded the possibility of a Franco-Dutch partition of the Netherlands and the Spanish Empire in which England should have no part, seized the opportunity to conclude on January 13, 1668, an alliance with Holland to force a peace on agreed terms between France and Spain and so bring an end to the French conquests.

1.INSTRUCTIONS TO SIR WILLIAM TEMPLE
[*Countersigned* 'Arlington']

January 1, 1667/8.

You shall transport yourself with all possible diligence into Holland upon the yacht we have assigned you for that purpose, which you are to detain there till you are ready to send to us an account of your success in the business upon which you are now employed.

Immediately upon your arrival you shall press the having an audience of the States General, and there deliver our letter of credence to them, accompanying it with such compliments that shall occur to you upon the occasion of your errand. But if you shall think it most proper to visit Monsieur de Witt first, as we think it may be, you shall begin with the assuring him of our accepting well the discourse and overtures that passed between him and you at your late conferences, and offer yourself to be directed by him in your Address to the States, adding the value and esteem we have constantly had for his person, and our dependence on his honour and integrity in the prosecution of your negotiations. And if you shall see cause for it, even in this entrance you shall endeavour to quiet all jealousy and apprehension he may have of our wishing to lessen his credit in that Government or of our concerning ourself for our nephew the Prince of Orange to the prejudice thereof, in the manner you were directed by your former instructions bearing date the 25th November last.

In this your conference with Monsieur de Witt, you shall let him know how willing we are to enter into a more strict Defensive League with the States General, in the manner he hath already specified to you in your late discourses together, according to which you shall offer him the project following:

Whereas in the 11th Article of the Treaty lately concluded at Breda between the King of Great Britain and the States General of the Netherlands, it is among other things agreed that the said King of Great Britain and the said States General remain friends, confederates, united, and allied, for the defence and preservation of the rights, liberties, and immunities of either Ally and their subjects against all whomsoever who shall endeavour to disturb the peace of either State by sea or land. . . . It is agreed between them that the said King of Great Britain and the said States General shall be and they are hereby united and confederated in a perpetual Defensive League. That is to say that in case any Prince, State or person whatsoever, whether Allies with the said King and the said States, or with either of them or others, shall upon any pretence whatsoever invade or attempt to invade the Dominions or countries of the said King of Great Britain, or do any act of hostility by sea or land against the said King or his subjects, that the said States General shall be and they are hereby obliged and bound to assist the said King for the suppressing, resisting, and repelling such attempts, invasion and hostilities. . . . And likewise that in occasion any Prince, State, or person whatsoever . . . shall upon any pretence whatsoever invade or attempt to invade the Dominions or countries of the said States General or do any act of hostility by sea or land against the said States or their subjects, that the said King of Great Britain shall be and is hereby obliged and bound to assist the said States and their subjects by the suppressing, resisting, and repelling such attempted invasion. . . .
. . . Item: It is therefore agreed by the said King of Great

Britain and the said States General, that they together with their Allies shall enter into a joint mediation between the most Christian and Catholic Kings, to the effect following, viz.: (1) To oblige France to accept the peace upon the terms already proposed by that King, both to the States, several Princes of Germany, and to the Empire, being either to retain the conquests of the last campaign, or to receive instead of them, Aire, St. Omer, Cambray, Douay, and either Luxembourg or the county of Burgundy. (2) To oblige France to stop all further progress of the war upon the first proposal of this mediation, and in case of a difficulty in Spain to accept it, that it shall be left wholly to the Mediators to persuade *or to force* them to. [*Note in Charles's own handwriting:* ' For the indecency of the word *force* I would willingly have it left out.—C.R.'] (3) That the Mediators shall become jointly the warranties of this agreement with a particular specification of what forces each of them shall furnish to maintain it against the first breach offered by either side. . . .

. . . And that this may be effected with all possible dispatch we have herewith caused to be delivered you a Power under our Great Seal of England, to conclude finally the aforesaid Treaty. . . .

Though extremely popular in England, and therefore a useful lever for getting the money from Parliament, the English treaty with Holland naturally did not commend itself to Louis, even though the terms of pacification were those already agreed between himself and Charles.

II. To Madame

Whitehall, January 23, 1667/8.

I believe you will be a little surprised at the treaty I have concluded with the States. The effect of it is to bring Spain to consent to the peace, upon the terms the King of France hath avowed he will be content with, so as I have done nothing to prejudice France in this agreement. And they cannot wonder that I provide for myself against any mischiefs this war may produce, and finding my propositions to France receive so cold an answer, which in effect was as good as a refusal, I thought I had no other way but this to secure myself. If I find by the letters that my Lord St. Albans is come away, I do intend to send somebody else into France to incline the King to accept of this peace.

I give you a thousand thanks for the care you take before-hand of James.[1] I will answer for him that he will be very obedient in all your commands, and your kindness to him obliges me as much as 'tis possible, for I do confess I love him very well. He was, I believe, with you, before your last letter came to my hands.

You were misinformed in your intelligence concerning the Duchess of Richmond. If you were as well acquainted with a little fantastical gentleman called Cupid as I am, you would neither wonder, nor take ill, any sudden changes which do happen in the affairs of his conducting, but in this matter there is nothing done in it. . . .

III. To Madame

Whitehall, January 30, 1667/8.

I cannot thank you enough for your goodness and kindness to James. His letter to me is almost nothing else but telling how much he is obliged to you and Monsieur for your care of him, and since you have taken the trouble of lodging him at the Palais Royal, I am sure he cannot be better. I am very glad that you have put the thought of going to the Army out of his head, for it were not proper that he should appear in any army, now that I have become a mediator by the treaty I have lately made with Holland. And I am now dispatching an envoy[2] to the King of France in order to the mediation, which I hope will hinder Monsieur's journey into Catalogna and save him from a hot campaign. And this is all I will trouble you with at present, only again thank you for your kindness to James; and beg of you to be assured that my kindness and tenderness to you is more than I can express.

[1] The young Duke of Monmouth, then on a visit to France.
[2] Sir John Trevor. He was appointed Secretary of State later in the year.

iv. To Louis XIV
[Translation from the French]

February 3, 1667/8.

Monsieur, my brother. The present posture of affairs not permitting me to deliberate a long time what part to take, I have chosen that which I thought most conformable to what I owe to the repose of Christendom, and have joined the States General of the United Provinces to bring about a peace between you and the Catholic King, my brother, in which I believe I have not done a disagreeable thing to you, as we have agreed to propose the said peace upon the conditions that you have often expressed yourself willing to accept, and more expressly in your last letter of the 27th past, in which (after having been so good as to communicate to me your intended march into the Franche Comte) you declare that, whatever the success may be, you still were willing to accept the beforementioned conditions; thus sacrificing your private interests to the public good. A most generous sentiment and worthy of you.

I have ordered the Chevalier Trevor, a gentleman of my bedchamber, whom I have sent to France in quality of my envoy extraordinary, to explain matters to you more at large and the desire I have to execute the treaty I have made with every possible regard for your satisfaction; to whom, if you please, you will give entire confidence, and more particularly when he assures you of the inviolable friendship which on all occasions I wish to preserve as, Monsieur, my brother, Your good brother.

v. To Madame

February 4, 1667/8.

I have dispatched this bearer, Sir John Trevor, into France as my envoy extraordinary, with power to negotiate the Peace between the two Crowns, according to the treaty I lately made with the States of the United Provinces.   I have given him orders to communicate all things with that freedom to you as I ought to do, from having that kindness for you which I cannot in words sufficiently express. I hope he will not find his work difficult, since I press nothing but the conditions of peace, which the King of France offered to agree with Spain upon. . . .

VI. To Madame

Whitehall, February 10, 1667/8.

I cannot enough thank you for your kindness to James. I hope he is as sensible of your goodness to him as I am. I do not intend to call him yet away from you, except Monsieur should go to the Army, but in that case I think it will not be decent for him to stay at Paris, when everybody will be in the field, and on the other side, as matters stand, it will not be convenient for me that he should go to the Army, for divers reasons, which I will not trouble you with in this letter. But I hope there will be no need of Monsieur's going thither.

I went this day to the Parliament, to acquaint them with the League I had lately made, and to put them in mind of my debts I had contracted in this last war, and to give me some money at this present. They have put off the consideration of it till Friday, and then I hope they will behave themselves as they ought to do. . . .

VII. Speech to both Houses

February 10, 1667/8.

My Lords and Gentlemen: I am glad to see you here again, to tell you what I have done in this interval, which I am confident you will be pleased with, since it is so much for the honour and security of this nation. I have made a League defensive with the States of the United Provinces, and likewise a League for an efficacious Mediation of Peace between the two Crowns; into which League that of Sweden, by its ambassador, hath offered to enter as a principal.

I did not at our last meeting move you for any aid, though I lie under great debts contracted in the last war; but now the posture of our neighbours abroad, and the consequence of the new alliance, will oblige me, for our security, to set out a considerable fleet to sea this summer. And besides I must build more great ships; and it is as necessary that I do some things in order to the fortifying some of our ports. I have begun something myself in order to these ends; but, if I have not your speedy assistance, I shall not be able to go through with it. Wherefore I do earnestly desire you to take it into your speedy consideration; for the loss of a little time now may beget a prejudice not to be repaired. And for the settling a firm Peace, as well at home as abroad, one thing more I hold myself obliged to recommend to you at this present; which is, that you would seriously think of some course to beget a better union and composure in the minds of my Protestant subjects in matters of religion, whereby they may be induced not only to submit quietly to the government, but also cheerfully give their assistance to the support of it.

But Charles's real hopes, as in the days before the war, were in favour of a French, and not a Dutch alliance, and though he had temporally annoyed Louis he knew that his move towards Holland had raised his price in the French King's eyes. Charles had no personal love for the Dutch, from whom he had suffered much, and saw in their sea power and commercial empire the real rival of his country; on the other hand, unlike the majority of his subjects, he liked the French and had no objection to their being predominant on land provided that they left him master of the seas. On that point he was always adamant: nor would he allow his desire to improve his relations with Louis to interfere for a moment with his interests or dignity at sea. At this moment he sent peremptory orders to the Duke of York to obtain immediate redress by force if necessary from a French sea captain who, in scouring the Channel for Spanish prizes, had defied international law by seizing two in English roadsteads. He did not even wait for the reply to the protest which he had sent to Louis.

VIII. TO THE DUKE OF YORK

[*Countersigned* ' By His Majesty's Command, Arlington ']

February 23, 1667/8.

Most dear brother, we greet you well. Whereas we have received information of great violences committed in several of our ports by certain French ships under the command of the

Sieur de la Roche, we have for the preventing the like for the future, as well as obtaining satisfaction for those already done, been pleased to signify our pleasure to you, that accordingly our will and pleasure is that you give orders unto Sir Thomas Allen, Knight, to sail towards those parts where it is probable he may find the said Sieur de la Roche, in performing of which he is carefully to observe the following instructions. . . .

. . . He is to look for the said Sieur de la Roche in all our ports, bays and roads of this our kingdom as far as Falmouth, and more particularly in Cowes Road, Torbay, Plymouth and Falmouth.   In case he finds him in any of them, he is to come to an anchor by the said Sieur de la Roche, and if he, the said Sir Thomas Allen, judge himself the stronger so as to be able to compel him, he is to require of him immediately to deliver to him all our subjects, whether seamen or others, who are on board any of the ships under his command. . . .

IX. To Madame

March 5, 1667/8.

I am extremely troubled that Trevor carried himself so like an ass to you.   I have sent him a chiding for it.   I can say nothing for him, but that it was a fault for want of good breeding, which is a disease very much spread over this country.

I received your long letter on the 7th inst. now, wherein I perceive you are very much alarmed at my condition, and at the cabals which are growing here.   I do take your concern for me very kindly, and thank you for the counsel you give me, but I do not think you have so much cause to fear as you seem to do in your letter.   There is no doubt but a House of Commons will be extravagant enough when there is need of them, and 'tis not much to be wondered at that I should be in debt after so expenseful a war as I have had, which undoubtedly will give me some trouble before I get out of it.   I will not deny but that naturally I am more lazy than I ought to be, but you are very ill informed if you do not know that my Treasury, and indeed all my other affairs, are in as good a method as our understandings can put them into.   And I think the peace [February 13,

1668] I have made between Spain and Portugal and the Defensive League [January 23, 1668] I have made with Holland, should give some testimony to the world that we think of our interest here. I do assure you that I neglect nothing for want of pains. If we fail for want of understanding, there is no help for it.

The gentleman by mistake gave Hamilton's letter to my Lord Arlington, who read it, without looking upon the superscription, and so brought it to me. I assure you that my Lord of Buckingham does not govern affairs here. I do not doubt but my Lord Clarendon, and some of his friends here, will discredit me and my affairs as much as they can, but I shall say no more upon that subject, for, if you knew how ill a servant he has been to me, you would not doubt but he would be glad things should not go on smoothly, now he is out of affairs. And most of the vexation and trouble I have at present in my affairs I owe to him.

The Parliament have voted me three hundred thousand pounds for the setting out of a fleet, and are now finding out the means of raising it.

You will hear great complaints from La Roche, who was taken in the ship called the *Ruby* last year, but Trevor will let you know the truth, and then you will see that I have reason to complain. I will add no more to this long letter, only again thank you for your good counsel, which I take very kindly from you as a mark of your concern for me. But pray do not be alarmed so soon by politique coxcombs, who think all wisdom lies in finding fault, and be assured that I have all the kindness and tenderness for you imaginable.

For the next few weeks the correspondence with Madame turned on personal rather than political matters. Her health, which was always frail, necessitated a visit to the waters at Bourbon, and Charles, ever anxious on her account, sent his personal physician, Dr. Alexander Fraizer, to attend her.

x. To Madame

Whitehall, March 10, 1667/8.

I am very sorry that your health obliges you to go to Bourbon, but undoubtedly 'tis the best course you can take to establish your health again, which is that which you ought to think of in the first place. I am sure I am more concerned for it than for anything in this world, and if I had no other reason but gratitude, I ought to love you more than I can express.

My Lord of Buckingham is so afraid that you should think that he is the cause that H. Killigrew[1] does not return hither, since you have desired him to forgive what is past, as he has again desired me to tell you there is nothing of what relates to him in the case; as in truth there is not, but he has offended so many of the Lady's relations in what concerns her, as it would not be convenient for him to show his face here. The truth is, both for his own sake and our quiet here, it will be no inconvenience for him to have a little patience in other countries.

The Parliament goes on very slowly in their money, but they advance something every day. However, I am preparing my ships to go to sea for the summer guard. We expect Don John every day here, on his way to Flanders. I hope his only business will be for the conclusion of the peace, which I wish may have a happy conclusion for many reasons. . . .

XI

April 4, 1668.

I send this express back again, with the return of what he brought from Trevor and Van Beuninghen, the particulars of which he will acquaint you with, so as I will only add upon that matter that I hope the peace will follow. I received yours of the sixth since the post went, so as I could not say anything to you then. I cannot tell whether the Duchess of Richmond will be much marked with smallpox; she has many, and I fear they will at least do her no good. For her husband, he cannot alter from what he is, let her be never so much changed.

But to turn my discourse to a matter which I am more concerned with than anything in this world. I see by your letter to James Hamilton that you are consulting your health with a

---

[1] Harry Killigrew, before flying to France from his creditors, had defamed the reputation of Lady Shrewsbury, in whose illicit favours he had been supplanted by the Duke of Buckingham.

physician which I have a very ill opinion of in that affair, which is yourself. I must confess I have not much better opinion of those you were governed by before, not believing they understand the disease you have so well as they do here. I have therefore sent Doctor Fraizer to you, who I will dispatch to-morrow, who is well acquainted with the constitution of your body, and I believe is better versed in those kind of diseases than any man in Paris, for those kind of obstructions are much more here than in France. And this is all I shall trouble you with at this time, but that I am entirely yours.   c.

XII

Whitehall, May 7, 1668.

I have so often asked your pardon for omitting writing to you, as I am almost ashamed to do it now. The truth is, the last week I absolutely forgot it till it was too late, for I was at the Duchess of Richmond's, who, you know, I have not seen this twelve months, and she put it out of my head that it was post day. She is not much marked with the smallpox, and I must confess this last affliction made me pardon all that is past, and cannot hinder myself from wishing her very well. And I hope she will not be much changed, as soon as her eye is well, for she has a very great defluction in it, and even some danger of having a blemish in it, but now I believe the worst is past.

I did receive your letter by Fitzgerald the same day that the physicians were doing the very prescriptions you advise in your letter. But now that matter is over, for my wife miscarried this morning.[1] And though I am troubled at it, yet I am glad that 'tis evident she was with child, which I will not deny to you till now I did fear she was not capable of. The physicians do intend to put her into a course of physic which they are confident will make her hold faster next time. . . .

I will not go about to decide the dispute between Mam's masses or Mr. de Mayerne's[2] pills, but I am sure the suddenness of your recovery is as near a miracle as anything can be. And

[1] Of a perfect child, Pepys heard, about ten weeks old.
[2] Sir Theodore Mayerne, the great physician and chemical experimentalist, whose pills Dr. Fraizer had recommended.

though you find yourself very well now, for God's sake have a care of your diet, and believe the plainer your diet is the better health you will have. Above all, have a care of strong broths and gravy in the morning.

I ask your pardon for forgetting to deliver your message to James,[1] but I have done it now. He shall answer for himself, and I am sure he has no excuse, for I have often put him in mind to acknowledge, upon all occasions, the great obligations he has to you for your goodness to him, which I assure you he expresses every day here. If he does fail in writing, I fear he takes a little after his father. And so I will end this long trouble with the assuring you that I cannot express the kindness and tenderness I have for you.

XIII

Whitehall, May 14, 1668.

Trevor was very much in the right to assure you that I would not take it ill that you did that part of *charité* for my Lord Clarendon, for my displeasure does not follow him to that degree as to wish him anywhere but out of England.[2]

I see Montbrun[3] does not change his humour; he always told every lady here that his daughter was not painted, and was believed as much as he is in France. For her two other qualities, I can only say that if she be as truly his daughter as I am confident she was honest here, he may be believed, for I am confident nobody here took the pains to ask her an indecent question. The truth is, James did maintain for some time that she was not painted, but he was quickly laughed out of it.

I am sorry to find that cuckolds in France grow so troublesome. They have been inconvenient in all countries this last year. I have been in great trouble for James his wife,[4] her thigh being as we thought set very well, for three days together.

---

[1] The Duke of Monmouth, who had returned to England in March.

[2] Madame had intervened to prevent Clarendon being expelled from France.

[3] The Marquis de Montbrun, then on a visit to England, a comic figure whose pride in his very ordinary daughters was inordinate.

[4] The young Duchess of Monmouth had broken her leg.

At last we found it was still out, so that the day before yesterday it was set with all the torture imaginable; she is now pretty
well, and I hope will not be lame. I have been to see some of
my ships, which are going out to sea, and am but newly returned,
so as I have not time to add any more but that I am entirely
yours. c.

XIV

Whitehall, June 14, 1668.

The bearer and James Hamilton will tell you all that passes
here. The sudden retreat of Madame Mazarin[1] is as extraordinary an action as I have heard. She has exceeded my Lady
Shrewsbury in point of discretion by robbing her husband. I
see wives do not love devout husbands, which reason this woman
had, besides many more, as I hear, to be rid of her husband,
upon any terms, and so I wish her a good journey.

I find, by the letters from Trevor, that they are alarmed in
France that I intend something against Denmark with the fleet
that I am now setting out. I do assure you there never was
any such intention, for I am now sending most of the great
ships into harbour, which are now only a charge, the peace at
Aix[2] being concluded, and I shall have this summer at sea only
the ordinary summer guard.[3] I shall say no more to you now,
only desire you to have the same goodness for James you had
the last time, and to chide him soundly when he does not that
he should do. He intends to put on a periwig again, when he
comes to Paris, but I believe you will think him better as I do,
with his short hair. And so I am entirely yours. c.

*The fears of his subjects as to the growing power of France
having been temporarily allayed by the pacification of Europe in*

[1] Hortense Mancini, Duchesse of Mazarin, Mazarin's beautiful niece
and heiress, had suddenly bolted from her religious and jealous husband,
the Marquis de la Meilleraye, to intrigue all Europe by her subsequent
behaviour. The jewels were actually her own.

[2] Between France and Spain.

[3] Charles was trying to put the bankrupt financial affairs of the Navy
straight by reducing naval expenditure to £200,000 per annum—a hopeless
attempt, as the event was to show.

*the Peace of Aix-la-Chapelle, Charles returned to his old project—
the traditional policy of Elizabeth and Cromwell—of strengthening the ties between England and France.   Hatred of Holland
and jealousy of Dutch sea power, admiration for Louis's absolute Government contrasted with his own Parliament-ridden,
money-starved state, and personal affection for his French
relations all prompted him.   Negotiations were now opened for
a definite understanding, and Louis, who since the events of
the beginning of the year had learnt to set more store on Charles's
friendship, sent Charles Colbert, Marquis de Croissy, brother of
his chief Minister, as ambassador to London with instructions
to break the Triple Alliance and substitute for it an offensive and
defensive alliance between England and France.*

xv. To Madame

Whitehall, July 8, 1668.

I cannot say much to you yet, in answer to the letters you
have writ to me, concerning the good correspondence you
desire there should be between the King of France and me.   I
am very glad to find, by your letters as well as Trevor's relations,
the inclinations there is to meet with the constant desire I have
always had to make a stricter alliance with France than there
has hitherto been.   And pray say all to the King you ought to
say from me in return of the kindness he expresses towards me,
and when Monsieur de Colbert comes, I hope he will have those
powers as will finish what we all desire.   And be assured that
whatsoever negotiation there is between France and me, you
shall always have that part in it as they shall see the value and
kindness I have for you.   One thing I desire you to take as much
as you can out of the King of France's head, that my Ministers
are anything but what I will have them, and that they have no
partiality but to my interest and the good of England. . . .

xvi. To Madame

Whitehall, July 27, 1668.[1]

I have been so faulty to you in matter of writing, as it is
impudence to expect pardon from you.   The truth is, I have got

---

[1] Attributed to 1667 in the volume of Charles's letters at the Quai
d'Orsay, but re-dated by Mr. Hartmann, I think rightly, to 1668.

into such a vein of hunting, and the game lies so far from this town, as I must spend one day entirely to kill one stag, and then the other days I have a great deal of business. So that all this, with my laziness towards writing, has been the cause of my fault towards you. I am but just now come from hunting, and am very weary, but I am resolved for the future to be very punctual in writing to you so that in time I hope to merit your pardon. For though I am faulty to you in letters, I am sure there is nothing can love another so well as I do you. c.

XVII. To Madame

Whitehall, August 3, 1668.

. . . I am very glad to find by you, and what James says to me, the inclination and intention the King, my brother, has to enter into a stricter friendship with me. I am sure I have all the inclinations towards it that either he or you can desire in that matter, and when Monsieur Colbert comes, he shall find nothing wanting on my part. I wish with all my heart that the propositions which Ruvigny sent, long since when he was here, had received that answer which I might reasonably have expected. They would have then seen that whatsoever opinion my Ministers had been of, I would and do always follow my own judgement, and if they take any other measures than that, they will see themselves mistaken in the end. I will say no more to you now but expect Monsieur Colbert, and I assure you the kindness I have for you will always make me do all I can to have a very good understanding with the country where you are, for there is nothing more at my heart than the letting you see, by all the ways I can, how truly I love you. c.

Before an Anglo-French alliance could be made, there were certain obstacles to be overcome. The almost certain opposition of most of his Ministers, and the hatred of his subjects for French Catholicism and their jealousy of every French success, Charles was confident he could overcome by wit and dissimulation. His existing alliance with the Dutch was a more serious obstacle, particularly as it was, on the whole, popular in England. But here Charles knew that he had only to play for time, for the recurrent tale of grievances suffered by English merchants and seamen at the hands of their Dutch rivals could be trusted to do their work. Meanwhile he could use public obligations to the Dutch as a bargaining point with Louis. But the greatest obstacle was Louis's scheme to create a great fleet and extend French commerce. It was to remove that obstacle that Madame's diplomatic services were now demanded, for not till the plan was abandoned could Charles join hands with the French King. On that point he would not yield an inch.

xviii. To Madame

Whitehall, September 2, 1668.

You judge very well when you conclude that I am satisfied with Monsieur Colbert, and I wish with all my heart that France had been as forward in their intentions towards us when Ruvigny was here, as I see they are now. I should not have been so embarrassed with the ties I am now under if the offers I then made had been accepted. My inclinations are still the same, and I hope in the end to bring all things to what I wish, but there are two impediments in the way, which at least do retard the inclinations there is, on both sides, to have an entire union.

The first is, the great application there is at this time in France to establish trade, and to be very considerable at sea, which is so jealous a point to us here, who can be only considerable by our trade and power by sea, as any steps that France makes that way must continue a jealousy between the two Nations, which will, upon all occasions, be a great hindrance to an entire friendship. And you cannot choose but believe that it must be dangerous to me at home to make an entire league till first the great and principal interest of this nation be secured, which is trade. The other difficulty is the treaties I am entered into of late, which I am sure the King, my brother, would not have me violate upon any terms, since he has given me the good example of being a martyr to his word.[1] But when I have said this, I do

---

[1] An ironical allusion to Louis's support of Holland during the second Dutch War.

believe we are not so tied, as if we received satisfaction on the principal matter of the sea, there is scope sufficient for a very near alliance. I am sure, as my inclinations carries me to it, so I will use all my endeavours to bring it to pass.

I have had some discourses with Mr. Colbert upon the subject of this letter, and have enlarged myself more fully to him than I can do in a letter, and now I must tell you that I am very well satisfied with him and think him as proper an ambassador for this place as could have been chosen. I have, upon all occasions, let him know the kindness I have for you, and that, if I had no other inclination to France but your being there, it would be a sufficient motive to make me desire passionately a strict union with them.

I am going to-morrow to Bagshot to hunt the stag, and shall not be here again till Saturday come sennight, intending likewise to take Portsmouth in my return, to see the fortifications that have lately been made there, and what is farther to be done. The Comte de Chappelle will tell you of all the little news here, so as I shall not trouble you with it. I have been as civil to him as I could, both upon your recommendations and the kindness Monsieur has for him, and besides that he hath a great deal of merit of his own. And I hope he is not ill satisfied with us here.

I hope you will not find fault with the shortness of this letter, and if you are but as sleepy at the reading of it as I am at the writing, I am certain you will think it long enough. And therefore, my dearest sister, I will only assure you that I am entirely yours. c.

XIX. To Madame

Whitehall, September 14, 1668.

At my return from Portsmouth, I found two of yours, one by the post, and the other by Mr. Lambert with the gloves, for which I thank you extremely. They are as good as is possible to smell. And in the other letter you accuse me most justly for my failing towards you, which I do ingeniously confess, as most people do to their ghostly father and as often fall into the same sin again. I hope I shall not be so faulty for the time to come, having now done stag-hunting for this year, which now and then made me so weary as, with the natural laziness I have towards writing, gave me occasion to miss oftener than otherwise I would have done.

The reason why I begin with the treaty of commerce is because I must enter first upon those matters which will render the rest more plausible here, for you know that the thing which is nearest the heart of the nation is trade and all that belongs to it. But I shall not enter further upon this matter now, because I have done it fully by de Chappelle, who will be with you before this time. And you may be sure that I will continue my care to let them see the power you have over me, and how much my kindness to you adds to my inclination to live always very well with France. . . .

. . . I do intend to go to Newmarket[1] the last day of this month, at which place and at Audley End, I shall stay near a month. My wife goes to the latter of these places at the same time, which is all I will trouble with at this time but to assure you that 'tis impossible to have more kindness and tenderness than I have for you.

One of Madame's greatest hopes was that her beloved brother should be reclaimed from the Protestant heresy in which he had been brought up and in which his subjects still imprisoned him. And though Charles was only received into the Catholic Church on his deathbed, his religious inclinations, so far as he had any, were all towards the ancient faith, whose practitioners had proved his staunchest friends during his early troubles, and whose doctrines suited monarchy so much better than Protestantism. He had already made one attempt to secure toleration for the English Catholics; now, probably at his sister's suggestion, he planned a bolder move to obtain them equal rights by declaring himself one of them. At least so he pretended, for it is impossible for anyone to say for certain whether Charles ever really intended to take such a perilous step. But since it was

---

[1] Where Charles paid the first of his regular visits that October, the Queen staying at Audley End, which Charles had taken for her.

perilous, and since Louis, thinking that it would increase his dependence on France, shared Madame's anxiety for the royal conversion, Charles saw that the idea could be made to pay. Into the negotiations for a treaty there crept a new element— an understanding that the alliance should be accompanied by a royal declaration of conversion and universal toleration, the hazard of which was to be balanced by the payment by Louis of a money subsidy. And in the burdened state of his finances, this was what Charles needed above everything else.

All this made the need for secrecy greater than ever: a cipher of names was agreed on between Charles and Madame, and elaborate deceptions were practised in order to allow the vain Buckingham, who could not be trusted, to initiate, or appear to initiate, a sham Anglo-French alliance through his agent, Sir Ellis Leighton. Meanwhile, Parliament, which had not met since May, 1668, was prorogued for another ten months.

xx. TO MADAME

Whitehall, December 14, 1668.

He that came last, and delivered me your letter of the 9th, has given me a full account of what he was charged with, and I am very well pleased with what he tells me. I will answer the other letter he brought to me very quickly. I am sure it shall not be my fault if all be not as you can wish. I will send you a cipher by the first safe occasion, and you shall then know the way I think most proper to proceed in the whole matter, which I hope will not displease you. I will say no more by the post upon this business, for you know 'tis not very sure.

I do intend to prorogue the Parliament till October next, before which time I shall have set my affairs in that posture as there will not be so many miscarriages to be hunted after as in the last sessions. I beg your pardon for forgetting, in my last, to thank you for the petticoat you sent me, 'tis the finest I ever saw, and thank you a thousand times for it. I can say no more to you now, for I am called to go to the play. . . .

XXI. To Madame

Whitehall, December 27, 1668.

You must yet expect a day or two for an answer to what Leighton brought, because I sent it by a safe way, and you know how much secrecy is necessary for the carrying on of the business. And I assure you that nobody does, nor shall know anything of it here but myself, and that one person more, till it be fit to be public, which will not be till all matters are agreed upon.

In the meantime I must tell you that I received yours of the 26th of this month, and the 2 of January just now. . . .

I must confess, I would rather have had you stayed some months before you had been with child, for reasons you will know shortly, but I hope it will be for your advantage, and then I shall be glad of it. I shall say no more now, only wish you a good new year, which, if it prove as happy to you as I wish, you will have no reason to complain.

On January 25, 1669, at a secret meeting in the Duke of York's lodgings, Charles revealed his ' grand design' to his brother, Lord Arlington, Sir Thomas Clifford, the daring Treasurer of his household, and Lord Arundell of Wardour. The latter, a leading Catholic, who as Queen Henrietta Maria's Master of Horse could travel between the two countries without suspicion, was selected to negotiate the religious-financial part of the alliance with Louis. He was to insist on a cessation of French shipbuilding and reserve the right of Charles to honour the letter of the law of his inconvenient treaty with the Dutch. At the same time Louis dispatched to England an Italian Abbé, of the name of Pregnani, with a fashionable reputation for casting horoscopes, in the belief that his carefully inspired predictions would hasten Charles into committing himself irretrievably to France and Catholicism. But here Louis was mistaken, for the Abbé never imposed for a moment on the English King, who derived a good deal of quiet amusement both from his pretensions and their effect on the members of his court. Meanwhile, the more practical aspects of the intended alliance were embodied in an Anglo-French commercial treaty, the terms of which both safeguarded English trading interests and occupied the energies of the unsuspecting Buckingham and the French ambassador, Colbert.

XXII. TO MADAME

Whitehall, January 20, 1668/9.

You will see, by the letter which I have written to the King, my brother, the desire I have to enter into a personal friendship with him, and to unite our interests so for the future as there may never be any jealousies between us. The only thing which can give any impediment to what we both desire is the matter of the sea, which is so essential a point to us here as a union upon any other security can never be lasting. Nor can I be answerable to my kingdoms if I should enter into an alliance, wherein their present and future security were not fully provided for.

I am now thinking of the way how to proceed in this whole matter, which must be carried on with all secrecy imaginable, till the particulars are further agreed upon. I must confess, I was not very glad to hear you were with child, because I had a thought by your making a journey hither, all things might have been adjusted without any suspicion. And as I shall be very just to the King, my brother, in never mentioning what has passed between us, in case this negotiation does not succeed as I desire, so I expect the same justice and generosity from him, that no advances which I make out of the desire I have to obtain a true friendship between us may ever turn to my prejudice. I send you, here enclosed, my letter to the King, my brother, desiring that this matter might pass through your hands, as the person in the world I have most confidence in. . . .

I had written thus far when I received yours by the Italian, whose name and capacity you do not know. And he delivered your letter to me in a passage, where it was so dark as I do not know his face again if I see him; so as the man is likely to succeed, when his recommendation and reception are so suitable to one another. But to return to the business of the letter, I assure you that there is no league entered into as yet with the Emperor. The only league I am in is the guarantee I am engaged in with the Hollanders upon the peace at Aix, which is equally binding towards both the Crowns. I think Monsieur de Lorraine deserves to be punished for his unquiet humour, but

I wish the King, my brother, do not proceed too far in that matter, least he gives a jealousy to his neighbours, that he intends a further progress than what he declared at first, which might be very prejudicial to what you and I wish and endeavour to compass.[1]

And you shall not want, upon all occasions, full informations necessary. But we must have a great care what we write by the post lest it fall into hands which may hinder our design, for I must again conjure you that the whole matter be an absolute secret, otherwise we shall never compass the end we aim at. I have not yet absolutely contrived how to proceed in this business, because there must be all possible precautions used, that it may not *éclat* before all things be agreed upon, and pray do you think of all the ways you can to the same end, and communicate them to me. I send you here a cipher, which is very easy and secure. The first side is the single cipher, and within such names I could think of necessary to our purpose. I have no more to add, but that I am entirely yours.   c.

XXIII. To Madame

Whitehall, March 7, 1668/9

I am to go, to-morrow morning, to Newmarket at three o'clock, and kept this express till now to know what the King, my brother, would do with Douglas his regiment, which I perceive, by yours that I received this day, does not go to Candia, which I take as a great mark of the King, my brother's, kindness to me.[2] And pray let him know so much from me, and assure him that it was not anything for Douglas his sake that I desired so earnestly his stay, but for reasons which he shall know within very few days.

[1] An expedition Louis was planning against Lorraine, which might have produced international complications and so have compelled Charles to honour his obligations to Holland.

[2] A Scots regiment in French service, commanded by Lord George Douglas, which Louis had been about to send to Candia against the Turks, and which Charles had successfully urged should remain in France lest its presence in Candia should cause Turkish reprisals against English merchants.

I have dispatched this night Lord Arundell[1] to Madame, who is fully instructed as you can wish. You will see by him the reason why I desired you to write to nobody here, of the business of France, but to myself; he has some private business of his own to dispatch before he leaves this town, but he will certainly set out this week. But pray take no notice of his having any commission from me, for he pretends to go only upon his own score to attend the Queen. . . .

. . . You may be sure that I will keep the secret of your prophet. I give little credit to such kind of cattle, and the less you do it the better, for if they could tell anything 'tis inconvenient to know one's fortune beforehand, whether good or bad, and so, my dearest sister, good night, for 'tis late, and I have not above three hours to sleep this night.

I had almost forgot to tell you, that I find your friend, l'Abbé Pregnani, a man very ingenious in all things I have talked with him upon, and I find him to have a great deal of wit, but you may be sure I will enter no further with him than according to your character.

XXIV. To Madame

Newmarket, March 12, 1668/9.

I have had very good sport here since Monday last, both by hunting and horse-races. L'Abbé Pregnani is here, and wonders very much at the pleasure everybody takes at the races. He was so weary with riding from Audley End hither, to see the foot-match, as he is scarce recovered yet. I have been a fox-hunting this day and am very weary. Yet the weather is so good, as my brother has persuaded me to see his fox-hounds run to-morrow, and at night I am to lie at Saxham, where I shall stay Sunday, and so come hither again, and not return to London till the latter end of next week.

This bearer, my Lord Rochester, has a mind to make a little journey to Paris, and would not kiss your hands without a letter from me; pray use him as one I have a very good opinion of.

---

[1] The significant names of this and the subsequent letters to Madame are in cipher.

You will find him not to want wit, and did behave himself in all the Dutch war as well as anybody, as a volunteer. I have no more to add, but that I am entirely yours.   c.

xxv. To Madame

Whitehall, March 22, 1668/9.

I came from Newmarket the day before yesterday, where we had as fine weather as we could wish, which added much both to the horse matches as well as to hunting. L'Abbé Pregnani was there most part of the time, and I believe will give you some account of it, but not that he lost his money upon confidence that the stars could tell which horse would win. For he had the ill luck to foretell three times wrong together, and James believed him so much as he lost his money upon the same score.

I had not my cipher at Newmarket when I received yours of the 16th, so as I could say nothing to you in answer to it till now. And before this comes to your hands, you will clearly see upon what score 363 [the Duke of York] is come into the business, and for what reason I desired you not to write to anybody upon the business of 271 [France]. 341 [Buckingham] knows nothing of 360 [Charles II] intentions towards 290, 315 [Catholic religion], nor of the person 334 [Charles II] sends to 100 [the King of France], and you need not fear that 341 [Buckingham] will take it ill that 103 [Madame] does not write to him, for I have told him that I have forbid 129 [Madame] to do it, for fear of intercepting of letters. Nor indeed is there much use of our writing much upon this subject, because letters may miscarry, and you are, before this time, so fully acquainted with all, as there is nothing more to be added till my messenger comes back.

You have counselled Monsieur very well in the matter of Mr. de Rohan. I never heard of a more impertinent carriage than his. I had not time to write to you by Father Patrick, for he took the resolution of going to France but the night before I left this place, but now I desire you to be kind to the poor man, for he is as honest a man as lives, and pray direct your physician to have a care of him, for I should really be troubled if he should not do well.

What you sent by Mercer is lost, for there are letters come that informs of his setting sail from Havre, in an open *challoupe*, with intention to come to Portsmouth, and we have never heard of him since, so he is undoubtedly drowned. I hear Mam[1] sent me a present by him, which, I believe, brought him the ill luck, so as she ought, in conscience, to be at the charges of pray-ing for his soul, for 'tis her fortune has made the man miscarry. And so, my dearest sister, I am yours, with all the kindness and tenderness imaginable.

With the progress of the negotiations grew the need for an elaborate series of deceptions to keep the less trustworthy Protestant Ministers, engaged in perfecting the outlying works of the proposed alliance, from penetrating its inner secrets. The most dangerous was Buckingham, whose restless vanity made him constantly suspicious—particularly of Madame's reported interviews with the French King and of old Lord St. Albans's rather ostentatious comings and goings, which set tongues wagging even in the streets of London. Another complication was caused by the necessary appointment of a new English ambassador at Paris—Ralph Montagu, who, as a Protestant, could not be let into the full secret. Madame was even inclined to distrust Charles's faithful Secretary of State, Arlington, who was regarded in France as pro-Spanish; but here she was wrong, as her brother assured her, for Arlington, though still a Protestant, was devoted to his master's interests. And on his own side, Charles had no love and little trust for the French ambassador, Colbert, whom Louis wished to entrust with the full secret of the negotiations.

XXVI. To Madame

Whitehall, April 25, 1669.

I find by 405 [Lord St. Albans] that he does believe there is some business with 271 [France], which he knows nothing of. He told 341 [Buckingham] that I had forbidden you to

[1] Henrietta Maria's ill-luck at sea was a family joke.

write to him, by which he believed there was some mystery in the matter, but 341 [Buckingham] was not at all alarmed at it, because it was by his own desire that I writ that to you, but how 379 [Lord St. Albans] comes to know that, I cannot tell. It will be good that you write sometimes to 393 [Buckingham] in general terms, that he may not suspect that there are further negotiations than what he knows of. But pray have a care you do not say anything to him which may make him think that I have employed anybody to 152 [Louis XIV], which he is to know nothing of, because by the messenger he may suspect that there is something of 290, 315 [the Catholic religion's] interest in the case, which is a matter he must not be acquainted with. Therefore you must have a great care, not to say the least thing that may make him suspect anything of it.

I had writ thus far before I had heard of your fall, which puts me in great pain for you, and shall not be out of it till I know that you have received no prejudice by it. I go to-morrow to Newmarket for six days, and shall be, in the meantime, very impatient to hear from you, for I can be at no rest when you are not well, and so, my dearest sister, have a care of yourself, as you have any kindness for me.

XXVII. To Madame

Whitehall, May 6, 1669.

You cannot imagine what a noise 353 [Lord St. Albans] coming has made here, as if he had great propositions from 152 [Louis XIV], which I beat down as much as I can, it being prejudicial, at this time, to have it thought that 360 [Charles II] had any other commerce with 126 [Louis XIV] but that of 280 [Treaty of Commerce]. And in order to that, I have directed some of the Council to treat with 112 [Colbert de Croissy], which in time will bring on the whole matter as we can wish. And pray let there be great caution used on the side of 271 [France] concerning 386 [Charles II] intentions towards 126 [Louis XIV], which would not only be prejudicial to the carrying on of the matters with 270 [England], but also to our further designs abroad. And this opinion I am sure you must be of, if you consider well the whole matter.

I believe Mr. Montagu has, before this, in some degree satisfied you concerning my Lord Arlington, and done him that justice to assure you that nobody is more your servant than he. For he cannot be so entirely mine as he is, and be wanting in you in the least degree, and I will be answerable for him in what he owes you. I find the poor Abbé Pregnani very much troubled for fear that the railleries about foretelling the horse matches may have done him some prejudice with you, which I hope it has not done, for he was only trying new tricks which he had read of in books, and gave as little credit to them as we did. And pray continue to be his friend so much as to hinder all you can any prejudice that may come to him upon that score, for the man has wit enough, and is as much your servant as is possible, which makes me love him.

My wife has been a little indisposed some few days, and there is hopes that it will prove a disease not displeasing to me. I should not have been so forward in saying thus much without more certainty, but that I believe others will write it to Paris, and say more than there is. And so I shall end with assuring you that 'tis impossible to be more yours than I am.

XXVIII. TO MADAME

Whitehall, May 24, 1669.

You have, I hope, received full satisfaction by the last post in the matter of Marsilly,[1] for my Lord Arlington has sent to Mr. Montagu his history all the time he was here, by which you will see how little credit he had here and that particularly my Lord Arlington was not in his good graces, because he did not receive that satisfaction in his negotiation he expected, and that was only in relation to the Swisers. And so I think I have said enough of this matter and shall give you now a particular account of my wife with that plainness you desire. She has

---

[1] A French traitor who had been plotting against Louis's life in England, and in whose possessions the French authorities had discovered documents that hinted at the complicity of Buckingham and Arlington.

missed *those* almost, if not altogether, twice about this time she
ought to have *them*, and she had a kind of a colic the day before
yesterday which pressed downwards and made her apprehend
she should miscarry, but to-day she is so well as she does not keep
her bed.   The midwives who have searched her say that her
matrix is very close, though it be a little low; she has now and
then some little shows of *them*, but in so very little quantity as
it only confirms the most knowing women here that there is a
fair conception.   I think this is sufficient to make you understand my wife's case, and if you desire any more of this kind
I will be instructed further by the women and send it to you.

The accident which befell the Prince of Tuscany and the
French ambassador[1] here made a great noise, but my Lady
Shrewsbury's business with Harry Killigrew has quite silenced
the other.[2]   My Lord Chief Justice is inquiring after the matter,
and what the Law will do I cannot tell; but the lady is retired
out of her house and not certainly known where she is.   And
so, my dearest sister, good night, for 'tis late and I have nothing
to add but that which I can never tell you too often, how truly
and passionately I love my dearest Minette.

XXIX. To Madame

Whitehall, June 6, 1669.

The opportunity of this bearer's going into France gives me
a good occasion to answer your letters by my Lord Allington,[3]
and in the first place to tell you that I am securing all the
principal ports of this country, not only by fortifying them as
they ought to be, but likewise the keeping them in such hands
as I am sure will be faithful to me upon all occasions.   And this
will secure the fleet, because the chief places where the ships lie
are Chatham and Portsmouth.   The first of which is fortifying
with all speed, and will be finished this year.   The other is in
good condition already, but not so good as I desire, for it will

---

[1] The usual kind of squabble about precedence.

[2] Killigrew, having returned to England and continued his insinuations
against Lady Shrewsbury, had been dangerously wounded in an attack
made on him by that lady's footmen.

[3] William, third Lord Allington of Killard.

cost some money and time to make the place as I have designed it. And I will not have less care both in Scotland and Ireland. As for that which concerns those who have church lands, there will be easy ways found out to secure them and put them out of all apprehension.

There is all the reason in the world to join profit with honour, when it may be done honestly, and 126 [Louis XIV] will find 360 [Charles] as forward to do 299 [Holland] a good turn as he can desire, and they will, I doubt not, agree very well in the point, for that country has used them both very scurvily.[1] I am sure 334 [Charles] will never be satisfied till he has had his revenge and is very willing to enter into an agreement upon that matter whensoever 152 [Louis XIV] please. And I will answer for 346 [Arlington] that he will be as forward in that matter as I am, and farther assurance you cannot expect from an honest man in his post, nor ought you to trust him if he should make any other professions than to be for what his master is for. I say this to you, because I undertook to answer that part of the letter you writ to him upon this subject, and I hope this will be full satisfaction as to him in the future, that there may be no doubt, since I do answer for him.

I had writ thus far when I received yours by Ellwies, by which I perceive the inclination there still is of trusting 112 [Colbert] with the main business, which I must confess, for many reasons, I am very unwilling to, and if there were no other reason than his understanding, which, to tell you the truth, I have not so great an esteem for, as to be willing to trust him with that which is of so much concern. There will be a time when both he and 342 [Montagu] may have a share in part of the matter, but for the great secret, if it be not kept so till all things be ready to begin, we shall never go through with it and destroy the whole business.

I have seen your letter to 341 [Buckingham] and what you write to him is as it ought to be. He shall be brought into all the business before he can suspect anything, except that which

---

[1] A reference to a secret proposal of De Witt's, contrary to the spirit of the Triple Alliance, that Holland and France should partition the decaying Spanish Empire between them without reference to England.

concerns 263 [religion], which he must not be trusted with. You will do well to write but seldom to him, for fear something may slip from your pen which may make him jealous that there is something more than what he knows of. I do long to hear from 340 [Arundell] or to see him here, for till I see the paper you mention which comes from 113 [Lionne] I cannot say more than I have done. . . .

I will end this with desiring you to believe that I have nothing so much at my heart as to be able to acknowledge the kindness you have for me. If I thought that making many compliments upon that matter would persuade you more of the sincerity of my kindness to you, you should not want whole sheets of paper with nothing but that. But I hope you have the justice to believe me, more than I can express, entirely yours.

xxx. To Madame

June 7, 1669.

I writ to you yesterday by Mr. de La Hilière upon that important point, whether 112 [Colbert de Croissy] ought to be acquainted with our secret, and the more I think of it, the more I am perplexed. Reflecting upon his insufficiency, I cannot think him fit for it, and therefore could wish some other fitter man in his station, but because the attempting of that might disoblige 137 [Colbert, the French minister], I can by no means advise it. Upon the whole matter I see no kind of necessity of telling 112 [Colbert de Croissy] of the secret now, nor indeed till 270 [England] is in a better readiness to make use of 297 [France] towards the great business. Methinks, it will be enough that 164 [Colbert de Croissy] be made acquainted with 100 [Louis XIV] security in 360 [Charles II] friendship, without knowing the reason of it. To conclude, remember how much the secret in this matter imports 386 [Charles II], and take care that no new body be acquainted with it, till I see what 340 [Arundell] brings 334 [Charles II] in answer to his propositions, and till you have my consent that 164 [Colbert de Croissy], or anybody else, have their share in that matter.

I would fain know (which I cannot do but by 336 [Arundell]) how ready 323 [France] is to break with 299 [Holland]. That is the game that would, as I conceive, most accommodate the interests both of 270 [England] and 297 [France]. As for 324 [Spain], he is sufficiently undoing himself to need any help from 271 [France], nay, I am persuaded the meddling with him would unite and make his counsels stronger. The sooner you dispatch 340 [Arundell], the more clearly we shall be able to judge of the whole matter.

One caution more I had like to have forgotten, that when it shall be fit to acquaint 138 [Colbert de Croissy] with 152 [Louis XIV] security in 386 [Charles II] friendship, he must not say anything of it in 270 [England]. And pray let the Ministers in 297 [France] speak less confidently of 360 [Charles II] friendship than I hear they do, for it will infinitely discompose 269 [Parliament] when they meet with 334 [Charles II] to believe that 386 [Charles II] is tied so fast with 271 [France], and make 321 [Parliament] have a thousand jealousies upon it. I have no more to add, but to tell you that my wife, after all our hopes, has miscarried again, without any visible accident. The physicians are divided whether it were a false conception or a good one, and so good night, for 'tis very late. I am entirely yours. c.

XXXI. To Madame

Whitehall, June 24, 1669.

It will be very difficult for me to say anything to you upon the propositions till 340 [Arundell] return hither. And if he makes many objections, which it may be are not altogether reasonable, you must not wonder at it, for, as he is not a man much versed in affairs of state, so there are many scruples he may have, which will not be so here. And I am confident, when we have heard the reasons of all sides we shall not differ in the main, having the same interest and inclinations. And for 372 [Arlington] I can say no more for him than I have already done, only that I think, being upon the place and observing everybody as well as I can, I am the best judge of his fidelity to me, and what his inclinations are. And, if I should be deceived in the opinion I have of him, I am sure I should smart for it most. I shall write to you to-morrow by l'Abbé Prégnani, so I shall add no more now. And, in truth, I am just now going to a new play that I hear very much commended, and so I am Yours. C.

That of June 24 is the last of Charles's letters to his sister that have come down to us: the vast majority were all returned to him after her death and almost certainly destroyed. Hence- forward the negotiations were conducted with even greater secrecy. The only surviving document by Charles is a letter of September 30, sent to Louis by Lord Arundell to introduce the demands which Charles asked of France—a million sterling with which to set out the English Fleet, the supreme control of the naval campaign, and a further £200,000 for his conversion. In return he promised to seize the first favourable opportunity of declaring war on Holland (since, were France to take the first step, England would be forced by her treaty obligations to assist the Dutch to repel invasion), and to assist Louis in obtaining his dynastic rights to the Spanish crown, when they accrued, on con- dition of receiving South America, Ostend and Minorca as the English share of the spoil.

xxxii. To Louis XIV
[*Translation from French*]

September 30, 1669.

Monsieur, my brother. The bearer is so well known to you, there needs no further recommendation for his being believed in the discourse he will hold to you on my part. My sister will at the time of his arrival deliver to you a paper which I thought proper should accompany him, in which you will see the most secret sentiments of my soul on the subject of the said discourse. I address the said paper to you by the hands of my sister to confirm you in the mutual confidence we both have in her discretion and zeal to unite us more strongly. I have charged the bearer to assure you of the entire satisfaction I have in your just and obliging proceeding with regard to myself, and of the real friendship with which I am. . . .

Meanwhile Charles was taking steps to safeguard his position at home. The chief forts and arsenals were placed in the hands of trustworthy officers, a Militia Act placing 22,000 Scottish troops at the royal disposal was coaxed through the Scottish Parliament, and an Act of Union between the two kingdoms prepared. To meet the pressing need of money, Parliament was called for October.

XXXIII. SPEECH TO PARLIAMENT

October 19, 1669.

My Lords and Gentlemen: I am very glad to see you here at this time, and I hope this will be a happy meeting, for I have had great experience of your affection and loyalty to me, and am very confident of your continuance of it. It is now almost a year and a half since your last sitting; and though my debts have pressed me very much, yet I was unwilling to call for your assistance till this time.

What you gave me last was wholly applied to the Navy and that extraordinary fleet for which it was intended. I desire that you will now take my debts effectually into your considerations. Something I have to propose to you of great importance, concerning the uniting of England and Scotland; but it will require some length; and I have left that, and some other things, to my Lord Keeper to open them fully to you.

Charles's appeal for more money was lost sight of by the Commons in the more attractive occupations of baiting unpopular officials, looking for defalcations in the royal accounts and disputing their privileges with the House of Lords. In December the King therefore prorogued them till February, 1670, when he met them again with his usual request.

XXXIV. SPEECH TO PARLIAMENT

February 14, 1669/70.

My Lords and Gentlemen: I sent forth my proclamation that there might be a good appearance at this meeting, having most confidence in full houses, where the well-being of the Church, and all other interests of the Crown and nation, are best secured. When we met last, I asked you a supply; and I ask it now again with greater instance. The uneasiness and straitness of my affairs cannot continue without very ill effects to the whole kingdom. Consider this seriously and speedily. It is yours and the kingdom's interest, as well as mine; and the ill consequence of a want of an effectual supply must not lie at my door. And that no misapprehensions or mistakes touching the expenses of the last war may remain with you, I think fit to let you know that I have fully informed myself in that matter; and do affirm to you that no part of those moneys that you gave me for that war have been diverted to other uses; but, on the contrary, besides all those supplies, a very great sum hath been raised out of my standing revenue and credit, and a very great debt contracted; and all for the war.

One thing I must earnestly recommend to the prudence of both Houses: that you will not suffer any occasion of difference between yourselves to be revived, since nothing but the unity of your minds and counsels can make this meeting happy, either to me or to the nation. . . .

This time Charles was successful in securing the grant of a seven years wine tax, calculated to bring in about £300,000 a year and so bridge the annual deficit which was still plunging the State deeper and deeper into debt.

In January, 1670, Charles met Louis's objections to his extravagant demands by a memorandum, showing the extent to which he was prepared to reduce them, but still insisting on the control of naval operations. The paper is in the writing of Sir Thomas Clifford[1] who was by now the controlling hand in the negotiations, but it expresses the King's views.

XXXV. STATEMENT OF POSITION IN REGARD TO FRANCE IN THE EVENT OF A WAR WITH HOLLAND

January 24, 1669/70.

As a war against Holland would in all respects suit with the interests of England and be very advantageous to it if the King

---

[1] It is still preserved at Ugbrooke in the possession of Clifford's descendant, Charles Clifford, and was recently printed for the first time by Cyril Hartmann in his brilliant work of scholarship, *Charles II and Madame.* I reprint it in part here by their kind permission.

of Great Britain had force ready to be master of the seas : so on the other hand if the Hollanders .should be strongest at sea nothing in the world could be so pernicious to England as that war.

All our trade, being considerable in many stations and parts in and out of Europe, would be exposed as a prey to our enemy, and particularly that of Gothenburgh and Norway, for masts, pitch tar and the other naval provisions with which England must perpetually be supplied, will be totally interrupted, and besides the trade of our plantations the plantations themselves would be in danger to be lost if there be not a naval force subsisting there to relieve them.

Beyond this, the affront to the nation of the Dutch laying upon our unfortified coasts and blocking up our open rivers would not be borne without a danger of mutinies and universal disorders, or if they should not happen the interruption only of the trade would cut off one of the best branches of His Majesty's revenue, viz., the customs valued at 500,000 sterling yearly, and this at a time when His Majesty would have most need of money. By this it is evident that the King of England can never think of consenting to a war against Holland unless he have in his prospect sufficient supplies to set out his whole naval force and to maintain it during the war; and consequently it must be an opinion very erroneously grounded that thirty or forty English ships joining with the French fleet can be sufficient to prosecute the war with advantage and security to England. . . .

. . . On the other side, if the King of England set out his whole fleet and be out before the Dutch all the forementioned advantages will accrue to England by destroying and interrupting their whole trade, taking their ships and blocking up their harbours, in a word totally disabling their Government, if the country be at the same time vigorously attacked by land while we are in a state of this pressing and molesting them by sea.

And these advantages upon them and disadvantages against ourselves were foreseen from the beginning that the war against Holland was mentioned, and therefore in our first paper . . . we ever mentioned the setting out of our whole fleet, and we do in the same paper mention the vast expense that this will necessarily require. It is expressly said it will cost a million of pounds sterling over and above the ordinary yearly expense that we usually allow our Navy. And in the same paper, after it had been shown how the last war had exhausted our treasure and emptied our store-houses and that there was little probability that the Parliament would give supplies proportionable to this occasion which was our only way of having money, we did yet notwithstanding say we would join in the war against Holland provided his most Christian Majesty would furnish us with supplies answerable to such an expense as was a million of pounds sterling. . . .

. . . But that the King of Great Britain might make his desires in this particular as agreeable to his most Christian Majesty as might be, and yet with safety and security to himself, a new proposition was offered to the French ambassador . . . which is to have in money only 300,000 sterling and the assistance of forty ships, the least to carry forty guns, and ten fire-ships which are to join with our fleet and we not to declare till their actual joining, a copy of which proposition is herewith also sent. But the French ambassador hath thought fit to refuse it, saying he hath already sent to the King his master the substance of it.

This is the full and true state of this matter at present and if this last proposition be as much disliked as the former which the ambassador thinks will be, the two Kings are far from a good conclusion. For it must be taken for a fundamental point from which the King of Great Britain cannot upon any terms be drawn : That if he declare a war against Holland he must set out his whole fleet and must have in prospect supplies sufficient to discharge the expense of it. . . .

All Louis's efforts to modify the naval articles of the proposed alliance proved unsuccessful. On May 22nd a treaty of perpetual alliance was signed between the two Crowns at Dover. War was to be declared by both kings on the United Provinces. Louis was to pay Charles three million livres Tournois (approximately £225,000) a year for the duration of the war and a further two million livres to aid his conversion whenever Charles should judge the moment ripe for that spiritual event.   France promised to preserve the conditions of the Peace of Aix-la-Chapelle, thus enabling Charles to continue to act in accordance with the terms of the Triple Alliance.   The conduct of the naval war was to be left in the charge of England, France assisting with an auxiliary squadron of thirty ships.   England was to have Walcheren, Cadzand, and the mouth of the Scheldt as her share of the conquered Dutch territory.

The necessary sequel to the treaty did not follow for nearly two years, though Madame's tragic life had ended within two months of its signature.   During the interval Charles was carefully preparing the ground at home, deceiving the Protestant members of his government by encouraging them to forward, as though on their own volition, elaborate plans for an anti-Dutch league with France, and using the fears conjured by his alternating religious ardours and scruples to screw a little more money out of Louis.   By the beginning of 1672 he felt himself ready. Downing, the old Cromwellian ambassador, was dispatched to the Hague with high-pitched demands, and the mortgaged royal revenues, now urgently needed to set out the Fleet, resumed by a suspension of Exchequer payments to State creditors.   When Downing exceeded his instructions, Charles severely reprimanded him, but war was none the less certain, and in February orders were given to the Fleet to seize Dutch ships, followed in March by the attempt to capture the Smyrna Fleet as it returned to Holland.

XXXVI. To Sir George Downing

January 16, 1671/2.

Sir George Downing.   I have seen all your letters to my Lord Arlington since your arrival in Holland.   And because I find you sometimes divided in your opinion betwixt what seems good to you for my affairs in the various emergencies and appearances there, and what my instructions direct you, that you may not err in the future, I have thought fit to send you my last mind upon the hinge of your whole negotiation, and in my own hand, that you may likewise know it is your part to obey punctually my orders, instead of putting yourself to the trouble of finding reasons why you do not do so, as I find in your last of the 12th current.   And first you must know I am entirely secure that France will join with me against Holland, and not separate from me for any offers Holland can make to them.   Next, I do allow of your transmitting to me the States's answer to your memorial concerning the flag, and that you stay there expecting my last resolution upon it, declaring that you cannot proceed to any new matter till you receive it.   But upon the whole matter you must always know my mind and resolution is not only to insist upon the having my flag saluted even on their very shore (as it was always practised), but in having my dominion of these seas asserted, and Van Gent exemplarily punished.   Notwithstanding all this, I would have you use your skill so to amuse them that they may not finally despair of me, and thereby give me time to make myself more ready and leave them more remiss in their preparations.

In the last place I must again enjoin you to spare no cost in informing yourself exactly how ready those ships of war are in all their ports, how soon they are like to put to sea, and to send what you learn of this kind hither with all speed.   I am your loving friend.   CHARLES R.

XXXVII. To the Duke of York
[*Countersigned* ' Arlington ']

March 5, 1671/2.

Most dear Brother, We greet you well. Having received many wrongs and indignities from the States General of the United Provinces of the Low Countries these late years, upon which they have given us no satisfaction . . . we have thought fit hereby to signify our pleasure to you, and accordingly we will that further upon receipt hereof you give order that such of our men-of-war as now lie ready at Portsmouth or elsewhere do immediately put to sea, to be followed with such others as can be soonest got ready, with instructions from you to seize and make stay of all such ships and vessels belonging to the said States General or their subjects as they shall meet with, and then to bring into port, and in safe custody keep and detain until our further orders, and such of them as shall make resistance to fight, sink, burn or otherwise destroy. Only our pleasure is that you give strict and severe command to the captains and commanders of our said men-of-war that they presume not in any wise to touch or meddle with the lading or whatever shall be on board the said vessels so seized and brought into port, whether in hold, or between decks and in the cabins, even though such vessels have made resistance in such their stay or seizure of them, our intention herein being for the present only to make and detain thereof without any violence more than what they shall unavoidably put themselves, and to be received in safe custody until further order. And therefore our pleasure is that you give strict charge that the commanders, officers and ship's company of the vessels so stayed and detained, be treated with all fairness and humanity.

At the same time Charles struck at the monopolistic power of the Anglican Church by a Declaration of Indulgence for Tender Consciences, issued on March 15th, 1672, suspending the penal laws against Nonconformists and allowing freedom of worship in their own houses to Catholics.

XXXVIII.DECLARATION OF INDULGENCE FOR TENDER CONSCIENCES

March 15, 1671/2.

Our care and endeavours for the preservation of the rights and interests of the Church have been sufficiently manifested to the world by the whole course of our government since our happy Restoration, and by the many and frequent ways of coercion that we have used for composing the unhappy differences in matters of religion, which we found among our subjects upon our return. But it being evident by the sad experience of twelve years, that there is very little fruit of all those forcible courses, we think ourself obliged to make use of that supreme power in ecclesiastical matters, which is not only inherent in us, but hath been declared and recognized to be so by several statutes and Acts of Parliament : and therefore we do now accordingly issue this our declaration, as well for the quieting the minds of our good subjects in these points, for inviting strangers in this conjuncture to come and live under us, and for the better encouragement of all to a cheerful following of their trade and callings, from whence we hope by the blessing of God to have many good and happy advantages to our government; as also for preventing for the future the danger that might otherwise arise from private meetings and seditious conventicles.

And in the first place, we declare our express resolution, meaning and intention to be, that the Church of England be preserved, and remain entire in its doctrine, discipline, and government, as now it stands established by law; and that this be taken to be, as it is, the basis, rule and standard, of the general and public worship of God, and that the orthodox conformable clergy do receive and enjoy the revenues belonging thereunto : and that no person, though of a different opinion and persuasion, shall be exempt from paying his tithes or other dues whatsoever.   And further, we declare, that no person shall be capable of holding any benefice, living, or ecclesiastical dignity or preferment of any kind in this our kingdom of England, who is not exactly conformable.

We do in the next place declare our will and pleasure to be, that the execution of all and all manner of penal laws in matters ecclesiastical, against whatsoever sort of Nonconformists or recusants, be immediately suspended.   And all judges, judges of assize and gaol-delivery, sheriffs, justices of the peace, mayors, bailiffs, and other officers whatsoever, whether ecclesiastical or civil, are to take notice of it, and pay due obedience thereunto.

And that there may be no pretence for any of our subjects to continue their illegal meetings and conventicles, we do declare, that we shall from time to time allow a sufficient number of places, as they shall be desired, in all parts of this our kingdom, for the use of such as do not conform to the Church of England, to meet and assemble in order to their public worship and devotion, which places shall be open and free to all persons.

But to prevent such disorders and inconveniencies as may happen by this our indulgence, if not duly regulated, and that they may be the better protected by the civil magistrate, our express will and pleasure is, that none of our subjects do presume to meet in any place, until such place be allowed, and the teacher of that congregation be approved by us.

And lest any should apprehend, that this restriction should

248

make our said allowance and approbation difficult to be obtained, we do further declare, that this our indulgence, as to the allowance of the public places of worship, and approbation of the teachers, shall extend to all sorts of Nonconformists and recusants, except the recusants of the Roman Catholic religion, to whom we shall in no wise allow public places of worship, but only indulge them their share in the common exemption from the execution of the penal laws, and the exercise of their worship in their private houses only.

And if after this our clemency and indulgence, any of our subjects shall presume to abuse this liberty and shall preach seditiously, or to the derogation of the established church, or shall meet in places not allowed by us, we do hereby give them warning and declare, we will proceed against them with all imaginable severity; and we will let them see we can be as severe to punish such offenders, when so justly provoked, as we are indulgent to truly tender consciences. . . .

Though aiming what he hoped would prove a mortal blow at Dutch commercial and maritime power, Charles was anxious to safeguard the position of his nephew, young William of Orange, who up till now had been little more than a cipher, the government of the United Provinces resting in the hands of the De Witt brothers and their fellow-republican magnates.

XXXIX. To William of Orange

Whitehall, April 22, 1672.

I could not omit writing one word to you by this bearer Flamann since I fear our correspondence must cease for some time upon this misunderstanding between the States and me, though I assure you my kindness shall never change to you in the heart. And though our interests seem to be a little differing at this present, yet I have done you that service, that if this war hath not fallen out, I am confident you had not so soon at least been in the post you are at present. This is all I have to say at this time, but I hope to live to be more useful to you, and you may be assured I will slip no opportunity to let you see how truly I am to you. CHARLES R.

*The war was not favoured by fortune. At home it was
unpopular from the first, for in his grandiose schemes for enhanc-
ing the greatness of his kingdom, Charles had made the mistake
of not taking his people into his confidence. And his policy of
securing national unity by the toleration foreshadowed in the
Declaration of Indulgence had exactly the opposite result to that
intended, for it ended in uniting his intensely anti-Catholic subjects against both the Papists and the royal prerogative which
had been used in their behalf. Nor did foreign affairs prosper.
True, the French Armies overran most of Holland, ' making all
Protestant hearts to tremble,' but though prizes came in at first,
the naval campaign of the summer was indecisive, the great
battle of Sole Bay on May 28 ending if anything in a victory for
the Dutch, for it left their fleet in being and so prevented the
threatened landing of English troops on their coast. Nor could
all Charles's careful instructions to the Duke of York give victory
to that cautious commander's ships.*

XL. To the Duke of York[1]

June 2, 1672.

I writ to you yesterday by my Lord Clifford, to give you my
opinion about your coming to the Buoy of the Nore as the fittest
place to refit.[2] But seeing the wind come more easterly and it
blowing very fresh, I thought it necessary to send this by land,
and the rather because I saw yours to my Lord Arlington this
morning wherein I perceive there is yet a doubt whether you
should come up or not. Pray consider that when you are in Sole
Bay the enemy may have the same advantage upon you they had
before; if you should retreat before them it would be a great
affront. And as the wind stands now (and I am afraid will
continue) all things will be long in coming to you. And the
Hollanders on the other side, being close under their own shore,
may refit as well at sea with this wind as in harbour, all things
coming out to them with ease. And what other ships they may
get out we know not, but still it will be in their power to attack
you as they please.

[1] In the Lansdowne MSS. this letter and several of those that follow
are without year dates and are stated to have been probably addressed to
Prince Rupert. But from their context they plainly belong to the year
1672, when the Fleet was still commanded by the Duke of York.
[2] After the Battle of Sole Bay.

In truth the arguments are so many and strong against the staying at Sole Bay as I believe this letter will be useless by not finding you there.   However, I could not be at ease till I had given you my opinion, it being the same with those here who understand the trade better than I do, which is all I have to say upon this matter.

But now I must tell you that there is a great noise made at Sheerness by the coxswain of the *Katherine* who says that all the misfortunes their ships suffered was by the volunteers who went into the pinnace on pretence to cut off the boat of the enemies' fireship that was coming up to them.   And instead of doing that, they forced the seamen to carry them away to another ship, as the *Katherine* had no way left in so small a gale to defend herself.   This is a matter ought to be examined, for if they durst not cut off the boat, they ought to have returned to the ship.   That is all I have to say but that I am truly yours.   C.R.

XLI. TO THE DUKE OF YORK[1]

July 14, 1672.

I have received yours by my Lord Peterborough this afternoon, but have not had time to speak with him upon the subject of Sir Barnard's letter.   I dispatched this bearer Skelton with what I know of the enemy's fleet, which you will find partly by the letters I received from Harwich this day which the Secretary does send you.   And besides I have spoken with one I sent unto Holland, who tells me that one of the Admiralty of Rotterdam did assure him the fleet had orders to go out.   Which if it be true, I cannot believe they intend to go directly to fight with you because their number of ships are too small, but will strive to slip by you if they can, and join to the northward their East India fleet, and then return all together, so as if they can by a running fight save their merchant ships with the loss some of their men-of-war they will think themselves happy.   I have sent orders to the *Portsmouth* to cruise over to the coast of Holland, and if he should meet with their fleet flying northwards then to make all the sail he can to advertise you of it, but if he finds them still in their old station to come hither again for further orders.

[1] See footnote to preceding letter.

The victuallers will be all ready by Wednesday, and as soon as wind and weather permits shall set sail and steer their course for Flamborough Head and then run along the Dogger Bank to find you out. The *Dunkirk* and another man-of-war will convoy them. You will do well to send a frigate or two to ply that way, with more particular directions where to find you, and pray keep always some good sailing frigates to watch de Ruyter's motion, for there is no danger but in his slipping by you. . . . I have no more to say but that I am truly yours.

XLII.TO THE DUKE OF YORK

July 26, 1672.

You will see by the note here enclosed the intelligence I have received this day from Plymouth by two East India ships newly arrived there, by which I begin to believe that the Dutch East India fleet must be stopped by the way. And I can guess at no place but Fero [*sic*] because as they tell me here there is a good port, and if they had either gone for Spain or Norway we should have heard of them before now. So as if they should be there in Fero, I believe their design is to stay there till the nights be longer and the weather worse, and then venture home. I propose to your consideration whether it would not be worth the sending a good sailing frigate thither to inquire after them; it may be in the going thither he may chop upon them and bring you intelligence of them, but I leave all this to your consideration.

In the meantime we are making all things ready in order to an attempt upon Holland or Zealand as shall be thought most feasible, and in three or four days I hope to send you a full account of how soon our preparations will be ready here. I have no more to say at present but to wish this last night's storm[1] may not have disabled some of your ships and so I am yours.

---

[1] 'The month ended in a storm such as was never seen before in any seaman's remembrance.'—*Journal of Sir Edward Spragge*, H. M. C. Dartmouth, III, 9.

XLIII. To the Duke of York

Whitehall, July 27, 1672.

I sent you yesterday the news we had received of the Dutch East India fleet, a copy of which goes here enclosed again. Upon consideration of which we have thought the said Dutch East India fleet may probably be stayed at Fero, by directions from their superiors, they seeing our fleet so much stronger than theirs, and consequently unwilling to hazard their coming home. If this be the case your stay where you are will be to no purpose, and in the meantime the season of the year will be past of attempting anything upon the Dutch fleet, or making a descent at land, without which we shall lose the reputation and advantage of this summer. To comply therefore as well as we can with all these ends, I have thought fit to dispatch this express to you, to direct you that immediately upon receipt hereof you detach fifteen good ships, ten English, five French and three fire ships, with orders to sail to Fero there to seek out the Dutch East India fleet. And at the same time you come away with the body of the fleet to the Galloper or thereabouts as you shall think fit. As soon as you send me notice of your being there, I will send to you the ships mentioned in the enclosed list to strengthen the fleet again in place of those you send away.

I am making ready, with all the speed I can, all the necessaries for a descent in the enemy's country which I hope may be ready by the time you shall be able to come to the Galloper. If you have learned by your intelligence that the number of fifteen ships be not sufficient to master the Dutch East India fleet, you shall do well to augment the number of them as you shall judge proper. I think Sir John Harman will be a proper man to command this squadron and to give a good account of the booty if it be taken.

Though there was in one of our letters from Holland some time since, intelligence that there were ten men-of-war sent from Amsterdam to convoy their East India men home, yet we never heard anything since to confirm that news; and I am confident there is no such thing. I send this bearer Ashton to give you an account of the commission I gave him to Zealand. You will find he has done his duty very well, and I hope there will come very good effects of it.   I have nothing more to say but to assure you that I am with all imaginable kindness, Yours.   c.r.

Although I send you these directions by way of an order, yet if you see a notorious inconvenience likely to follow upon it, I allow you to suspend the execution, and to represent to me your opinion, which do not fail to do with all speed.

xliv.To the Duke of York

August 8, 1672.

I have received yours of the 3rd giving an account of the necessities of your coming to the Buoy of the Nore to refit your ships, in which I think you have taken a very good resolution, and the sooner you are there the better.   There shall be orders given for the providing cables and anchors, but the sooner you send the number that is wanting and the qualities of them, the readier the Commissioners of the Navy will be able to furnish them.   I would also be glad to be informed by the first occasion what kind of damage is done to particular ships, that I may judge thereby whether anything be feasible according to what I laid before you in my letter by Ashton.

We hear nothing with any certainty of de Ruyter, the common opinion is that he lies in or about his old station, though there be a report that he is gone to the mouth of the Ems there to shelter their East India fleet.   We are not altogether without a belief that there may be quickly a Treaty, the Dutch preparing new ambassadors for France and for us. Nothing can get us a better peace than the appearing ready to continue the war, and continuing the alarm of a descent, which cannot be done either in show or in reality but by keeping all officers and seamen aboard.   And that there may be no pretence for their coming on shore, when we know your particular wants, we will double our diligence and pains here to send all things to you, and this is all I have to say but that I am truly yours.

There is nothing of that you hear of James Hamilton.

xlv. To the Duke of York

August 10, 1672.

I writ two days since to you approving your resolution of coming to the Buoy of the Nore, in order to the more speedy repairing of those defects the bad weather have caused in the fleet, but finding by your letter which this bearer Griffin brought me, that you intended to come no farther up at farthest than the Gunfleet, I thought fit to dispatch him to you again to desire you that you will continue your resolution of making the best of your way to the Buoy of the Nore, where undoubtedly you will sooner fit again than at a greater distance. And besides I perceive I have not expressed myself well by Ashton, because I find you make a little mistake about the ships which are here in the river. Upon the whole matter undoubtedly the greatest dispatch will be made at the Buoy of the Nore, both in order to the repair of the ships and the adjusting all matters for our design both by sea and land, of which I shall say no more to you now because we will be with you as soon as I know you are at the Nore to acquaint you with my thoughts and preparations in order to the carrying on of the rest of this summer service. . . .

xlvi. To the Duke of Lauderdale

August, 1672.

I am ashamed to have been so long without writing to you. I assure you it has not been for want of kindness, but you may easily believe I have had much business. And I confess I am a little slow in expressing my kindness this way.

We are making all things ready here in order to a descent in Holland, if it be feasible after the enemy's fleet be either beaten or driven into their harbours. The greatest want I foresee will be a supply of men in case our first attempt succeed; therefore if it were possible to have two thousand men ready in Scotland upon such an occasion, it might be of the last importance.

Just as I had writ this far, news is come out of Holland

255

that de Witt and his brother are torn in pieces by the people, the particulars of which you will receive by my Lord Kincairn.

I expect my brother with the fleet to come to the Buoy of the Nore in a day or two, there to mend those small damages he has received by the foul weather at sea, and likewise to adjust our design for the rest of this summer, which I hope will not be the less prosperous for what has befallen De Witt;[1] this accident causing great tumults there which undoubtedly will not rest with this disorder only. I have no more to say at present but to thank you for the good service you do me in your station, and to assure you I am and ever will be your true friend. C.R.

Pray remember me very kindly to my Lady Duchess.

When the Fleet put in at the Buoy of the Nore, it was so damaged by the great storms of that autumn, and its over-crowded crews so decimated by sickness that all further hope of an invasion of Holland in 1672 was at an end.

XLVII.To THE DUKE OF YORK

[*Whitehall, Tuesday night.*]
(*Probably end of August, 1672*)

For my dear brother the Duke of York.

I received yours by Nicholas just now, by which I perceive the Dutch fleet is drawn in, so that I think you have nothing to do but to come hither, after you have left the orders necessary for the ships which remain at the Nore. So as I have nothing now to say, but that you shall be very welcome to him that can never be otherwise than entirely yours. C.R.

Meanwhile Charles had continued his attempts to gain his ends by bribing William of Orange to accept a peace that, while abandoning the commercial and political interests of the United Provinces, should strengthen his dynastic rights.

---

[1] Murdered by the angry burghers of the Hague.

XLVIII. To William of Orange

Whitehall, July 12, 1672.

My dear nephew, I have heard this bearer, Monsieur Reede,[1] at large upon all you have directed him to impart to me, and have had many conversations with him about your affairs as matters now stand in Holland; in all which he will assure you that my kindness to you is not in the least diminished. The advice I give you by him I am certain is impartial, and most for your good, which you will not often hear from those that I find are about you, who will have ends very much contrary to your interest. But if you will follow my advice I make little doubt by the blessing of God of establishing you in the power there, which your forefathers always aimed at. And I hope your ambition is not less for being my nephew. I will say no more on this subject having so fully instructed the bearer, only tell you that though you may put it out of my power to express the kindness I have for you, I can never change in my heart from being, my dear nephew, your most affectionate uncle. CHARLES R.

Unfortunately for Charles's calculations, William proved a better Dutchman than a Stuart. When the French armies overran Holland that summer, the young man put himself at the head of a hard-pressed nation, which turned to him in its hour of need, and, declaring that he would ' die in the last dyke' sooner than yield, let in the sea as his great ancestor had done.

XLIX. To William of Orange

Whitehall, July 31, 1672.

My dear nephew. I received yours by Silvius[2] and heard from him what you directed him to say to me, which falls infinitely short of what I expected from you, not only in that you suppose I can or will make conditions without France, but even in the conditions themselves, which I do not demand only for

[1] Van Reede van Schonouwen whom William had sent to Charles to try to secure a peace.

[2] Sir Gabriel Silvius, whom Charles had sent to William with an offer of the hereditary sovereignty of the Seven Provinces in return for acceptance of the Anglo-French terms, and whom William had now sent back to England.

my own security, but for yours also. I pray therefore bethink yourself well what will become of you when the war shall be ended if I have not a good footing in that country to stand by you against the designs and machinations of those that shall find themselves thrown out of the government to which they have been so long accustomed, or what you will do with them even in the continuance of a war amongst strangers, whom they are willing to call in, if it be but to disappoint you of being their master.

I have discoursed freely to Dr. Rompfe[1] of all these matters because I know you trust him, and likewise in what manner I will be content to qualify my demands of cautionary places,[2] that you may see that I am willing to be easy in that point as far as it can consist with my security and yours. The time is come that either we must seek a peace, or the prospect of a long war. Therefore I pray bethink yourself well upon it, for though nothing shall make me withdraw my kindness or concernment from you, it is in your own hands to make it valuable to you. I am ever, my dear nephew, your most affectionate uncle.

CHARLES R.

L. To William of Orange

Whitehall, August 20, 1672.

My dear nephew. The last letters having brought us the news of the people having murdered De Witt and his brother as the authors and occasion of the war, makes it plain to me they are infinitely desirous of a peace and being very apprehensive of your person, if they shall imagine you have repugnance to it. The tender love I have for you makes me again mind you of it, and reflecting upon the length of time it will take up for you to send ambassadors to the King of France and myself as I formerly insinuated to you, I have bethought myself of a way of shortening it; which is that if you will send ambassadors to Dunkirk, I will undertake to you not only to send mine thither,

---

[1] Dr. Rompfe, William's confidential physician, whom he had sent to England with Silvius with offers of a separate peace, which he hoped would be sufficiently favourable to detach Charles from France.

[2] Dutch ports which Charles was asking for as guarantees till a large indemnity should be paid.

but to prevail with the King of France to dispatch thither his plenipotentiaries, where a peace may be speedily concluded. Such a one as in the bad condition of your affairs will be much better for you and that poor people than any war can be, whereby they may be eased of their burdensome payments, and be for ever beholding to you for so good a change in their condition. Let nobody prevail with you to believe that what I say to you proceeds from any other motive than my kindness to your person and my goodwill to the people that expresses so great an affection for you. I no more to say but that I am and ever will be, my dear nephew, your most affectionate uncle.   CHARLES R.

LI. TO WILLIAM OF ORANGE

September 20, 1672.

My dear nephew. I was very much surprised to find myself so long without an answer to my two letters recommending to you sentiments of peace, and showing you a ready way to it, by an assurance of a moderation in the demands of France as well as England, and naming a place for the Treaty so near you. But I must confess to you, I was much more surprised when after so long an expectation I had your answer by Monsieur de Reede without the least signification that my offers were acceptable to you, upon which I have taken the liberty to speak my mind freely to Monsieur de Reede. And I hope you will take it for a great mark of my kindness to you that I have done so. I assure you, if I loved you less I would have taken another course. After all, you are best judge what is good for you and that poor people for whom I cannot but be concerned, for their great good will towards you, and for peace sake, which all good men ought to desire. Whatever your thoughts or resolutions are, I shall not willingly hear or believe anything that may give me cause to change the kindness I have to you, and which you shall find the effects of in all occasions relating to your good, if you yourself do not prevent me therein. I am, my dear nephew, Your most affectionate uncle.

CHARLES R.

There, as William would not abandon his country, nor Charles his ally, the matter was left.

Meanwhile the state of the Treasury was such that there was nothing for it but to pay off the main fleet and call Parliament, adjourned since the spring of 1671, to meet in February, 1673. The members, angry alike at the Declaration of Indulgence and the French alliance, and suspicious of still worse things, were in an ill humour, and Charles, though he greeted them with his usual easy politeness, knew it.

LII. Speech to both Houses

February 4, 1672/3.

My Lords and Gentlemen: I am glad to see you here this day. I would have called you sooner together, but that I was willing to ease you and the country till there were an absolute necessity.

Since you were last here, I have been forced to a most important, necessary, and expensive war; and I make no doubt but you will give me suitable and effectual assistance to go through with it. I refer you to my declaration for the causes, and indeed the necessity of this war; and shall now only tell you, that I might have digested the indignities to my own person, rather than have brought it to this extremity, if the interest as well as the honour of the whole kingdom had not been at stake. And if I had omitted this conjuncture, perhaps I had not again ever met with the like advantage.

You will find that the last supply you gave me did not answer expectation for the ends you gave it, the payment of my debts: therefore I must, in the next place, recommend them again to your especial care.

Some few days before I declared the war, I put forth my Declaration for Indulgence to Dissenters, and have hitherto found a good effect of it, by securing peace at home when I had war abroad. There is one part in it that hath been subject to misconstruction, which is that concerning the Papists; as if more liberty were granted them than to the other recusants, when it is plain there is less; for the others have public places allowed them, and I never intended that they should have any, but only have the freedom of their religion in their own houses without any concourse of others. And I could not grant them less than this, when I had extended so much more grace to others, most of them having been loyal and in the service of me and of the King, my father. And in the whole course of this indulgence, I do not intend that it shall any way prejudice the Church, but I will support its rights and it in its full power. Having said this, I shall take it very ill to receive contradiction in what I have done. And, I will deal plainly with you, I am resolved to stick to my Declaration.

There is one jealousy more that is maliciously spread abroad, and yet so weak and frivolous that I once thought it not of moment enough to mention, but it may have gotten some ground with some well-minded people; and that is, that the forces I have raised in this war were designed to control law and property. I wish I had more forces the last summer; the want of them then convinces me I must raise more against this next spring; and I do not doubt but that you will consider the charge of them in your supplies.

I will conclude with this assurance to you, that I will preserve the true Reformed Protestant Religion and the Church as it is now established in this kingdom, and that no man's property or liberty shall ever be invaded. I leave the rest to the Chancellor.

The Commons, who though they hated the French had little love for the Dutch, voted an eighteen months' assessment of £70,000 per month, but before the Bill for raising it was engrossed, demanded that the Declaration of Indulgence should be withdrawn, claiming in their petition that penal laws in religious matters could only be suspended by Parliament. Charles took ten days to reply, and then, while promising them satisfaction on other points (they demanded a Bill for easing Protestant as opposed to Catholic Nonconformists) evaded the main issue.

LIII. REPLY TO THE HOUSE OF COMMONS' ADDRESS

February 24, 1672/3.

His Majesty hath received an Address from you: and he hath seriously considered of it; and returneth you this answer:

That he is very much troubled that that Declaration, which

he put out for ends so necessary to the quiet of his kingdom, and especially in that conjuncture, should have proved the cause of disquiet in his House of Commons and give occasion to the questioning of his power in ecclesiastics : which he finds not done in the reigns of any of his ancestors. He is sure he never had thoughts of using it otherwise than as it hath been entrusted to him, to the peace and establishment of the Church of England, and the ease of all his subjects in general. Neither doth he pretend to the right of suspending any laws, wherein the properties, rights, or liberties of any of his subjects are concerned; nor to alter anything in the established doctrine or discipline of the Church of England. But his only design in this was to take off the penalties the Statutes inflict upon Dissenters; and which he believes when well considered of, you yourselves would not wish executed according to the rigour and letter of the law. Neither hath he done this with any thought of avoiding or precluding the advice of his Parliament. And if any Bill shall be offered him, which shall appear more proper to attain the aforesaid ends, and secure the peace of the Church and kingdom, when tendered in due manner to him, he will show how speedily he will concur in all ways that shall appear good for the kingdom.

But the Commons were insistent. On February 26 they presented a second Address complaining that the King's answer as to the suspensory power was equivocal: and two days later resolved that all who refused to take the Oaths of Allegiance and Supremacy and to receive the Anglican Sacrament should be declared incapable of public employments. It was a blow aimed directly at Charles's closest advisers, for he knew that neither his brother, the Lord High Admiral, nor his Treasurer, Lord Clifford, both now Catholics, could take the Test. On March 1 Charles appealed to the Lords. It was in vain. A week later, faced by the alternative of abandoning his ally and making an unsatisfactory peace for lack of money, he withdrew his Declaration of Indulgence, promised to accept the Test Act, and begged for the supplies which alone could enable him to set out his fleet for the summer. Content with a great constitutional victory, the Commons engrossed the Money Bill, and Charles gave his assent to the Test Act on March 29.

LIV. SPEECH TO BOTH HOUSES

March 8, 1672/3.

My Lords and Gentlemen: Yesterday you presented me an Address, as the best means for the satisfying and composing the minds of my subjects; to which I freely and readily agreed. And I shall take care to see it performed accordingly.

I hope, on the other side, you, gentlemen of the House of Commons, will do your part; for I must put you in mind it is near five weeks since I demanded a supply; and what you voted unanimously upon it, did both give life to my affairs at home, and disheartened my enemies abroad. But the seeming delay it hath met withal since, hath made them take new courage; and they are now preparing for this next summer a greater fleet (as they say) than ever they had yet; so that, if the supply be not very speedily dispatched, it will be altogether ineffectual; and the safety, honour, and interest of England must of necessity be exposed. Pray lay this to your heart; and let not the fears and jealousies of some draw an inevitable ruin upon us all.

My Lords and Gentlemen: If there be any scruple remain with you concerning the suspension of penal laws, I here faithfully promise you that what hath been done in that particular shall not for the future be drawn either into consequence or example. And as I daily expect from you a Bill for my supply, so, I assure you, I shall as willingly receive and pass any other you shall offer me, that may tend to the giving you satisfaction in all your just grievances.

By sacrificing his dream of religious toleration and a Catholic throne at home, Charles purchased a last throw for his greater dream of a British Empire founded on the ruins of imperial Holland and Spain. Once more, with the money voted by the triumphant Commons, he set out his fleet and mustered his troops for the invasion of Holland. But the sea campaign of 1673 was no more successful than that of 1672. Prince Rupert, who succeeded to the command of which the Test Act deprived the Duke of York, proved no match for de Ruyter, despite the care the King (whose naval acumen, had he been in actual command of the fleet, might well have changed the fortunes of the campaign) took to prompt and advise him.

LV. TO PRINCE RUPERT

May 5, 1673.

To my dear Cousin Prince Rupert.

I received yours of yesterday just now, and have seen your other letters. There is all diligence used in sending down all sorts of ships to you, and you will receive from my brother and my Lord Arlington the account of what directions we sent both to Haddock[1] and to those ships in the Downs. So, as I have nothing to add but to wish you a good westerly wind, and desire you to be assured that I am with all imaginable kindness. Yours.

C.R.

LVI. TO PRINCE RUPERT

May 10, 1673.

The letters which Charles Bertie carried you on Thursday were written with an assurance that the French Fleet were in sight of the Isle of Wight: yesterday I received a letter from the Comte d'Estrees dated the 17th S.N. that they were in sight of Dartmouth. And because I suppose he will make the best of his way to join you, I have advised this gentleman to go straight to Rye. I send a duplicate of my letter to the Comte d'Estrees to Portsmouth that he may make all the haste he can to join you at Dungeness, which I think a very good station for you till he be come up to you.

I received yours by Dowcett this morning and I sent immediately for the Master of the Ordnance and he tells me all the materials are on board small vessels and gone down four days since, but I have ordered him to send an express to hasten them to you by the Downs. My letters from Ostend give me the same account that your frigates do of the Dutch Fleet's being off West Capelle, but they say that they intend to come upon our coast again as soon as the Zealand squadrons come out, which they tell me is now ready. I pray leave writing to me with ceremony, for I will use none to you, but to assure you that I am truly yours. C.R.

---

[1] Captain Richard Haddock, that summer appointed a Commissioner of the Navy.

LVII. To Prince Rupert

May 12, 1673.

There shall be no diligence omitted in the getting out the ships in the river, though I am afraid we shall not be able to get seamen for the *Sovereign* till Narborough[1] be come home. I hope the Comte d'Estrees[2] is with you before this time, for he passed the Isle of Wight three days since, and the wind has been here all northerly so as he has had a good start. I desire you would make all convenient haste with the list of the strength of every company now on board, for I intend to recruit every company to a hundred men, as well those on board as the eight regiments here on shore, and to that end it will be well you send an officer or two hither of those regiments that are entirely on shipboard to make the recruits of the companies with you. This is all I have to say at present but that I am yours.   C.R.

LVIII. To Prince Rupert

May 14. '*Eight at night.*'

Perceiving by yours of the 13th to my Lord Arlington that the French squadron is likely to join you this day, and that you must take in some water, I thought it a good time to make you a visit, to the end we may adjust our measures together, so that I send this by an express to know where you will be on Friday. I do intend to set out that morning for Dover, and if you should not water at Folkestone, but where you were at the writing of your letter, 'tis but my riding twenty miles more. Pray let me know as soon as you can where you will be, and so I am yours.

C.R.

LIX. To Prince Rupert

May 24, 1673.

Our letters from Dover and Deal told us when you passed with the fleet in their sight with a good gale, by which we conclude you in sight of the enemy. The question is whether

---

[1] Captain, afterwards Admiral Sir John Narborough.
[2] Commander of the French squadron in co-operation with the English Fleet.

they will stand to fight you, and if it please God to give you success, what will be fit to be done next upon the coast, whether you shall make an attempt upon Goree, the Brill, Helvoetsluys, Flushing or Trevere. I must confess I incline more to this last, by what I heard the pilots say when I was with you of the depth of water just to the very key of the town. But I should be glad to know your mind that we may take our measures from hence of giving you all the assistance we can accordingly.

I am making all the haste we can in marching the regiments up this way, bearing the recruits if they be not ready to follow. I have also taken care to have in readiness all other particulars to make and secure a descent, which is all I can yet say to you from hence till I hear from you, of which you may judge I am very impatient in such a conjuncture. The *Sovereign*, *Victory*, and I think the *Diamond* sailed from the Nore the day before yesterday, so as by this time they are with you, which is all I have now to say, only wish you good luck, and assure you that I am yours. c.r.

lx. To Prince Rupert

June 1, 1673.

Having had the news of an engagement the last week by the guns heard from all parts on the 28th,[1] you may easily guess in what pain I was till I received yours of the 29th, which was brought me on the 31st in the morning, whereby I see you have done all that was possible with those circumstances the enemies afforded you. I assure myself that when our letters come from the other side of the water, we shall know in spite of their teethes [*sic*] that they have had a considerable loss. In a word, I am very well pleased with your success.

Immediately upon the receipt of your letters I gave order for all those things which you writ for, and I hope the ten fire ships will be ready very soon. The Straights fleets are in the Downs, and as fast as they come up these men shall be sent to you. The particular account of all these things, you will receive from my brother and the officers of the navy, so I shall add

[1] The first of the two battles off the Schonveld.

266

nothing to this only to thank you for what you have done and to wish you more success, assuring you of the continuance of my kindness to you in all occasions.

I hope you will punish those captains of the fireships who did ill, as severely as you can. And pray send those Englishmen who were taken in the Dutch service in some safe vessel that they may be sure to be hanged here, but there must be sent two or three witnesses with them.

LXI. INSTRUCTIONS GIVEN TO PRINCE RUPERT AT A COUNCIL OF FLAG OFFICERS ABOARD THE 'ROYAL SOVEREIGN' AT THE BUOY OF THE NORE.[1]

July 26, 1673.

Resolved—

That His Highness Prince Rupert do immediately, wind and weather permitting, sail away with His Majesty's fleet under his command out of the river of Thames, taking with him several ships and vessels in which the land-forces with their ammunition, provision and baggage, etc., are embarked.

That being at sea, His Highness do in the first place take care to send under sufficient convoy the said land-forces, with their ammunition, provision, baggage, etc., to Yarmouth; there to be disposed of according to such directions as His Majesty has on that behalf given to the Count de Schomberg.

That this being done, His Highness with the fleet shall sail to the coast of Flanders, and there show himself (nearer or farther off) to the enemy's fleet lying within the Schonveld, as upon consideration had of the posture of the enemy, condition of the weather, and other circumstances shall be by him judged most advisable. But that he do not for any consideration whatever adventure upon attacking the enemy within the Schonveld— until upon further knowledge of the condition of the Treaty and His Majesty's other affairs he shall receive directions from His Majesty for his so doing.

That His Highness having thus shown himself to the Dutch fleet shall make the best of his way to the Texel, whither it is

[1] In the hand of Samuel Pepys, that June appointed Secretary of the new Admiralty Commission.

to be hoped the enemy will be drawn (and give an opportunity of fighting them where there is sea-room) for the preventing a descent upon their coast and securing their East India ships— now expected home—and His Highness being arrived there, shall proceed in the further employing and disposing of the fleet as he shall from time to time judge to be best for His Majesty's service. C.R.

LXII. To Prince Rupert

August 4, 1673.

I send you by this bearer in a letter of form the answer to all those questions in your letter to my Lord Arlington. I shall only add that the reason that makes me so cautious at this time, is, that if we have no ill luck and keep masters at sea, I am confident we shall have a good conclusion of our treaty at Cologne. And if any accident should happen to our fleet though but small, it would so puff up that party in Holland who do not desire a peace, as we should see no good conclusion of the Treaty for a long time.

I am very glad the *Charles* does so well; a girdling this winter when she comes in will make her the best ship in England next summer. I believe if you try the two sloops that were built at Woolwich which have my invention in them, they will outsail any of the French sloops. Sir Samuel Morland[1] has now another fancy concerning weighing anchor, and the resident of Venice has made a model also to the same purpose. We have not yet consulted them with Mr. Tippetts nor Mr. Deane,[2] but I hope when they are all well considered we may find one out of them that will be good. I have no more to say at this time but that I am yours. C.R.

LXIII. To Prince Rupert

August 20, 1673.

I have seen the letter the Lord Commissioners of the Admiralty writ to you by this occasion which is sufficient for the

[1] The great inventor of the age, formerly Pepys's tutor at Cambridge.
[2] Anthony Deane, the naval architect, and Pepys's friend and colleague.

particulars mentioned therein. That which I have further to say is, considering the treaty at Cologne, the condition in which ours and the enemies fleets are, and that we expect home a considerable fleet of merchant ships, some of them East India men, I think it is our part to avoid coming to the hazard of a battle all we can. On the other side I think we ought to keep the sea with the fleet as long as the weather will suffer the great ships to be abroad with safety. And therefore I think the best station for the fleet will be about Boulogne Bay and Dungeness as the wind will permit, and when the wind is westerly the Downs is as good for all these purposes as either of them, and even for fighting the enemy if they will come into the Channel. My directions therefore to you are that upon receipt of this you make the best of your way towards the Channel, keeping yourselves about the stations I have mentioned according as the wind and weather will permit you.

I am sorry to hear of the jealousies fallen into the fleet concerning the French. I hope they have not given so much cause for them as is publicly discoursed. Whatever the matter hath been it will warn you to suppress the effects of them all you can, lest the enemy come to gain a greater advantage upon us that way than they can possibly have by fighting. . . .

LXIV. TO PRINCE RUPERT

August 24, 1673.

I have received your letters by Tom Daniell, Colte and Beckman all together, they all arriving here almost at the same instant. On Thursday night I dispatched Tom Howard to you by way of Yarmouth, who I hope has met you before now, and yesterday I sent the Kitchen Yacht with a duplicate of his dispatch. By all which you will see my directions are for you to go into the Channel, to secure the riches the merchants and I have coming home.

I send this bearer, Sir Jeremy Smyth, to you that you may order him where the victuallers that come to you in order to that design, and though in my former letters I mentioned the Downs, Boulogne road or Dungeness according as the wind lay proper for them, yet if you shall think any other station in the Channel more proper for the security of those merchant ships, I do leave it to your judgements upon the place as the best judges. And I hope they will be very soon in the Channel, for I have sent an express to Kinsale (where they are all) to make the best of their way to Plymouth, and there they shall receive further orders according to the intelligence we shall have when they come there. If my Lord Ossory do make use of the leave I have given him to come hither, I desire you that Narborough may not lose his right, but that he may have the rear admiral's flag of the Red.

I have given order for the Commissions for Potts and Beckman as you desire, which is all I have to say now but that I am yours. C.R.

The summer ended with the Dutch still in possession of their Fleet and their liberties, and the English government several hundreds of thousands of pounds more bankrupt than before. War at such a rate could no longer be maintained. Moreover, the discontent of the country had been fanned to fury by the apparent reluctance of the French naval commanders to share the same perils as their English allies and by the secret anti-Catholic propaganda of Dutch agents in England. When Parliament reassembled at the end of October, Charles's usual appeal for supply fell on deaf ears. Within four days the resolutions of the angry Commons against the standing army and the King's ministers (particularly against the hated Lauderdale who was successfully engaged in taming Scotland), proved so threatening that to save them Charles was forced to prorogue the Houses till the New Year.

LXV. SPEECH TO BOTH HOUSES

October 27, 1673.

My Lords and Gentlemen: I thought this day to have welcomed you with an honourable Peace. My preparations for the war and condescensions at the Treaty gave me great reason to believe so: but the Dutch have disappointed me in that expectation, and have treated my ambassadors at Cologne with the contempt of conquerors, and not as might be expected from men in their condition. They have other thoughts than peace.

This obligeth me to move you again for a supply, the safety and honour of the nation necessarily requiring it. It must be one proportionable to the occasion; and I must tell you besides, that if I have it not speedily, the mischief will be irreparable in my preparations for the next spring. The great experience I have had of you, gentlemen of the House of Commons, will not suffer me to believe that the artifices of our enemies can possibly divert you from giving me this supply, or that you can fail of adjusting the proportion of it.

I hope I need not use many words to persuade you that I am steady in maintaining all the professions and promises I have made you concerning Religion and Property; and I shall be very ready to give you fresh instances of my zeal for preserving the Established Religion and laws, as often as any occasion shall require.

In the last place, I am highly concerned to commend to your consideration and care the Debt I owe the Goldsmiths,[1] in which very many other of my good subjects are involved. I heartily recommend their condition to you, and desire your assistance for their relief. There is more that I would have you informed of, which I leave to the Chancellor.

LXVI. SPEECH TO BOTH HOUSES

November 3, 1673.

My Lords and Gentlemen: I need not tell you how unwillingly I call you hither at this time, being enough sensible what advantage my enemies both abroad and at home will reap by the least appearance of a difference between me and my Parliament; nay, being assured they expect more success from such a breach (could they procure it) than from their arms.

This, I say, shall (whilst I live) be my chief endeavour to prevent; and for that reason I think it necessary to make a short

---

[1] The debt to the bankers, which in 1672 had anticipated the entire revenue and whose interest the Government had been forced temporarily to suspend in the Stop of the Exchequer of that year.

recess, that all good men may recollect themselves against the next meeting and consider whether the present posture of affairs will not rather require their applications to matters of Religion and support against our only competitors at sea than to things of less importance.   And in the meanwhile, I will not be wanting to let all my subjects see that no care can be greater than my own in the effectual suppressing of Popery.   And it shall be your faults if, in your several countries, the laws be not effectually executed against the growth of it.

I will not be idle neither in some other things which may add to your satisfaction; and then I shall expect a suitable return from you.   And so I shall give order to the Lord Chancellor to prorogue you to the 7th January next.

LXVII. To the Duke of Lauderdale

Whitehall, November 29, 1673.

I have constantly read all your letters to your brother, and do very well approve of your proceedings for the laying of those heats I see was endeavoured to be stirred there. If the Parliament continue in that good temper as I find by your last letter, in the going on quietly in the right way in the Articles, I think you ought to continue the sessions and so redress those matters which may give any pretence for grievances, which I hope will give good example to the Parliament here against our next meeting. Some of those persons who had a great hand in the extravagances here were in great hopes of making a flame in that kingdom also, but now they are not so pert on that subject as they were, and your son Yester[1] (who comes but seldom in my eye) looks but melancholy upon it. I know you will omit nothing whereby you may keep the boroughs right to me, and then I do not doubt but this will prove a good sessions. That is all I have to say now, only to assure you of the continuance of my constant friendship to you.   C.R.

---

[1] John Hay, Lord Yester, Lauderdale's son-in-law.

LXVIII. TO THE DUKE OF LAUDERDALE

Whitehall, December 21, 1673.

I have had a full account from my Lord Kincardine of all you instructed him with. And though this bearer Hatton will more at large tell of my approbation of all your proceedings there, yet I thought it necessary to tell you under my own hand how sensible I am of the service you do me in that kingdom, and the rather because I see the great artifices has been used both here and there to hinder your endeavours to serve me. All I shall add at this time is to tell you that you may be most assured of my constant kindness to you, and that it shall not be in anybody's power to do you the least prejudice with me. For I have had too long experience of your abilities and faithfulness to serve me, ever to change from being your true friend.

There was nothing left for penniless Charles to do but to make peace and abandon Louis, with as little inconvenience to that monarch and as much respect to his own honour as was under the circumstances possible. The reassembling of Parliament in January, 1674, made the inevitability of this course obvious. The 'cheerful aid' asked for was again ignored, and the King's Ministers were again attacked.

LXIX. SPEECH TO BOTH HOUSES

January 7, 1673/4.

My Lords and Gentlemen: When I parted with you last, it was but for a little time, and with a resolution of meeting suddenly again. That alone was enough to satisfy my friends that they need not fear, and my enemies that they could not hope for, a breach between us. I then told you that the time of this short recess should be employed in doing such things as might add to your satisfaction: I hope I have done my part towards it. And if there be anything else which you think wanting to secure Religion or Propriety, there is nothing which you shall reasonably propose, but I shall be ready to receive it. I do now expect you should do your parts too; for our enemies make vigorous preparations for war; and yet their chief hopes are to disunite us at home.   'Tis their common discourse, and they reckon upon it as their best relief.

My Lords and Gentlemen : It is not possible for me to doubt your affections at any time, much less at such a time as this, when the evidences of your affection are become so necessary to us all.   I desire you to consider that as the war cannot be well made without a supply, so neither can a good peace be had without being in a posture of war.   I am very far from being in love with war for war's sake but, if I saw any likelihood of peace, without dishonour to myself and damage to you, I would soon embrace it.   But no proposals of peace have yet been offered, which can be imagined with intent to conclude, but only to amuse. Therefore the way to a good peace is, to set out a good fleet. . . .

I cannot conclude without showing the entire confidence I have in you.   I know you have heard much of my alliance with France; and I believe it hath been very strangely misrepresented to you, as if there were certain secret Articles of dangerous consequence; but I will make no difficulty of letting the Treaties and all the Articles of them, without any the least reserve, to be seen by a small Committee of both Houses, who may report to you the true scope of them; and I assure you, there is no other Treaty with France, either before or since, not already printed, which shall not be made known.[1]   And having thus freely trusted you, I do not doubt but you will have a care of my honour and the good of all the kingdom.

The rest I refer to my Lord Keeper.

Charles preferred to cut his losses rather than abandon his Ministers or face civil war.   He wrote to Lauderdale assuring him of his continued support, and on January 24, throwing precedent to the winds, revealed to the Houses the terms of peace which he was offering to Holland and asked their advice. They replied by counselling a speedy peace.   This, with the acknowledgement of the right of the flag and a moderate indemnity of 800,000 crowns, he was able to present to them a few weeks later.   It was all the substance he ever grasped of his

---

[1] In the telling of this deliberate lie, Charles was seen to fumble with his notes.

grandiloquent dream of 1668.   And even for that the price he had to pay was overwhelmingly heavy; for a once loyal Parliament and an obstinate, liberty-loving Protestant community were now united in suspicion of their King, his advisers and his measures.

LXX. TO THE DUKE OF LAUDERDALE

1673/4.

You may easily believe that I do not want business at this time, but yet I could not let this express go to you without a line under my own hand, to assure you of the continuance of my kindness to you, which nothing shall alter.   My Lord K. will give you a particular account of what was done yesterday upon your subject, and, though it is hot at present, yet I do not despair when they have taken their swing round, and come to examine particulars, that reason and justice will have the credit it ought to have.   I assure you I find the honest country gentlemen begin to understand some of the great leaders, which gives me hopes that this session may end better than some wish it should.   I am called away, and therefore can say no more but that I will ever be your true friend.

LXXI. SPEECH TO BOTH HOUSES

January 24, 1673/4.

My Lords and Gentlemen : At the beginning of this session, I told you, as I thought I had reason to do, that the States General had not yet made me any proposals which could be imagined with intend to conclude, but only to amuse.

To avoid this imputation, they have now sent me a letter by the Spanish ambassador, offering me some terms of peace, upon conditions formally drawn up, and in a more decent style than before.   It is upon this that I desire your speedy advice; for, if you shall find the terms such as may be embraced, your advice will have great weight with me; and if you find them defective, I hope you will give me your advice and assistance how to get better terms.   Upon the whole matter, I doubt not but you will have a care of my honour, and the honour and safety of the nation, which are now so deeply concerned.

LXXII.Speech to both Houses

February 11, 1673/4.

My Lords and Gentlemen : I have pursued your advice, and am come hither to tell you, that, according to your desires, I have made a speedy, honourable, and, I hope, a lasting peace, signed already.

Mr. Speaker, and you gentlemen of the House of Commons : I told you yesterday in the Banqueting House that I would give you a speedy answer to your address about disbanding the Forces therein mentioned. And I do assure you that before you made your address, I had given orders for the doing of it as soon as I should be sure of the peace; and I shall reduce them to a less number than they were in the year 1663, and shall give direction for the march of those who are to return to Ireland, who were brought from thence. And as our forces are lessened at land, it will be necessary to build more great ships; for we shall not be safe, unless we equal the strength of our neighbours at sea. Therefore I shall recommend it to your care to give me means for the effectual doing thereof. And this is all I have to say to you at this time.

CHAPTER VIII

STRUGGLE AND FINAL TRIUMPH

The last ten years of Charles's reign is the story of his struggle to resist the flood of suspicion and hostility which his daring design had loosed against his government. Of those ten years, four saw the flood growing till it burst its banks and all but over-whelmed the monarchy in the torrent of terror and hatred called the Popish Plot. For three more years Charles with consummate skill contended against those pent-up waves of angry national feeling. The last three saw him, through his own extraordinary skill and political sense, again at peace with his people and wielding a power that no English sovereign had possessed since the death of Elizabeth.

For the history of those years there are comparatively few letters. Charles had learnt his lesson, and kept his political secrets not only from paper, but from the ears of his Ministers, his closest friends, his very mistresses. The key to his policy, so far as it is to be found at all in the written word, must be sought in the periodical declarations of policy which he made to his Parliaments and people.

When at the close of 1673 Charles realized the utter defeat of his grandiloquent aims and the peril to which they had brought him, he abandoned them for ever and fell back on the one party who were still ready to support his threatened throne —the Cavalier country gentlemen. Their price was an end of the French alliance, rigid intolerance, and an Anglican cabinet. Their leader, Sir Thomas Osborne, whom Charles created Lord Treasurer and Earl of Danby, proved a financial genius, and under his management the royal revenue began to expand with the growing trade of the country, so that the disastrous gap between governmental income and expenditure was partly bridged. The result was four and a half years of comparative peace.

But it was peace at a cost. Charles had no love for a rigid Anglican system, and, though he appears to have abandoned all hope of a Catholic throne, he still dreamed of national toleration. Nor did he like to abandon France, at war with a European league, or to have his foreign policy dictated to him by an assembly of country squires. Secretly, to Danby's discomfiture, he continued to correspond with Louis and even to coax small subsidies out of him—mostly expended on the needs of his Navy —in return for periodic adjournments of his anti-French Parliament.

The history of the years 1674-8 turns largely on Danby's efforts to woo Charles from this spasmodic dependence on Louis by persuading the Cavalier majority in the Commons to vote the Crown sufficient money to liquidate its debts and maintain a strong navy. Unfortunately for him, the squires, being the chief tax-payers, were reluctant to loosen the purse strings, while their majority over their opponents was increasingly small and precarious. For the Grand Design and the third Dutch War had created a strong Parliamentary and even republican Opposition, which did all in its power to harass Danby's government and precipitate a general election which it believed would transform its minority into a majority. This party was led by two fallen Ministers, Lord Shaftesbury, the ex-Chancellor, a political manager of genius, and the erratic but powerful Duke of Buckingham, both of whom were in touch with the dissatisfied republican and Nonconformist elements in the country.

The first round in this complicated political duel came in the spring of 1675 when Charles, in pursuance of Danby's advice, called Parliament, prorogued since February 1674, to ask for a supply for a much-needed naval building programme.

1.Speech to Parliament

April 13, 1675.

My Lords and Gentlemen : The principal end of my calling you now is to know what you think may be yet wanting to the securing of religion and property, and to give myself the satisfaction of having used the uttermost of my endeavours to procure and settle a right and lasting understanding between us. For, I must tell you, I find the contrary so much laboured, and that the pernicious designs of ill men have taken so much place under specious pretences, that it is high time to be watchful in preventing their contrivances; of which it is not the least, that they would, by all the means they can devise, make it unpracticable any longer to continue this present Parliament. For that reason, I confess, I cannot think such have any good meaning to me; and therefore, when I consider how much the greatest part of this Parliament has, either themselves, or their fathers, given me testimony of their affections and loyalty, I should be extreme loath to oblige those enemies, by parting with such friends. . . .

I must needs recommend to you the condition of the Fleet, which I am not able to put into that state it ought to be; and which will require so much time to repair and build, that I should be sorry to see this summer (and consequently a whole year) lost without providing for it. The season of the year will not admit any long session; nor would I have called you now, but in hopes to do something that may give content to all my subjects, and lay before you the consideration of the Fleet; for I intend to meet you again at winter. In the meantime, I earnestly recommend to you all such a temper and moderation in your proceedings, as may tend to unite us all in counsel and affection, and disappoint the expectation of those who hope only by violent and irregular motions to prevent the bringing of this session to a happy conclusion. The rest I leave to the Lord Keeper.

Danby's hope to secure the King's whole-hearted support of his policy by presenting him with a liberal Parliamentary grant proved vain. The Opposition, though forestalled by a Governmental proclamation against Catholic priests from raising the time-honoured cry of 'Ware Popery', tried to impeach the Ministers, demanded the recall of all British volunteers serving in the French Army, and insulted the King by trying to earmark his Customs receipts for the Navy. And when Danby retaliated with a No-Resisting Bill aimed at excluding all but ardent Anglicans from membership of Parliament, they brought the session to an untimely end by a cleverly fostered and furious dispute between the two Houses over their privileges.

II. SPEECH TO BOTH HOUSES AT THE BANQUETING HOUSE

June 5, 1675.

My Lords and Gentlemen : You may remember that, at the meeting of this session, I told you no endeavour would be wanting to make the continuance of this Parliament unpracticable. I am sorry that experience hath so quickly showed you the truth of what I then said; but I hope you are well convinced that the intent of all these contrivances is to procure a dissolution. I confess, I look upon it as a most malicious design of those who are enemies to me and the Church of England; and, were the contrivers known, I should not doubt but the dislike of their practices would alone be a means of bringing the Houses to a good understanding.   But, since I cannot prescribe any way how to arrive to the discovery of it, I must tell you plainly my opinion, that the means to come to any composure between yourselves cannot be without admitting of such free conferences as may convince one another by the reasons then offered, or enable me to judge rightly of the differences, when all hath been said on both sides which the matter will afford. . . . But I must let you know, that whilst you are in debate about your privileges, I will not suffer my own to be invaded. . . .

III.Speech at the Prorogation of Parliament

June 9, 1675.

My Lords and Gentlemen : I think I have given sufficient evidence to the world, that I have not been wanting on my part, in my endeavours to procure the full satisfaction of all my subjects, in the matters both of religion and property; I have not only invited you to those considerations at our first meeting, but I have been careful through this whole session that no concern of my own should divert you from them. . . . But I must confess, the ill designs of our enemies have been too prevalent against those good ones I had proposed to myself in behalf of my people; and those unhappy differences between my two Houses are grown to such a height, that I find no possible means of putting an end to them but by a prorogation. . . .

It is perhaps symptomatic of the more permanent results of Charles's rule that the summer that witnessed this fruitless and ill-tempered session, saw also the issue of the royal orders for commencing the building of Wren's St. Paul's.

IV.To the Commissioners for rebuilding St. Paul's

May 14, 1675.

Whereas we have been informed that a portion of the imposition laid upon coals, which by an Act of Parliament is appointed and set apart for the rebuilding of the Cathedral Church of St. Paul's in our capital city of London; doth at present amount to a considerable sum, which though not proportionable to the greatness of the work is notwithstanding sufficient to begin the same . . . and whereas amongst divers designs which have been represented to us we have particularly pitched upon one, as well because we found it very artificial, proper and useful, as because it was so ordered that it might be built and finished by parts, we do therefore by these presents signify our royal approbation of the said design hereunto annexed, and do will and require you forthwith to proceed according to the said design, beginning with the east end or choir and accomplishing the same with the present stock of money. . . .

The autumn session was as unsuccessful as that of the spring. A majority in the Commons, not uninfluenced by the bribes of the Spanish ambassador who was doing all he could to fan anti-French feeling, refused to make provision for the Crown's debts and, by attaching to the Subsidies Bill a clause which the Crown could not accept without humiliation, left the King without supply.   On November 22 Charles again prorogued the Houses.

v.Speech on opening the Session

October 13, 1675.

My Lords and Gentlemen. . . .

The causes of the last prorogation, as I, for my part, do not desire to remember, so I hope no man else will, unless it be to learn from thence how to avoid the like occasions for the future. And I pray consider how fatal the consequence may be, and how little benefit is like to redound to the people by it.   However, if anything of that kind shall arise, I desire you would defer those debates till you have brought such public Bills to perfection as may conduce to the good and safety of the kingdom; and particularly I recommend to you whatever may tend to the security of the Protestant religion, as it is now established in the Church of England.

I must likewise desire your assistance in some supplies, as well to take off the anticipations which are upon my revenue as for building of ships. And though the war has been the great cause of these anticipations, yet I find, by a late account I have taken of my expenses, that I have not been altogether so good a husband as I might have been and as I resolve to be for the future: although, at the same time, I have had the satisfaction to find that I have been far from such an extravagancy in my own expense as some would have the world believe. I am not ignorant that there are many who would prevent the kindness of my Parliament to me at this time; but I as well know that your affections have never failed me: and you may remember, it is now above three years since I have asked you anything for my own use. . . .

In spite of Danby's failure to obtain a parliamentary aid, the King had still enough faith in his Minister to resist the pressure that both Louis and the Opposition leaders were putting on him to dissolve the Cavalier Parliament. Instead he accepted a small subsidy from Louis to keep it prorogued for a year.

Actually the Houses remained prorogued for fifteen months. During that time the government of the country was carried on much as usual, for Parliament was still no part of the regular administration of the country. Charles's attention in matters political was mainly focused on the maritime and commercial development of the country: not only did his natural bent lie that way, but his principal revenue from Customs and Excise was dependent on trade. The plans, drawn up by himself and Pepys, to strengthen the Navy, the fitting out of an expedition to discover the North-East passage, and the royal attempts to encourage the study and science of navigation are all examples of this. Two letters of 1676 illustrate the last: the one concerning the apprenticeship of the boys from the Mathematical School at Christ's Hospital which Charles had founded to raise up English navigators, and the other in assistance of young Edmund Halley, the astronomer, then nineteen years of age.

VI.CIRCULAR LETTER TO THE EAST INDIA COMPANY, THE MUSCOVY COMPANY, THE EAST LAND COMPANY, THE ROYAL AFRICAN COMPANY AND THE LEVANT COMPANY

[*Countersigned* ' Williamson ']

January 11, 1675/6.

Whereas we have thought fit out of pious regard to the hospital of our royal predecessor, King Edward VI, commonly called Christ's Hospital, and to the general interests of our subjects in whatever may conduce to the advancing of the navigation of this our kingdom, by our Letters Patents bearing date the 19th day of August, 1673 to establish a distinct foundation within the said hospital and endowed the same with a maintenance for forty poor boys therein, who, having attained to a competent skill in the grammar and the ordinary parts of arithmetic in other schools within the said hospital, shall become fit to be further educated in a Mathematical School and there taught and instructed in the art of navigation and the whole science of arithmetic, until their age and proficiency therein shall have qualified them for the being initiated into the practice of navigation, and bound forth to some able Commanders or Masters of ships as apprentices. . . . And whereas we reflecting with great satisfaction upon the proof which . . . has been already given of the effects of this our royal bounty in the extraordinary proficiency of fifteen of the aforesaid number of the children first chosen into the said school (as the same has upon strict examination and inquiry thereunto lately made by the Master, Wardens and Assistants of the Trinity House of Deptford Strand been by them largely represented unto us) have out of our further gracious inclination to the perfecting this so pious and public a work, by providing encouragement for a constant supply of able and sober masters for the entertaining the said children as apprentices, as fast as they shall be ripened to a proficiency in the aforesaid studies . . . been pleased to grant to the Governors of the said hospital for ever by our further Letters Patents now passing to that effect, an allowance of common seamen's pay, being 19s. per month for each lunary month (amounting to £12 7s. per annum) to be by them given to each master who shall take one of the said children as an apprentice, the same to continue for the said Master for the first three years of each child's apprenticeship. . . .

VII.TO THE EAST INDIA COMPANY
[*Countersigned* ' Williamson ']

September 14, 1676.

Whereas we are humbly informed that Edmund Halley, a student of Queen's College in Oxford (who for several years hath been a diligent observer of the Planets and Stars), hath an intention in order to the making observations for rectifying and finishing the Celestial Globe, to pass and remain for some time in the Isle of St. Helena (which place he conceives very fit and proper for such a design). We being graciously willing to give all encouragement and protection to whatever may tend to the improvement of navigation and be beneficial to the public, have thought fit hereby most particularly to recommend him to you, that you will give order, that he, his friend and their necessaries may be transported to the said island upon the first of your ships which shall go thither, and that he be received and entertained there and have such assistance and countenance from your officers as he may stand in need of. And we not doubting of your readiness to contribute on your parts what fairly may be expected for his encouragement to proceed in so useful an undertaking, we bid you farewell.

Parliament met again on February 15, 1677. Though French conquests abroad and Catholic ones among the courtiers at home filled the country with vague alarms, sedulously fanned by the Opposition leaders and their paid rumour-mongers, the Commons proved more amenable than before.

VIII.SPEECH ON OPENING PARLIAMENT

February 15, 1676/7.

My Lords and Gentlemen : I have called you together again, after a long prorogation, that you might have an opportunity to repair the misfortunes of the last session, and to recover and restore the right use and end of Parliaments. . . . For I declare myself very plainly to you that I come prepared to give you all the satisfaction and security in the great concerns of the Protestant religion, as it is established in the Church of England, that shall reasonably be asked, or can consist with Christian prudence. And I declare myself as freely, that I am ready to gratify you in a further securing of your liberty and property (if you can think you want it) by as many good laws as you shall propose, and as can consist with the safety of the government; without which, there will neither be liberty nor property left to any man.

Having thus plainly told you what I am ready to do for you, I shall deal as plainly with you again, and tell you what it is I do expect from you. First, I do expect and require from you, that all occasions of difference between the two Houses be carefully avoided. . . . And let all men judge who is most for arbitrary government, they that foment such differences as tend to dissolve all Parliaments, or I, that would preserve this and all Parliaments from being made useless by such dissensions. In the next place, I desire you to consider the necessity of building more ships, and how much all our safeties are concerned in it. And since the additional revenue of excise will shortly expire, you that know me to be under a great burden of debts, and how hard a shift I am making to pay them off as fast as I can, I hope will never deny me the continuance of this revenue and some reasonable supply to make my condition more easy. . . .

To conclude : I do recommend to you the peace of the kingdom, in the careful prevention of all differences; the safety of the kingdom, in providing for some greater strength at sea; and the prosperity of the kingdom, in assisting the necessary charge and support of the government. And if any of these good ends should happen to be disappointed, I call God and men to witness this day, that the misfortune of that disappointment shall not lie at my doors.

Encouraged thereafter by Pepys's patriotic eloquence and Danby's money bags, Parliament voted a much-needed £600,000 for building thirty new warships.

For a moment it looked as though Danby's plan to give the Crown independence and power through a Cavalier majority in Parliament had succeeded.   But the opening of the spring campaign in Flanders spoilt all.   Fortress after fortress fell to the French armies, and the Opposition, backed now by the almost universal opinion of the country, was easily able to procure a Parliamentary address to the King to enter the war against Louis. On May 28 Charles, refusing to abandon his acknowledged royal prerogative of decision in foreign affairs, once more prorogued Parliament.

But though Charles refused to let Parliament dictate foreign policy, he was fully aware that Louis, alarmed at his new naval programme, and anxious to cripple England by dissension at home, had been bribing the Opposition against him.   Anxious himself at Louis's victories over the Spanish, he now resolved to double-cross him.   While continuing to coax money from him for a further adjournment, he secretly made arrangements to marry his niece, Mary, daughter of the Catholic Duke of York, to the Protestant William of Orange.   It was an adroit move, calculated both to allay national fears of a Catholic dynasty and to redress the balance of power on the Continent.   The marriage, which took place on November 4, 1677, was followed by a new alliance with Holland for the pacification of Europe and the security of the Netherlands.   Louis was asked to accept peace with his enemies on terms agreed between Charles and William, who announced their readiness to enforce them if necessary by armed intervention.   When Louis refused, Charles summoned his Parliament and asked for supplies.

IX. Speech to both Houses

January 28, 1677/8.

My Lords and Gentlemen : When we parted last, I told you, that before we met again, I would do that which should be to your satisfaction.   I have accordingly made such alliances with Holland as are for the preservation of Flanders; and which cannot fail of that end, unless prevented either by the want of due assistances to support those alliances, or by the small regard the Spaniards themselves must have to their own preservation.

The first of these I cannot suspect, by reason of your repeated engagements to maintain them. . . . Besides, it will not be less necessary to let our enemies have such a prospect of our resolutions, as may let them see certainly that we shall not be weary of our arms till Christendom be restored to such a peace as shall not be in the power of any prince alone to disturb.

I do acknowledge to you that I have used all the means possible, by a mediation, to have procured an honourable and safe peace for Christendom; knowing how preferable such a peace would have been to any war, and especially to this kingdom, which must necessarily own the vast benefits it has received by peace, whilst its neighbours only have yet smarted by the war. But, finding it no longer to be hoped for by fair means, it shall not be my fault if that be not obtained by force which cannot be had otherwise.

For this reason I have recalled my troops from France; and have considered, that although the Dutch shall do their parts, we cannot have less on ours than ninety sail of capital ships constantly maintained, nor less than thirty or forty thousand land men . . . to be employed upon our fleets and elsewhere. And because there shall be no fear of misemploying what you shall give to these uses, I am contented that such money be appropriated to those ends as strictly as you can desire.

I have given testimony enough of my care in that kind, by the progress I have made in building the new ships; wherein, for the making them more useful, I have directed such larger dimensions, as will cost me above £100,000 more than the Act allows.[1] I have gone as far as I could, in repairing the old fleet, and in buying of necessary stores for the Navy and Ordnance; and in this, and other provisions for better securing both my foreign plantations and the islands nearer home, I have expended a great deal more than the £200,000 you enabled me to borrow upon the Excise, although I have not found such a credit as I expected upon that security. I have borne the charge both of a rebellion in Virginia and a new war with Algiers. I stand

---

[1] An example, fully illustrated by Pepys's Naval MSS. at Magdalene College, Cambridge, and in the Bodleian, of Charles's close interest in the technicalities of shipbuilding.

engaged to the Prince of Orange for my niece's portion, and I shall not be able to maintain my constant necessary establishments, unless the new impost upon wines, etc., be continued to me. . . .

I hope these things will need little recommendation to you, when you consider your promises in some and the necessity of the rest. And to let you see that I have not only employed my time and treasure for your safety, but done all I could to remove all sorts of jealousies, I have married my niece to the Prince of Orange, by which I hope I have given full satisfaction that I shall never suffer his interest to be ruined, if I can be assisted as I ought to preserve them. Having done all this, I expect from you a plentiful supply, suitable to such great occasions; whereon depends not only the honour, but (for aught I know) the being of an English nation, which will not be saved by finding faults afterwards, but may be prevented by avoiding the chief fault of doing weakly and by halves what can only be hoped from a vigorous and thorough prosecution of what we undertake. . . .

But if Charles had again shown Louis that he was not to be trifled with, Louis could retaliate. Encouraged by French bribes, the Opposition, who had hitherto been clamouring for war, now did everything possible to withhold supplies. Though Charles's declaration on his foreign policy had won him a vote for ninety ships and thirty-two regiments, the Poll Bill to raise the wherewithal to equip them was delayed and its value largely mitigated by the loss to the Customs revenue involved in a Parliamentary prohibition of French imports. In the meantime Charles, at the cost of running himself once more heavily into debt, was pouring troops into Flanders under his son Monmouth.

x. To the Duke of Monmouth

March 3, 1677/8

To our dearly beloved son James, Duke of Monmouth.

We desiring to preserve the town of Bruges (unless that place be so invested as that you cannot with reasonable probability of success attempt the going in) command that you march with the two battalions under your command at Ostend to Bruges, and there comport yourself according to the same instructions you received for the governing yourself at Ostend.

The further Charles proceeded towards war, the clearer became the nature of the trap into which he was falling. At home the Opposition, utilizing the popular suspicion that the army which was being raised was intended against not French but English liberties, continued to starve him of adequate supplies, and at the same time to urge him publicly to attack France, while abroad William of Orange, faced by a similar combination of French gold and factious deputies, warned his uncle that active support from Holland was not to be expected. Under these circumstances Charles met treachery with dissimulation and prepared his retreat by re-opening secret negotiations with Louis. On March 25 Danby, on royal instructions, wrote to Ralph Montagu, the English ambassador at Paris.

XI. THE EARL OF DANBY TO THE HON. RALPH MONTAGU

London, March 25, 1678.

Since my writing to you by Mr. Brisbane[1] the resolutions have been altered as to the sending you instructions as yet for the proposing anything to the French King. The particulars which will be consented to on the part of the Confederates and of which this is a copy will be communicated to you by Mr. Secretary Coventry, but you will have no other direction from him about them, but only thereby to be enabled to find the pulse of the King (or his Ministers at least) against the time that you shall receive orders to make the proposals to him. That you may know from whence the nicety of this affair proceeds, it is necessary to inform you that, for the fear of its being ill resented by the Parliament here, the King will not make any proposal at all of peace unless he shall be pressed to it by the confederates. . . . To supply this defect, therefore, and to prevent the King's sending again into Holland before he knows the mind of France, I am commanded by His Majesty to let you know that you are to make the propositions enclosed to the

---

[1] The Secretary of the Embassy.

King of France, and to tell him that the King will undertake for the seeing them made good on the part of Spain and Holland in case they shall be accepted by him. . . . For the more dexterous management of this matter the King is advised to show these propositions to Monsieur Barillon, but not to give him a copy, so that by the strength of memory it is expected he shall write to his Master, and by that means only are we to hope for an answer to a matter of this vast importance. And consequently you may imagine what a satisfaction we are like to reap from it when it comes. I doubt not but by your conduct it will be brought to a speedier issue, which is of as great importance as the thing itself, there being no condition worse for His Majesty than his standing unresolved betwixt peace and war.

I find by Monsieur Barillon that 'tis like some places, which are dependencies upon greater towns, may be demanded by the King of France, but if he intend the peace (which you will do very well to know his mind fully in), you may justly say you hope he will neither stand upon one single place (though a fortified one), nor upon any place unfortified, which is a dependant upon those which are to be restored to Spain. And if anything should be mentioned about Sicily to remain in the French hands until the peace of Sweden were concluded, you are only to say that you are not empowered to say anything upon it, and you are confident the King has done all he could to get the utmost propositions they could consent to. . . . In case the conditions of the peace shall be accepted, the King expects to have six millions of livres a year for three years from the time that this agreement shall be signed betwixt His Majesty and the King of France, because it will probably be two or three years before the Parliament will be in humour to give him any supplies after the making of any peace with France, and the ambassador here has always agreed to that sum, but not for so long time. If you find the peace will not be accepted, you are not to mention the money at all. And all possible care must be taken to have this whole negotiation as private as possible, for fear of giving offence at home, where for the most part we hear in ten days after of anything that is communicated to the French Ministers. I must again repeat to you, that whatever you write upon this subject to the Secretary (to whom you must not mention a syllable of the money) you must say only as a thing you believe they would consent to, if you had power formally to make those propositions. Pray inform yourself to the bottom of what is to be expected from France and assure them that you believe this will be the last time that you shall receive any propositions of a peace, if these be rejected, as indeed I believe it will, so that you may take your own measures as well as the King's upon it.

At the foot of this draft appears in Charles's handwriting this note:

I approve of this letter.—c.r.

Meanwhile Charles and Danby continued to try and obtain from Parliament a sufficient measure of support to convince Louis that if he refused to accept their terms England meant business. Such an appearance of strength had now become all the more necessary owing to the renewed successes which the opening of the spring campaign brought to the French in Flanders.

But Parliament was not to be wooed. The Commons by narrow majorities voted that they would give no more money until they were secured against Popery, that the alliances which Charles had made at their request with Holland were not consistent with their safety, and that the Ministers should be impeached. By May 13 their proceedings had become so threatening that Charles was forced to prorogue them for ten days. Meanwhile, as the only way to secure both himself and what remained of Flanders, he pursued his negotiations with Louis, reaching a definite agreement with him that, if the terms of peace that France was now ready to offer her enemies (which had already been approved by William of Orange) were not accepted by Spain and her confederates, England should refrain from further action. But the money bribe that Louis offered him to disband his army and dissolve Parliament he refused, though characteristically he secured a secret promise of its payment should he ever elect to change his mind and accept such humiliation.

XII.To Louis XIV
[*Translation from French*]

May 17, 1678.

Monsieur, my brother. It is an extreme joy to me to find that the occasion of renewing that friendship which seemed likely to be interrupted, presents itself so favourably and certainly, and that I have had the happiness to contribute to the peace of Christendom so much as I have done by the articles which the Sieur de Ruvigny carries to you. As you act entirely in this peace for your glory, I receive it also as the most particular effect that could have been shown me of your good will towards me, seeing it lays the foundations of a friendship which I hope will last as long as it shall please God to let us live.

The circumstances of my affairs have obliged me to finish with your ambassador in an extraordinary manner, because the secret is of the greatest importance to me and to my affairs. I therefore earnestly pray that nothing be said of it, till I let your ambassador know that the whole may be public without prejudice to me. I have desired the Sieur de Ruvigny to speak to you upon all my concerns, for which I depend on your friendship, knowing how much and how fully you ought to be assured of mine. So, I pray God, Monsieur, my brother, to keep you in His holy protection. Your good brother. CHARLES.

Charles's appeal to Parliament at its reassembly on May 23 for money to support his forces till peace was concluded was met by a vote for an immediate disbandment of the Army—a gratuitous sotisse which he himself had just refused to commit at Louis's bidding.

XIII.Speech to Parliament on opening the Session

May 23, 1678.

My Lords and Gentlemen: When I met you last, I asked your advice upon the great conjunctures abroad. What return you gentlemen of the House of Commons made me, and whether it was suitable to the end I intended (which was the saving of Flanders), I leave it to yourselves, in cold blood, to consider.

Since I asked your advice, the conjunctures abroad and our distempers (which influenced them so much) have driven things violently on towards a peace; and where they will end, I cannot tell; but will say this only to you, that I am resolved, as far as I am able, to save Flanders, either by a war or a peace, which way soever I shall find most conducing towards it; and that must be judged by circumstances, as they play from abroad. For my own part, I should think, being armed were as necessary to make peace, as war; and therefore, if I were able, would keep up my Army and my Navy at sea for some time till a peace were concluded, if that must be.   But, because that will depend upon your supplies, I leave it to you to consider whether to provide for their subsistence so long, or for their disbanding sooner, and to take care, in either case, not to discourage or use ill so many worthy gentlemen and brave men, who came to offer their lives and service to their country upon this occasion; and in pursuit of your own advices and resolutions. . . .

Charles, having, as he thought, secured a Treaty that both preserved the Flemish ports from French occupation and gave his old ally a profitable and reasonable peace, gave way to his Parliament gracefully.   His speech to the Houses on June 18, asking for new taxes to make good the loss to the national revenue by the expiry of old, was conciliatory and, since Danby had now been able to secure a slight majority, well received.

xiv. Speech to both Houses

June 18, 1678.

My Lords and Gentlemen: I know very well that the season of the year requires this session should be short; and that both for my health and your occasions, we may all have liberty to go into the country by the middle of the next month at the farthest.   I think it a matter of yet more importance, that we part not only fairly but kindly too, and in perfect confidence one of another; since nothing else can render us either safe and easy at home, or considered so far abroad as this Crown has ever been, and is now more necessary than ever, both for the safety of Christendom and our own. Therefore I shall at this time open my heart freely to you, in some points that nearest concern both you and me; and hope you will consider them so, because I am sure our interest ought not to be divided; and for me they never shall be.

I told you at the opening of this session, how violently things abroad were driving on towards a peace, and that I could not tell where they would end; but that I was resolved to save Flanders, either by a war or a peace; in which I am still fixed, as in the greatest foreign interest of this nation. I must now tell you, that things seem already to have determined in a peace, at least as to Spain and Holland; who have so far accepted the terms offered to France, that my ambassador at Nimuegen writes me word he expected to be called upon to sign it by the last of this month. My part in it will be not only of a mediator, but to give my guarantee to it, which the Confederates will call upon me for. And I am resolved to give in the strongest manner they themselves will desire, and I am able. How far this will go, I cannot tell; but they send me word already, that unless England and Holland will both join in the charge of maintaining Flanders, even after the peace, the Spaniards will not be in condition of supporting it alone and must fall into other measures. On the other side, they think France will be left so great, that nothing abroad can treat with them hereafter upon an equal foot, without the hopes of being supported by this Crown. And, to this end, I am sure, it will be necessary not only to keep our Navies constantly strong at sea, but to leave the world in some assurance of our being well united at home, and thereby in as great an opinion of our conduct hereafter as they are already of our force. Upon this occasion, I cannot but say that though, after our joint resolutions of a war, and the supplies you have given towards it, you may think the peace an ill bargain, because it will cost you money, yet perhaps you will not believe it so, if you consider that by it so great a part of Flanders is like to be saved. Whereas, without the paces we made towards war, there is nothing so certain as that the whole of it would have been absolutely lost this campaign, if not by this very time; and I believe you would give much greater sums than this will cost you, rather than the single town of Ostend should be in the French hands, and forty of their men-of-war in so good a haven over against the river's mouth. Besides, both you and I (as we are true Englishmen) cannot but be pleased, and understand the importance of that reputation we have gained abroad, by having in 50 days raised an Army of near 30,000 men, and prepared a Navy of 90 ships, which would have been now ready at sea, if we had gone into a war.

Now, my Lords and Gentlemen, I know that in so great conjunctures you desire that I should keep the honour of my crowns, and look to your safety, by some balance in the affairs abroad; and I should be very glad I were able to do it. But I do not see how it will be possible for me, even in a time of peace, with a revenue so impaired as mine is by my debts long since contracted, and the present anticipations, and at the best so disproportioned, not only to that of the Kings, my neighbours, but even to that of the United Provinces themselves (though of no larger extent than two or three of our counties). Therefore, as I said I would open my heart freely to you, so I must tell you that if you would see me able in any kind to influence the great conjunctures abroad, wherein the honour and safety of the nation are so much concerned, and wherein the turns are sometimes so short as not to give me leave to call in time either for your advice or assistances; if you would have me but to pursue such a war as this of Algiers[1] with honour, and at the same time keep such fleets about our own coasts as may give our neighbours the respect for us that have been always paid this Crown; if you would have me pass any part of my life in ease or quiet, and all the rest of it in perfect confidence and kindness with you and all succeeding Parliaments; you must find a way of settling for my life, not only my revenue, and the additional duties as they were at Christmas last, but of adding to them, upon some new funds, £300,000 a year. Upon which I shall consent that an Act may pass for appropriating £500,000 a year to the constant maintenance of the Navy and Ordnance, which I take to be the greatest safety and interest of these kingdoms : and I will at the

---

[1] With the Algerian pirates who were constantly harassing English trade in the Mediterranean.

same time (as I do now) assure you that I shall not only, this or any other session of Parliament, consent to such reasonable and Public Bills as you shall offer me, but shall employ my whole life to advance the true and public good and safety of my people, and endeavour, while I live, that none else shall ever be able to do them harm. . . .

But the consequence of Parliament's decision to get rid of the Army raised to intimidate him was that Louis demanded better terms than those he had promised Charles he would accept. At the end of June Flanders and the peace of Europe were again threatened. Charles acted promptly and gave orders to suspend further demobilization. His action was effective. Parliament supported him by voting supply for the emergency, reinforcements were hurried to Flanders and, faced by an immediate war with England, Louis gave way. On July 31 peace was signed at Nimuegen.

The events of the summer may have caused Charles and Danby to believe that they had at last triumphed over the Opposition. A letter written by Charles that July to the Cavalier Lord Chancellor Finch shows him taking a strong line towards his opponents.

xv. To Lord Chancellor Finch

Windsor, July 24, 1678.

I do find by what my Lord Yarmouth[1] hath showed me, that the commission is not yet gone forth for the Justices of peace in Norfolk, therefore I see no inconvenience in leaving Sir J. Hobart, Sir J. Holland and Sir R. Kempe out of the peace, at least the two first. For there is no objection against it but in disobliging those sort of people who will never be obliged, and any countenance I give them is only used against myself and Government.

[1] Lord Lieutenant of Norfolk and formerly Sir Robert Paston, a Cavalier squire, whose long-delayed elevation to the peerage in 1673 had created a vacant seat in Parliament for Samuel Pepys.

The events which occurred before Parliament's reassembly in October showed that the Opposition was very far from being subdued. In August before leaving for Windsor Charles was stopped in St. James's Park and warned of a Catholic plot against his own and his Protestant subjects' lives. On his return to London in September the alleged plot again reappeared, this time in the form of detailed information made before the Council by a brazen-faced scoundrel named Titus Oates. Though Charles never believed in Oates's lies, his subjects were more credulous. The story, admirably attuned to their religious prejudices, was already spreading over the kingdom, when in the middle of October the public was electrified by the mysterious murder of a Protestant magistrate, Sir Edmund Berry Godfrey. Out of this the Opposition leaders and their pamphleteers and mob-managers fomented a panic. Such was the juncture of affairs on October 21, when Charles, by this time apparently the only calm man in the nation, greeted his Parliament.

XVI. SPEECH TO PARLIAMENT

October 21, 1678.

My Lords and Gentlemen : I have thought the time very long since we parted last; and would not have deferred your meeting by so many prorogations, if I could well have met you sooner. The part which I have had this summer in the preservation of our neighbours, and the well-securing what was left of Flanders, is sufficiently known and acknowledged by all that are abroad : and though for this cause I have been obliged to keep up my troops (without which our neighbours had absolutely despaired), yet both the honour and interest of the nation have been so far improved by it, that I am confident no man here would repine at it, or think the money raised for their disbanding to have been ill employed in their continuance. And I do assure you, I am so much more out of purse for the service, that I do expect you should supply it. . . .

I now intend to acquaint you (as I shall always do with anything that concerns me), that I have been informed of a design against my person by the Jesuits; of which I shall forbear any opinion, lest I may seem to say too much, or too little. But I will leave the matter to the law; and, in the meantime, will take

299

as much care as I can to prevent all manners of practices by that sort of men, and of others too, who have been tampering in a high degree by foreigners, and contriving how to introduce Popery amongst us.

I shall conclude with the recommending to you my other concerns. I have been under great disappointments by the defect of the Poll Bill. My revenue is under great anticipations, and at the best was never equal to the constant and necessary expense of the government, whereof I intend to have the whole state laid before you; and require you to look into it, and consider of it with that duty and affection which I am sure I shall always find from you. The rest I leave to the Chancellor.

But if Charles appeared calm, he had no doubts as to the strength of the storm or of the ill-will of the forces which were behind it. He wrote to his old Cavalier Lord Lieutenant in Ireland, Ormonde, to be on his guard, remembering how the disasters of that kingdom had hastened his father's downfall forty years before, and set himself to clear the decks of the ship of State for the hurricane.

XVII. To the Marquess of Ormonde

Whitehall, November 5, 1678.

You may easily believe that I have not a little business now upon my hands. This bearer will inform you so particularly of all as I need not tell you my opinion of it nor enter farther upon the matter. I am sure you will put things into the best posture where you are, that may be upon all events; so as I shall say no more to you, only to assure you that I have that confidence in you and kindness for you, as you may be assured of my constant friendship.

The aim of the Opposition was to destroy the hereditary monarchial principle by striking at its weakest part, the Catholic successor. On November 2nd Lord Shaftesbury, in a fiery speech, urged that the Duke of York should be dismissed from the Council. Charles, resolved to concentrate all his scanty strength on safeguarding essentials, parried by persuading his

*brother to withdraw from the principal Committees of State:
then came down to the Lords to inform Parliament that he was
ready to agree to all reasonable safeguards against abuse of power
by a Catholic successor provided that nothing was done to impair
the ancient legal principle of hereditary succession. And following the same plan of yielding in inessentials, he gave the Houses
the right to decide whether the plan urged by the Spanish
ambassador for the further preservation of Flanders should be
adhered to or whether the forces maintained for that purpose
should be immediately abandoned, as the Commons demanded.*

XVIII.SPEECH TO BOTH HOUSES RELATING TO THE SUCCESSION

November 9, 1678.

My Lords and Gentlemen : I am so very sensible of the great
and extraordinary care you have already taken, and still continue
to show for the safety and preservation of my person in these
times of danger, that I could not satisfy myself without coming
hither on purpose to give you all my most hearty thanks for it.
Nor do I think it enough to give you my thanks only, but I hold
myself obliged to let you see withal, that I do as much study
your preservation, too, as I can possibly; and that I am as ready
to join with you in all the ways and means that may establish
a firm security of the Protestant religion as your own hearts
can wish. And this not only during my time, of which I am
sure you have no fear, but in future ages, even to the end of the
world.

And therefore I am come to assure you that whatsoever Bills
you shall present, to be passed into laws, to make you safe in the
reign of my successor (so they tend not to impeach the right of
succession, nor the descent of the Crown in the true line; and so
as they restrain not my power, nor the just rights of any
Protestant successor) shall find from me a ready concurrence.

And I desire you withal, to think of some more effectual
means for the conviction of Popish recusants, and to expedite
your councils as fast as you can, that the world may see our
unanimity; and that I may have an opportunity of showing you
how ready I am to do anything that may give comfort and satisfaction to such dutiful and loyal subjects.

XIX. SPEECH TO BOTH HOUSES

November 25, 1678.

My Lords and Gentlemen : I told you in the beginning of this session how much I had been obliged to keep up my Forces in Flanders; that without it our neighbours had absolutely despaired, and by this means, whatever has been saved of Flanders, is acknowledged to be wholly due to my interposition. And I showed you withal, that I had been forced to employ that money, which had been raised for the disbanding those troops, in the continuance of them together; and not only so, but that I had been much more out of purse for that service. . . .

I have now undergone this expense so long that I find it absolutely impossible to support the charge any longer; and did therefore think of putting an end to that charge, by recalling my troops with all possible speed, who are already exposed to the utmost want and misery, being without any prospect of further pay or subsistence. But whilst I was about to do this, I have been importuned by the Spanish Ministers to continue them a little longer, until the ratifications of the peace be exchanged; without which, all that hath been hitherto saved in Flanders, will inevitably fall into the hands of their enemies. And now, between this importunity to keep up those troops, and my own inability to pay them any longer, I find myself in great difficulties what to resolve.

If you do not think that the public safety may require the continuance, I do wish as heartily as any man, that for the public ease they may be speedily disbanded and paid off. I have thought fit to lay the matter before you. And having acquitted myself to all the world, by asking your advice and assistance, I desire it may be speedy, and without any manner of delay.

On essentials Charles would not yield an inch. At the end of November he rejected a Bill for placing the Militia under Parliamentary control—he would not, he told the Houses, let that command leave his hands for even half an hour—and on December 30th, taking advantage of a quarrel between the two Houses, prorogued them to save Danby, who had been im-

peached as a result of the Opposition's production of his letter of
March 25th (see p. 291) to Ralph Montagu. And an attempt
on the part of Oates and his managers to involve the Queen in
the pretended plot against the King's life was met by the sternest
royal disapproval.

xx. SPEECH TO BOTH HOUSES

December 30, 1678.

My Lords and Gentlemen: It is with great unwillingness
that I come this day to tell you, I intend to prorogue you. I
think all of you are witnesses that I have been ill used; the
particulars of it I intend to acquaint you with at a more convenient time. In the meantime, I do assure you that I will
immediately enter upon the disbanding of the Army, and let all
the world see that there is nothing that I intend but for the
good of the kingdom, and for the safety of religion. I will likewise prosecute this plot, and find out who are the instruments in
it: and I shall take all the care which lies in my power, for the
security of religion, and the maintenance of it as it is now established. I have no more to say to you at this time, but leave the
rest to my Lord Chancellor to prorogue you.

xxi. TO DOM PEDRO OF PORTUGAL

January, 1678/9.

We doubt not but that your Highness hath already heard of
the unhappy reflection that hath been lately raised against our
dear consort the Queen, and do believe your Highness hath
taken a sensible part with us in that indignation wherewith we
have resented the same. We brought the matter (as soon as it
was known) unto our Council Board, and the reception which
there it had we are sure will not sound unpleasing to your
Highness, because it gave satisfaction to us, and did let the
Queen clearly see that all was done for her present vindication,
which the time would permit. But this misfortune arising while
the States of our kingdoms were assembled, who by their
constitution may take cognizance of whatever happens of an

extraordinary nature, they drew the inquiry before them. And even then such of them as took but time to deliberate and to consider how the Queen hath lived, found motives to reject the complaint, and instead of favouring the accusation the time was only spent in magnifying of her virtues. . . .

To save Danby, Charles decided in January, 1679, to face the risk of a general election. The Cavalier Parliament was accordingly dissolved and writs issued for a new Parliament. But in the existing state of popular opinion, the republican ' Whigs ' or ' Mutineers ', as they were called, who were already a well-organized party (which their opponents were far from being), had no difficulty in controlling the antiquated electoral machinery of the country. Before Parliament met it was known that Shaftesbury would have a well-disciplined majority under his orders in the Commons, and that both the succession and the King's Ministers would be fiercely attacked.

Charles had to recast his plans. After a vain attempt to persuade his brother to abandon his unpopular creed, he commanded him to leave England, coupling his public letter to this effect with a Declaration in Council that he had never married any woman but the Queen, in order to safeguard the succession against his own son, Monmouth, whom the Opposition was now insinuating was legitimate.

XXII. TO THE DUKE OF YORK

February 28, 1678/9.

For my most dear friend the Duke of York.

My dear Brother. I have already fully told you the reasons which oblige me to send you from me for some time beyond sea.

As I am truly sorry for the cause of our separation, you may also assure yourself that I shall never wish your absence to continue longer than is absolutely necessary for your good and my service. I find it, however, proper to let you know under my hand that I expect you will satisfy me in this; and that I wish it may be as soon as your conveniency will permit. You may easily believe that it is not without a great deal of pain I write

you this, being more touched with the constant friendship you
have had for me than with anything else in the world; and I
also hope that you will do me the justice to believe for certain,
that neither absence, nor anything will hinder me from being
truly and with affection yours.

*Having taken these steps indicative of modern constitutional
practice, Charles, on March 6, welcomed his new and obviously
hostile Parliament with fitting politeness.*

XXIII. Speech on opening the Session

March 6, 1679.

My Lords and Gentlemen : I meet you here with the most
earnest desire that man can have to unite the minds of all my
subjects, both to me, and to one another.   And I resolve it shall
be your faults, if the success be not suitably to my desires.   I
have done many great things already in order to that end; as, the
exclusion of the Popish Lords from their seats in Parliament; the
execution of several men, both upon the score of the Plot and of
the murder of Sir Edmund Berry Godfrey.   And it is apparent
that I have not been idle in prosecuting the discovery of both, as
much further as hath been possible in so short a time.

I have disbanded as much of the Army as I could get money
to do; and I am ready to disband the rest, so soon as you shall
reimburse what they have cost me, and will enable me to pay
off the remainder.   And, above all, I have commanded my
brother to absent himself from me, because I would not leave
the most malicious man room to say I had not removed all
causes which could be pretended to influence me towards Popish
Counsels.   Besides that end of union which I aim at (and which
I wish could be extended to Protestants abroad, as well as at
home), I propose, by this last great step I have made, to discern
whether Protestant religion and the peace of the kingdom be as
truly aimed at by others, as they are really intended by me; for,
if they be, you will employ your time upon the great concerns
of the nation, and not be drawn to promote private animosities
under pretence of the public.   Your proceedings will be calm

and peaceful, in order to those good ends I have recommended to you; and you will curb the motions of any unruly spirits, which would endeavour to disturb them. I hope there will be none such amongst you; because there can be no man that must not see how fatal differences amongst ourselves are like to be at this time, both at home and abroad.

I shall not cease my endeavours daily to find out what more I can, both of the plot and murder of Sir Edmund Berry Godfrey; and shall desire the assistance of both my Houses in that work. I have not been wanting to give orders for putting all the present laws in execution against Papists; and I am ready to join in the making such further laws as may be necessary for securing of the kingdom against Popery.

I must desire your assistance also in supplies, both for disbanding the Army (as I have already told you) and for paying that part of the fleet which hath been provided for by Parliament but till the 5th of June last; as also that debt for stores which was occasioned by the Poll Bill's falling short of the sum which that Act gave credit for. I must necessarily recommend to you likewise the discharging of those anticipations which are upon my revenue, and which I have commanded to be laid before you; and I have just cause to desire such an increase of the revenue itself, as might make it equal to my necessary expenses. But, by reason of those other supplies which are absolutely necessary at this time, I am contented to struggle with that difficulty a little longer; expecting for the present only to have the additional duties upon customs and excise to be prolonged to me; and that you will some way make up the loss I sustain by the prohibition of French wines and brandy, which turns only to my prejudice and to the great advantage of the French.

I must needs put you in mind how necessary it will be to have a good strength at sea this summer, since our neighbours are making naval preparations. And, notwithstanding the great difficulties I labour under, I have taken such care as will prevent any danger which can threaten us, if your parts be performed in time. And I do heartily recommend to you, that such a constant establishment might be made for the Navy as might make this kingdom not only safe, but formidable; which can never be whilst there remains not enough besides to pay the necessary charges of the Crown.

I will conclude, as I began, with my earnest desire to have this a healing Parliament; and I do give you this assurance, that I will with my life defend both the Protestant religion and the laws of this kingdom. And I do expect from you to be defended from the calumny, as well as danger, of those worst of men, who endeavour to render me and my Government odious to my people. . . .

There was another point in which Charles anticipated modern constitutional practice. Perceiving the inevitability of the attack by the Whig majority in the Commons on his old Cavalier Ministers, and fully aware of the crippling effects on governmental action which such attacks involved, he adopted the expedient of offering office to the leaders of his adversaries. By reconstituting his Council and partly filling it with Whig grandees, he countered the outcry of the Commons against ' evil counsellors' and to some extent circumscribed the activities of his most powerful adversaries: at the same time he secretly reserved to himself the right to ignore the advice of his new Ministers as often as he chose.

XXIV. SPEECH TO BOTH HOUSES

April 21, 1679.

My Lords and Gentlemen : I thought it requisite to acquaint you with what I have done now this day; which is, that I have established a new Privy Council, the constant number of which shall never exceed thirty.

I have made choice of such persons as are worthy and able to advise me; and am resolved, in all my weighty and important affairs, next to the advice of my Great Council in Parliament (which I shall very often consult with), to be advised by this Privy Council.

I could not make so great a change without acquainting both Houses of Parliament. And I desire you all to apply yourselves heartily, as I shall do, to those things which are necessary for the good and safety of the kingdom, and that no time may be lost in it.

Yet against the fury of faction and the strength of the religious terror behind it, Charles's moderation seemed almost fatuous. To James, watching anxiously across the water, it appeared that his brother was taking the same slippery path to disaster as his father. But when he wrote to him urging his own return and the adoption of strong policy, Charles's reply was not encouraging.

xxv. To the Duke of York

Probably May, 1679.

. . . I am sorry to tell you that the temper of the people is such in all places, especially in London, that the Lords in the Tower being not yet tried (by which men's minds (are) as full as ever with the apprehension of the plot and Popery) that if you should come over at this time, it would be of the last ill consequence both to you and me. I am sure there is nothing troubles me more than to be deprived of your company, nor can I write anything more against my heart than this. But when I consider it is the last stake, I would not let my inclinations sway me so far as to give a counsel so much to the prejudice of our interest as matters stand at present.

The proceedings in the House were such as to lend support to James's worst fears. On May 8th the Commons voted an Address for the removal of Lauderdale; two weeks later a Bill for disabling the Duke of York from succeeding passed its second reading by a majority of ninety-two. Meanwhile debts were piling up, the officers were unpaid and the scanty royal garrisons without stores. In Scotland there was open rebellion on the part of the Covenanters, only suppressed by the hasty dispatch of Monmouth. Yet Charles, by delaying, knew that every day in which he remained calm brought nearer the time when England must regain her normal sanity. And on May 26, seeing that nothing but trouble could be hoped for from it, he prorogued his third Parliament. A few weeks later he dissolved it and issued writs for a new election.

Though the result of the general election that followed showed that the Whigs were still in possession of the electoral machinery, Charles was right in supposing that the tide of

*popular opinion was beginning to turn in his favour. A
dangerous illness that August hastened the process, and he felt
strong enough in the autumn to allow his brother to leave his
exile in Flanders and take over the government of Scotland,
and at the same time to deprive Monmouth, whom the
republican leaders were using as a puppet successor, of his
command of the Army.*

XXVI. To the Duke of Monmouth

[*Countersigned* ' Sunderland ']

September 12, 1679.

Right trusty and well-beloved Cousin and Counsellor, we
greet you well. Whereas we did some time since constitute you
Captain-General of all our land forces in this our kingdom, and
whereas we intend to revoke your commission of Captain-
General as thinking it for our service at this time; we have
thought fit by these presents to signify the same to you, and
accordingly do hereby require you to deliver up your commission
and send it forthwith to us. . . .

*When Shaftesbury protested at these marks of the royal
initiative, Charles dismissed him from his Presidency of the
Council. Moreover, in spite of the Opposition's attempt to
revive popular fears by the decoy Meal Tub Plot and Shaftesbury's vigorous campaign of rumours and monster petitions and
processions, Charles was able, during the winter of 1679/80,
quietly but steadily to strengthen his position. The new
Parliament was prevented from meeting by a succession of
prorogations, young Ministers favourable to the King's views
were appointed, and Republicans and Nonconformists everywhere
dismissed from the Commissions of Peace. And both to keep
malcontents from key positions and allay popular fears, the
various Acts disqualifying Nonconformists and Papists from
office were vigorously enforced.*

XXVII. To the Lord Mayor and Common Council of London

[*Countersigned* ' Sunderland ']

December 17, 1679.

Right trusty and well-beloved and trusty and well-beloved, we
greet you well. Whereas by an Act of Parliament, made in the

thirteenth year of our reign, entituled an Act for the well governing and regulating of Corporations, it is enacted that no person shall for ever hereafter be placed, elected or chosen into the office of Mayor, Alderman or Common Council man, that shall not within one year next before such election or choice have taken the Sacrament of the Lord's Supper according to the rites of the Church of England; and that each person or persons so placed, elected and chosen shall likewise take the oaths of Allegiance and Supremacy, and the oath in the said Act mentioned against the unlawfulness of taking arms against ourself, and subscribe the Declaration concerning the illegality of imposing the oath commonly called the Solemn League and Covenant upon our subjects of England.   And it being our pleasure that particular and exact care be taken that the said Act should be duly put in execution for the prevention of the many mischiefs that may otherwise be designed by persons ill affected to the government and the public peace thereof both in Church and State, and the time for electing of new Common Council men for our said city of London now approaching. . . . We have therefore thought fit to require you to take especial care that the said Act be duly put in execution and that no Common Council men be admitted in Council, or presume in any respect whatsoever to act as a Common Council man but such as have pursued the said Act of Parliament. . . .

In the spring of 1680 Shaftesbury renewed his attack on the monarchy by unearthing a new plot, an Irish one this time, directed against the loyal Lord Lieutenant, old Ormonde, and by sedulously circulated rumours of a legendary black box said to contain proof of the King's marriage with Lucy Walter, Monmouth's mother. Charles issued a public denial of the latter, and showed Ormonde his confidence by appointing his gallant son, Lord Ossory, to command his troops in Tangier, then in danger from the Moors—an appointment turned to tragedy by Ossory's untimely death from a fever on the eve of setting sail.

XXVIII. DECLARATION TO ALL LOVING SUBJECTS

Whitehall, June 2, 1680.

We cannot but take notice of the great industry and malice wherewith some men of a seditious and restless spirit do spread abroad a most false and scandalous report of a marriage or contract of marriage supposed to be had and made between us and one Mrs. Walter, alias Barlow, now deceased, mother of the present Duke of Monmouth, aiming thereby to fill the minds of our loving subjects with doubts and fears, and, if possible, to divide them into parties and factions, and as much as in them lies, to bring into question the clearly undoubted right of our true and lawful heirs and successors to the Crown. We have therefore thought ourself obliged to let our loving subjects see what steps we . . . have already made, in order to obviate the ill consequences that so dangerous and malicious a report may have in future times upon the peace of our kingdoms.

In January last was twelve month, we made a Declaration written with our own hand in these words following:

' There being a false and malicious report industriously spread abroad by some, who are neither friends to me nor the Duke of Monmouth, as if I should have been either contracted or married to his mother; and though I am most confident that this idle story cannot have any effect in this age, yet I thought it my duty in relation to the true succession of the Crown, and that future ages may not have any pretence to give disturbance upon that score, or any other of this matter, to declare, that I do here declare in the presence of Almighty God, that I never was married nor gave any contract to any woman whatsoever but to my wife, Queen Catherine, to whom I am now married. In witness thereof I set my hand at Whitehall 6th January, 1678/9.
' CHARLES R.'

To strengthen which Declaration, we did in March following (which was March last was twelve month) make a most public Declaration in our Privy Council, written likewise with our own hand; and having caused a true transcript thereof to be entered in our Council books, we signed it, and caused the Lords of our Privy Council then attending us in Council to subscribe the same likewise, and we ordered the original to be kept in the Council chest, where it now lies. The Declaration whereof in the Council book is in these words following:

'*March* 3, 1678/9. For the avoiding of any dispute which may happen in time to come, concerning the succession of the Crown, I do here declare in the presence of Almighty God that I never gave nor made any contract of marriage, nor was married to any woman whatsoever, but to my present wife, Queen Catherine, now living. Whitehall. 3rd March, 1678/9. c.r.'

In April last we found the same rumour not only revived again, but also employed with new additions. To wit, it was given out, that there was a writing yet extant, and lately produced before several persons, whereby the said marriage, or a contract at least (for the report was various), did appear, and that there are several Lords and others yet living, who were pretended to be present at the said marriage. We knew full well that it was impossible that any of this should be true (being nothing more groundless and false than that there was any such marriage or contract between us and the said Mrs. Walter, alias Barlow), yet we proceeded to call before us, and caused to be interrogated in Council, such Lords and other persons as the common rumour did surmise to have been present at the pretended marriage, or to know something of it, or of the said writing. And though it appeared to all our Council, upon the hearing of the said Lords and other persons severally interrogated, and upon their denying to have been present at any such marriage, or to know anything of it . . . that the raising and spreading of such a report, so incoherent in the several parts of it, was the effect of a deep malice in some few, and of loose and idle discourse in others. Yet we think it requisite at this time to make our Declaration above recited more public, and to order the same . . . to be forthwith printed, and published. And we do again upon this occasion call Almighty God to witness, and declare upon the faith of a Christian, and the word of a King, that there was never any marriage or contract of marriage had or made between us and the said Mrs. Walter, alias Barlow, the Duke of Monmouth's mother, nor between us and any woman whatsoever, our Royal Consort Queen Catherine, that now is, only excepted. . . .

XXIX. TO THE MARQUESS OF ORMONDE

Windsor, July 16, 1680.

For my Lord Lieutenant of Ireland.

I do not write so often to you with my own hand as I would, yet I cannot now omit the letting you know how kindly I take it of my Lord Ossory that he hath accepted of the employment I have given him to go to defend Tangier from the Moors, till I can do better for the place than my present condition permits me to do, and to assure you I will in my memory add this to the many marks you and your family have given me of your affection and zeal to my service.

XXX. TO THE MARQUESS OF ORMONDE

Windsor, August 3, 1680.

I do write this letter to you and my Lady Duchess upon the great loss you have had of your son Ossory, in which I take myself to be an equal sharer with you both. You know I do not love to use more words than are necessary at any time, much less upon so melancholy a subject as this, wherein all I can say is too little to express the great loss we have had. And therefore will only desire you to take it as patiently as 'tis possible and submit all to the good pleasure of God Almighty.

It was the peril of Tangier, combined with the situation on the Continent, where France was once more threatening the Netherlands and the balance of power, that gave Shaftesbury his opportunity. Needing money urgently, Charles decided to allow his fourth Parliament to meet in October and, despite its unpromising complexion, to appeal to it to save Tangier and Europe.

XXXI. Speech to both Houses

October 21, 1680.

My Lords and Gentlemen: . . . The several prorogations I have made have been very advantageous to our neighbours, and very useful to me; for I have employed that time in making and perfecting an alliance with the Crown of Spain, suitable to that which I had before with the States of the United Provinces, and they also had with that of Spain, consisting of mutual obligations of succour and defence. . . .

. . . And as these are the best measures that could be taken for the safety of England, and the repose of Christendom; so they cannot fail to attain their end, and to spread and improve themselves farther, if our divisions at home do not render our friendship less considerable abroad.

To prevent these as much as may be, I think fit to renew to you all the assurances which can be desired, that nothing shall be wanting on my part to give you the fullest satisfaction your hearts can wish, for the security of the Protestant religion . . . and to concur with you in any new remedies which shall be proposed, that may consist with preserving the succession of the Crown in its due and legal course of descent.

. . . I need not tell you what danger the city of Tangier is in, nor of what importance it is to us to preserve it : I have, with a mighty charge and expense, sent a very considerable relief thither. But constantly to maintain so great a force as that war will require and to make those new works and fortifications without which the place will not long be tenable, amounts to so vast a sum, that without your support it will be impossible for me to undergo it. Therefore I lay the matter plainly before you, and desire your advice and assistance.

But that which I value above all the treasure in the world, and which I am sure will give me greater strength and reputation both at home and abroad than any treasure can do, is a perfect union amongst ourselves. Nothing but this can restore the kingdom to that strength and vigour which it seems to have lost; and raise us again to that consideration which England hath usually had. All Europe have their eyes upon this assembly;

and think their own happiness or misery, as well as ours, will depend upon it. If we should be so unhappy as to fall into such a misunderstanding amongst ourselves as would render our friendship unsafe to trust to; it will not be wondered at if our neighbours should begin to take new resolutions, and perhaps such as may be fatal to us. Let us therefore take care that we do not gratify our enemies, and discourage our friends, by any unseasonable disputes. If any such do happen, the world will see it was no fault of mine; for I have done all that was possible for me to do to keep you in peace while I live and to leave you so when I die. But from so great prudence, and so good affections as yours, I can fear nothing of this kind; but do rely upon you all that you will use your best endeavours to bring this Parliament to a good and happy conclusion.

The appeal was in vain. Shaftesbury and the republican leaders, aided by French gold, had their flock in the Commons well in hand. During the ensuing weeks, their proceedings were such as to make it seem that '41 had come again. On November 4th the Bill for excluding the Duke of York received its first reading; eleven days later it was carried triumphantly to the Lords. But here the Opposition received a check, for the King's unexpected firmness and the eloquence of Lord Halifax heartened the doubting peers to reject the measure. Thereafter the Commons voted furious resolutions against Halifax and the King's Ministers, and imprisoned all who dared petition or vote against them, while Shaftesbury talked of Civil War and an Association of his followers to take over the principal fortresses of the kingdom.

The King made one last appeal to his Commons to lay aside faction and save Tangier and the balance of power.

XXXII. SPEECH TO BOTH HOUSES

December 15, 1680.

My Lords and Gentlemen: At the opening of this Parliament I did acquaint you with the alliances I had made with Spain and Holland, as the best measures that could be taken for the safety of England, and the repose of Christendom.

But I told you withal, that if our friendship became unsafe to trust to, it would not be wondered at if our neighbours should begin to take new resolutions, and perhaps such as might be fatal to us.

I must now tell you, that our allies cannot but see how little has been done since this meeting to encourage their dependence upon us. And I find by them that unless we can be so united at home as to make our alliance valuable to them, it will not be possible to hinder them from seeking some other refuge; and making such new friendships as will not be consistent with our safety. . . .

I did likewise lay the matter plainly before you, touching the estate and condition of Tangier. I must now tell you again, that, if that place be thought worth the keeping, you must take such consideration of it that it may be speedily supplied; it being impossible for me to preserve it at an expense so far above my power.

I did promise you the fullest satisfaction your hearts could wish for the security of the Protestant religion; and to concur with you in any remedies, which might consist with preserving the succession of the crown in its due and legal course of descent. I do again with the same reservations renew the same promises to you; and being thus ready on my part to do all that can reasonably be expected from me, I should be glad to know from you, as soon as may be, how far I shall be assisted by you, and what it is you desire from me.

When the appeal was rejected the King took his own measures. On January 10, 1681, while the Commons were voting that whoever should advise a prorogation was a betrayer of the kingdom, a promoter of Popery and a pensioner of France, he appeared in their midst and prorogued them. A week later he dissolved Parliament. In the meantime he took his measures with Louis: the balance of power might be important to England, but in Charles's view the preservation of the hereditary monarchy was more so. In return for a promise of English neutrality on the Continent, Louis promised to pay Charles a subsidy of approximately £400,000 and to guarantee that he would not attack the Netherlands. With this promise

*in his pocket the King of England knew that he could make shift
to govern without Parliament.*

*Before he finally decided, Charles made one last effort to
obtain an honourable peace with the Opposition. On January
19 a new Parliament was summoned to meet in March at
Oxford, where the disturbing influence of the London mob could
not be felt. But though the monarchial tide was now setting
in fast in the country, it had not yet penetrated to the electoral
corporations, where the Whig party managers were still firmly
entrenched. It was therefore as hostile a Parliament as its
predecessors that Charles greeted at Oxford on March 20, 1681,
with an offer of all reasonable expedients against abuse of power
by a Catholic successor (even to a regency under Mary of Orange),
but with a stern reminder that he intended to abide by the
fundamental laws of the land.*

XXXIII.SPEECH TO BOTH HOUSES ON OPENING THE SESSION

March 20, 1680/1.

My Lords and Gentlemen : The unwarrantable proceedings
of the last House of Commons were the occasion of my parting
with the last Parliament. For I, who will never use arbitrary
government myself, am resolved not to suffer it in others. I am
unwilling to mention particulars, because I am desirous to forget
faults; but whosoever shall calmly consider what offers I have
formerly made, and what assurances I renewed to the last
Parliament: how I recommended nothing so much to them
as the alliances I had made for preservation of the general peace
in Christendom, and the further examination of the Popish Plot,
and how I desired their advice and assistance concerning the
preservation of Tangier; and shall then reflect upon the strange,
unsuitable returns made to such propositions . . . perhaps may
wonder more, that I had patience so long, than that at last I grew
weary of their proceedings.

I have thought it necessary to say thus much to you, that I
may not have any new occasion given me to remember more of
the late miscarriages. It is as much my interest, and it shall be
as much my care as yours, to preserve the liberty of the subject;
because the Crown can never be safe when that is in danger.

And I would have you likewise be convinced, that neither your liberties nor properties can subsist long, when the just rights and prerogatives of the Crown are invaded, or the honour of the government brought low and into disreputation.

I let you see, by my calling this Parliament so soon, that no irregularities in Parliament shall make me out of love with them; and by this means offer you another opportunity of providing for our security here, by giving that countenance and protection to our neighbours and allies, which you cannot but know they expect from us, and extremely stand in need of at this instant; and at the same time give one evidence more that I have not neglected my part to give that general satisfaction and security which, by the blessing of God, may be attained, if you, on your parts, bring suitable dispositions towards it : and that the just care you ought to have of religion be not so managed and improved into unnecessary fears as may be made a pretence for changing the foundation of the government. . . .

But I must needs desire you not to lay so much weight upon any one expedient against Popery as to determine that all others are ineffectual : and, among all your cares for religion, remember, that without the safety and dignity of the monarchy, neither religion nor property can be preserved.

What I have formerly, and so often declared touching the succession, I cannot depart from. But to remove all reasonable fears that may arise from the possibility of a Popish successor's coming to the Crown; if means can be found that in such a case the administration of the government may remain in Protestant hands, I shall be ready to hearken to any such expedient, by which the religion might be preserved, and the monarchy not destroyed. I must therefore earnestly recommend to you, to provide for the religion and government together, with regard to one another, because they support each other. And let us be united at home, that we may recover the esteem and consideration we used to have abroad.

I conclude with this one advice to you, that the rules and measures of all your votes may be the known and established laws of the land; which neither can, nor ought to be departed from, nor changed, but by Act of Parliament. And I may the more reasonably require, that you make the laws of the land your rule, because I am resolved they shall be mine.

It was in vain. Supported by armed retainers, the Commons seemed to be heading straight for civil war. On Sunday, March 27th, the King, in secret conference with his Council in Merton College, took his decision. Next morning, to the surprise of his people, who supposed him on the point of surrender, he went down to the Lords, summoned the Commons, and, donning his crown and robes, which had been hastily fetched in a sedan chair, commanded the Chancellor to dissolve Parliament.

XXXIV.SPEECH TO BOTH HOUSES ON DISSOLVING PARLIAMENT FOR THE LAST TIME

March 28, 1681.

My Lords and Gentlemen : That all the world may see to what a point we are come, that we are not like to have a good end, when the divisions at the beginning are such : therefore, my Lord Chancellor, do as I have commanded you.

The King had counter-attacked at exactly the right moment. His opponents, by their violence and ever-growing ambitions, had finally alienated the goodwill of the nation. Charles now followed up his Oxford victory by a Declaration, which was read in every church in England, and which, by showing how arbitrary had been the proceedings of his last two Houses of Commons, started a great avalanche of monarchial feeling that in the next four years all but destroyed the Whig Party.

XXXV.DECLARATION TO BE READ IN ALL THE CHURCHES

April 8, 1681.

It was with exceeding great trouble that we were brought to the dissolving of the two last Parliaments without more benefit to our people by the calling of them.   But having done our part, in giving so many opportunities of providing for their good, it cannot be justly imputed to us that the success hath not answered our expectations.   We cannot at this time but take notice of the particular causes of our dissatisfaction, which at the beginning of the last Parliament we did recommend to their care to avoid, and expected we should have had no new cause to remember them.

We opened the last Parliament, which was held at Westminster, with as gracious expressions of our readiness to satisfy the desires of our good subjects and to secure them against all their just fears, as the weighty consideration either of preserving the Established Religion and the liberty and property of our subjects at home, or of supporting our neighbours and allies abroad, could fill our heart with, or possibly require from us. And we do solemnly declare, that we did intend, as far as would have consisted with the very being of the Government, to have complied with anything that could have been proposed to us to accomplish those ends. We asked of them the supporting the alliances we had made for the preservation of the general peace in Christendom. We recommended to them the further examination of the Plot. We desired their advice and assistance concerning the preservation of Tangier. We offered to concur in any remedies that could be proposed for the security of the Protestant religion, that might consist with preserving the succession of the Crown in its due and legal course of descent. To all which we met with most unsuitable returns from the House of Commons:—addresses, in the nature of remonstrances rather than of answers; arbitrary orders for taking our subjects into custody for matters that had no relation to privileges of Parliament; strange illegal votes, declaring divers eminent persons to be enemies to the King and kingdom, without any order or process of law, any hearing of their defence, or any proof so much as offered against them.

Besides these proceedings, they voted as followeth on the 7th January . . . [the two resolutions against lending of money and buying any tally of anticipation] which votes, instead of giving us assistance to support our allies and enable us to preserve Tangier, tended rather to disable us from contributing to either, by our revenue or credit; not only exposing us to all dangers that might happen either at home or abroad; but endeavouring to deprive us of the possibility of supporting the government itself, and to reduce us to a more helpless condition than the meanest of our subjects. And on the 10th of the same month they passed another vote [against the prosecution of Protestant dissenters upon the Penal Laws], by which vote, without any regard to the laws established, they assumed to themselves a power of suspending Acts of Parliament. Whereas our Judges and Ministers of Justice neither can nor ought, in reverence to the votes of either or both the Houses, break the oaths they have taken for the due and impartial execution of our laws; which by experience have been found to be the best support both of the Protestant interest and of the peace of the kingdom. These were some of the unwarrantable proceedings of the House of Commons, which were the occasion of our parting with that Parliament.

Which we had no sooner dissolved but we caused another to be assembled at Oxford; at the opening of which we thought it necessary to give them warning of the errors of the former, in hopes to have prevented the like miscarriages. And we required of them to make the laws of the land their rule; as we did, and do resolve, they shall be ours. We further added, that what we had formerly and so often declared concerning the succession we would not depart from; but to remove all reasonable fears that might arise from the possibility of a Popish successor's coming to the Crown, if means could be found that in such a case the administration of the Government might remain in Protestant hands, we were ready to hearken to any expedient by which the religion established might be preserved, and the monarchy not destroyed. But contrary to our offers and expectation, we saw that no expedient would be entertained but that of a total exclusion, which we had so often declared was a point that in our own royal judgement so nearly concerned us both in honour, justice and conscience that we could never consent to it. . . .

But notwithstanding all this, let not the restless malice of ill men who are labouring to poison our people, some out of fondness for their old beloved Commonwealth principles, and some out of anger at their being disappointed in the particular designs they had for the accomplishment of their own ambition and greatness, persuade any of our good subjects that we intend to lay aside the use of Parliaments. For we do still declare that no irregularities in Parliament shall ever make us out of love with Parliaments; which we look upon as the best method for healing the distempers of the kingdom, and the only means to preserve the monarchy in that due credit and respect which it ought to have both at home and abroad.   And for this cause we are resolved, by the blessing of God, to have frequent Parliaments; and both in and out of Parliament to use our utmost endeavours to extirpate Popery and to redress all the grievances of our good subjects, and in all things to govern according to the laws of the kingdom.   And we hope that a little time will so far open the eyes of all our good subjects that our next meeting in Parliament shall perfect all that settlement and peace which shall be found wanting either in Church or State.   To which, as we shall contribute our utmost endeavours, so we assure ourself, that we shall be assisted therein by the loyalty and good affections of all those who consider the rise and progress of the late troubles and confusions, and desire to preserve their country from a relapse.   And who cannot but remember that religion, liberty and property were all lost and gone when the monarchy was shaken off; and could never be revived till that was restored.

Charles had no more Parliaments.   Nor are there many letters of importance in the remaining three and a half years of his life.   Perhaps the most significant, symptomatic of his ceaseless interest in the expansion of English trade and empire overseas which was the dominant fact of his reign, is that in which he defined the boundaries of the great tract of land in America which he granted to William Penn the Quaker.

XXXVI. To Lord Baltimore
[*Countersigned* ' Conway ']

April 2, 1681.

Right trusty, etc. . . . Whereas by our letters patent bearing date the 4th day of March last past we have been graciously pleased out of our royal bounty and the singular regard which we have to the merits and services of Sir William Penn, deceased, to give and grant to our trusty, etc. . . . William Penn, Esq., son and heir to the said Sir William Penn, a certain tract of land in America by the name of Pennsylvania, as the same is bounded on the east by Delaware River from twelve miles distant northwards of New Castle town unto the forty-third degree of northern latitude, if the said river doth extend so far northwards, and if the said river shall not extend so far northward, then by the said river so far as it doth extend, and from the head of the said river the eastern bounds to be determined by a meridian line to be drawn from the head of the said river unto the said forty-third degree; the said Province to extend westwards five degrees in longitude to be computed from the said eastern bounds and to be bounded on the north by the beginning of the forty-third degree of northern latitude, and on the south by a circle drawn at twelve miles distance from New Castle northwards and westwards unto the beginning of the fortieth degree of northern latitude, and then by a straight line westwards to the limit of longitude above mentioned, as by our said letters patent doth particularly appear.   And to the end that all due encouragement be given to the said William Penn in the settlement of a plantation within the said country, we do hereby recommend him his deputies and officers employed by him, to your friendly aid and assistance, willing and requiring you to do him all the offices of good neighbourhood and amicable correspondence which may tend to the mutual benefit of our subjects within our provinces under your respective proprieties.   And more especially we do think fit that in order hereunto you do appoint with all convenient speed some person or persons who may in conjunction with the agent or agents of the said William Penn make a true division and separation of the said provinces of Maryland and Pennsylvania, according to the bounds and degree of northern latitude expressed in our said letters patent, by settling and fixing certain landmarks, where they shall appear to border upon each other for the preventing and according all doubts and controversies that may otherwise happen concerning the same. . . .

The struggle with Shaftesbury lasted till the autumn of 1682;
then with the capture by the Tories of his great stronghold, the
Corporation of London (which for two years the Whigs had
held with such effect that its very juries had become picked

republican committees), the fallen statesman fled from England
to die in exile. The discovery of the Rye House Assassination
Plot in the summer of 1683 completed the discomfiture of his
foes, which Charles at once followed up with a further public
Declaration.

XXXVII. DECLARATION

July 28, 1683.

It hath been our observation, that for several years last past
a malevolent party hath made it their business to promote sedition by false news, libellous pamphlets, and other wicked arts,
whereby they endeavoured not only to render our Government
odious, and our most faithful subjects suspected to the people,
but even to incite them to a dislike and hatred of our royal
person.   Whereupon it was evident to us that the heads of this
party could have no other aim but the ruin of us and our
Government.

And whilst, by our utmost care, we manifested to all our
subjects our zeal for the maintenance of the Protestant religion,
and our resolutions to govern according to law; it was a great
trouble to us, to find that evil persons, by misrepresenting our
actions to the people, should so far insinuate themselves into the
affections of the weaker sort, as that they looked upon them as
the only patriots and assertors of their religion and liberties, and
gave themselves up entirely to their conduct.

As their numbers increased, so did their boldness, to that
height, that by often showing themselves in tumults and riots,
and unlawful and seditious conventicles, they not only engaged,
but proclaimed an impunity to their own party, who thought
themselves already too strong for the laws; and they seemed to
believe, that in a short time they should gain upon the people,
so as to persuade them to a total defection from the Government.

But it pleased God, by these their violent ways, to open the
eyes of our good subjects, who easily foresaw what troubles these
methods would produce; and thereupon, with great courage, as
well as duty and affection towards us, upon all occasions, did
manifest their resolution and readiness in defence of our person,
and support of our Government, and the religion established;

324

and did likewise convince the common people of the villainous designs of their factious leaders, and the miseries that would befall them, in pursuing such courses.

By these means the factious party lost ground daily; and finding that it was impossible to keep up the spirits of their followers against the religion established and the laws, whilst we were steady in the maintenance and execution of them, became desperate, and resolved not to trust any longer to the slow methods of sedition, but to betake themselves to arms; not doubting but that they remained still strong enough, by force, to overrun the Government which they could not undermine.

It is hard to imagine how men of so many different interests and opinions could join in any enterprise; but it is certain they readily concurred in the resolution of taking arms to destroy the Government, even before they had agreed what to set up in the place of it.

To which purpose they took several ways: for whilst some were contriving a general insurrection in this kingdom, and likewise in Scotland, others were conspiring to assassinate our royal person and our dearest brother, and to massacre the magistrates of our city of London and our officers of State, that there might be no appearance of Government nor any means for our subjects to unite for their defence. In case it had pleased God to permit these wicked designs to have taken effect, there could have been nothing in prospect but confusion. For instead of the reformation they pretended, their success would have produced divisions and wars amongst themselves; until the predominant party would have enslaved the rest, and the whole kingdom.

But the Divine Providence, which hath preserved us through the whole course of our life, hath at this time, in an extraordinary manner, showed itself in the wonderful and gracious deliverance of us, and our dearest brother, and all our loyal subjects, from this horrid and damnable conspiracy. . . .

During the last years of his reign Charles was able to live in peace and leave the bulk of his subjects free to do the same. Five letters written between 1682 and 1684 to his natural daughter, the young Countess of Lichfield[1] *(who sometimes, tradition has it, used to tickle his bald pate as he slept after his dinner), must suffice to show Charles enjoying the comparative peace of his last years.*

XXXVIII. TO THE COUNTESS OF LICHFIELD

Whitehall, October 2, 1682.

I have had so much business[2] since I came hither that I hope you will not think that I have neglected writing to you out of want of kindness to my dear Charlotte. I am going to Newmarket to-morrow,[3] and have a great deal of business to dispatch to-night. Therefore I will only tell you now that I have five hundred guineas for you which shall be either delivered to yourself or any whom you shall appoint to receive it, and so, my dear Charlotte, be assured that I love you with all my heart being your kind father. C.R.

XXXIX. TO THE COUNTESS OF LICHFIELD

Whitehall, October 22, 1682.

I should not have been so long in writing to you, my dear Charlotte, but that I was at Newmarket where too all day about business I had little time to spare. And though I have very much business now, yet I must tell you that I am glad to hear you are with child, and I hope to see you here before it be long, that I may have the satisfaction myself of telling you how much I love you, and how truly I am your kind father. C.R.

XL. TO THE COUNTESS OF LICHFIELD

April 3, 1684.

I think it a very reasonable thing that other houses should not look into your house without your permission, and this note

---

[1] She was the daughter of the termagant Castlemaine, now Duchess of Cleveland, but, unlike her mother, a pattern of modesty and wifely virtue.

[2] The London electoral battle of September 1682 which ended in the election of a Tory Lord Mayor.

[3] Charles was at Newmarket that autumn from October 3 to 21.

will be sufficient for Mr. Surveyor[1] to build up your wall as high as you please and you may show it to him. The only caution I give you, is not to prejudice the corner house which you know your sister Sussex[2] is to have, and the building up the wall there will signify nothing to you, only inconvenience her. I shall be with you on Saturday next, and so, my dear Charlotte, I shall say no more but that I am your kind father.

C.R.

XLI. To the Countess of Lichfield

Whitehall, August 11, 1684.

I received yours, my dear Charlotte, just now, concerning the desire you make about Mrs. Young's reversion, but I was engaged in that matter some days since, so as I can only tell you that I am very glad to hear that I shall see you, and 'tis the greater satisfaction to me, because I did not expect it so soon. And be assured that I am as kind to you as you can expect from your kind father.

XLII. To the Countess of Lichfield

Winchester, September 5, 1684.

Your excuse for not coming hither is a very lawful one, though I am sorry I shall be so long deprived of seeing my dear Charlotte. Your brother Harry[3] is now here and will go in a few days to see Holland, and by the time he returns he will have worn out in some measure the redness of his face so as not to fright the most part of our ladies here. His face is not changed, though he will be marked very much. I will give order

[1] Sir Christopher Wren.
[2] Anne Fitzroy, Countess of Sussex, another daughter of Charles by the Duchess of Cleveland.
[3] The Duke of Grafton, the nominal Vice-Admiral of England, whom Charles was bringing up as a sailor at sea, and who had recently suffered from an attack of smallpox.

for the two hundred pounds for your building and the reason that you have had it no sooner is the change I have made in the treasury,[1] which now in a little time will be settled again.   And so, my dear Charlotte, be assured that I am your kind father.

C.R.

Charles died on the 6th February, 1685, after a brief though painful illness, at the age of fifty-four

[1] The celebrated kicking of the High Tory, Lord Rochester, ' up-stairs ' from the Treasury Commission into the magnificent but comparatively powerless position of Lord President of the Council, to make way for a nominee of the moderate Lord Privy Seal, Lord Halifax.

APPENDICES

APPENDIX I

GENEALOGICAL TABLE OF THE STUART KINGS OF ENGLAND

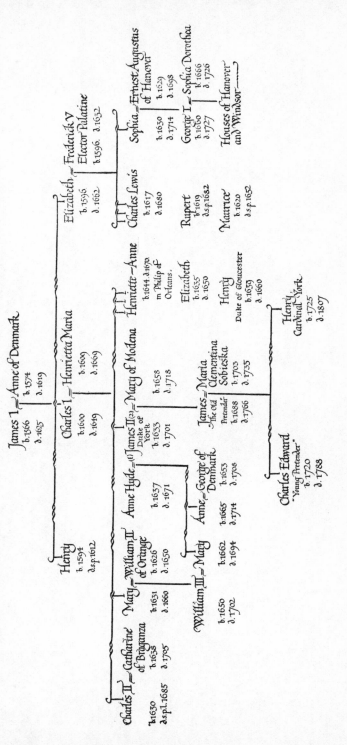

APPENDIX II

LIST OF ABBREVIATIONS USED

Add. MSS. . .	Additional Manuscripts, British Museum.
Bodley	Bodleian Library.
B.M.	British Museum.
Carte	Carte, Thomas. *Collection of Original Letters and Papers, 1641-60.* 1739.
Cartwright . .	Cartwright, Julia. *Madame.* 1894.
Clar. S.P. . . .	Clarendon State Papers, 1786.
Clar. MSS. . . .	Clarendon Manuscripts. Bodleian Library.
C.J.	Commons, Journals of the House of.
Hartmann . . .	Hartmann, Cyril Hughes. *Charles II and Madame.* 1934.
H.M.C. Rep. . .	Historical Manuscripts Commission, Reports of.
Lansdowne MSS. .	Lansdowne Manuscripts, British Museum.
Lauderdale Papers	*The Lauderdale Papers* (ed. O. Airy). Camden Society. 1884-5.
L.J.	Lords, Journals of the House of.
Macray	Macray, W. D. *Notes which passed at Meetings of the Privy Council between Charles II and the Earl of Clarendon.* Roxburghe Club. 1896.
Misc. Aul. . . .	*Miscellanea Aulica* (ed. Brown), 1702.
Nijhoff	Nijhoff. *Bijdragen voor Vaderlandsche Geschiednis. Nieuwe Reeks.* Part iv.
S.P.	State Papers, Foreign and Domestic. At the Public Record Office.
Thurloe . . .	Thurloe, John. *State Papers* (ed. T. Birch), 1742.

CHAPTER I
THE PRINCE OF WALES

I. B.M. Harleian MSS. 6988, f. 101.

II. H.M.C. Rep. 9, part ii, appendix, p. 243. From the MSS. at Traquair House.

III. S.P. 16/510, f. 115. (French translation of this letter is printed in Thurloe's State Papers, vol. i, p. 72.)

IV. S.P. 16/516, f. 75.

V. *Calendars of State Papers (Domestic Series)—1649-50*, p. 5.

CHAPTER II

THE SCOTTISH ADVENTURE

I. Carte, vol. ii, p. 363.

II. S.P. 18/2, f. 109.

III. H.M.C. Rep. 12, appendix, part ix, p. 47. From the MSS. of the Duke of Beaufort.

IV. H.M.C. Rep. 6, appendix, p. 612. From the MSS. of the Duke of Argyll.

V. Napier, M., *Memorials of Montrose*, 1856, vol. ii, p. 752.

VI. H.M.C. Rep. 10, appendix, part iv, p. 147. From N. S. Maskelyne's MSS.

VII. Gardiner, S. R., *Charles II and Scotland in 1650*, p. 57. (Printed by Dr. Wijnne in *De Geschillen over de Afdanking van 't Krigsvolk*, p. 112.)

VIII. H.M.C. Rep. 6, appendix, p. 694. From the MSS. in the possession of Sir Robert Menzies.

IX. Carte, vol. ii, p. 397.

X. Evelyn, John, *Diary and Correspondence*, vol. iv, p. 194. Ed. Bray, 1895. (The names and secret strictures in the original letters are in cipher.)

XI. H.M.C. Rep. 12, appendix, part viii, p. 11. From the MSS. of the Duke of Atholl.

XII. H.M.C. Rep. 12, appendix, part viii, p. 11. From the MSS. of the Duke of Atholl.

XIII. H.M.C. Rep. 3, appendix, p. 401. From the MSS. of the Duke of Montrose.

XIV. Carte, vol. ii, p. 433.

XV. Bodley, Rawlinson MSS. 115, f. 99.

XVI. H.M.C. Rep. 10, appendix, part iv, p. 148. From the MSS. of N. S. Maskelyne.

CHAPTER III

IN EXILE

I. H.M.C. Various Collections, vol. ii, p. 350. From the MSS. of Mrs. Harford, of Holm Hall, Yorks.

II. Seward, *Anecdotes of Some Distinguished Persons* (ed. 1798), vol. ii, p. 11.

III. Clar. S.P., vol. iii, p. 141.

IV. Clar. MSS., vol. 45, 21 March, 1653.

V. Thurloe, vol. i, p. 495.

VI. Pythouse Papers, p. 34. Ed. W. A. Day, 1879. (Also Clar. MSS., vol. 49, f. 187.)

VII. Misc. Aul., p. 108.

VIII. B.M. Lansdowne MSS. 1236, f. 113. (Printed in Ellis, *Letters in English History*, 2nd Series, vol. iii, p. 376.)

ix. Clar. MSS., vol. 49, f. 135.

x. Clar. MSS., vol. 49, f. 136.

xi Clar. MSS., vol. 49, f. 137.

xii. Clar. MSS., vol. 49, f. 137.

xiii. Misc. Aul., pp. 109-110.

xiv. H.M.C. Rep. ix., part ii, appendix, p. 234. From the MSS. of Sir R. A. O. Dalyell.

xv. H.M.C. Rep. 6, appendix, p. 613. From the MSS. of the Duke of Argyll, in the Argyll archives.

xvi. H.M.C. Rep. 14, appendix, part vii, p. 14. From the MSS. of the Marquis of Ormonde.

xvii. Clar. MSS., vol. 49, f. 387.

xviii. Thurloe, vol. i, p. 662.

xix. H.M.C. Rep. 6, appendix, p. 473. From the MSS. in the possession of T. Raffles, Esq.

xx. Misc. Aul., pp. 119-20.

xxi. Misc. Aul., p. 115.

xxii. Misc. Aul., p. 116.

xxiii. Misc. Aul., p. 117.

xxiv. Misc. Aul., p. 120.

xxv. Misc. Aul., p. 123.

xxvi. Misc. Aul., p. 124.

xxvii. H.M.C. Rep. 14, part vii, p. 18. From the MSS. of the Marquis of Ormonde.

xxviii. Thurloe, vol. i, p. 663.

xxix. Thurloe, vol. i, p. 663.

xxx. Clar. S.P., vol. iii, p. 288.

xxxi. Clar. MSS., vol. 51, f. 106.

xxxii. Clar. S.P., vol. iii, p. 292.

xxxiii. Clar. S.P., vol. iii, p. 292.

xxxiv. Clar. S.P., vol. iii, p. 296.

xxxv. Clar. S.P., vol. iii, p. 298.

xxxvi. B.M. Lansdowne MSS. 1236, f. 115.

xxxvii. Misc. Aul., p. 126.

xxxviii. Misc. Aul., p. 127.

xxxix. Misc. Aul., p. 118.

xl. Misc. Aul., p. 128.

xli. Misc. Aul., p. 129.

xlii. Thurloe, vol. i, p. 661.

xliii. Camden Miscellany, vol. v, p. 10.

xliv. Clar. S.P., vol. iii, p. 317.

xlv. Clar. S.P., vol. iii, p. 332.

xlvi. Clar. S.P., vol. iii, p. 346.

xlvii. Clar. MSS., vol. 55, f. 50.

xlviii. Clar. S.P., vol. iii, p. 351.

xlix. Clar. S.P., vol. iii, p. 363.

l. Thurloe, vol. i, p. 662.

LI. H.M.C. Rep. 10, appendix, part vi, p. 188. From Lord Braye's MSS.
LII. Clar. S.P., vol. iii, p. 403.
LIII. Clar. S.P., vol. iii, p. 403.

CHAPTER IV

THE RESTORATION

I. Clar. S.P., vol. iii, p. 417.
II. H.M.C. Rep. 10, appendix, part vi, p. 190. From Lord Braye's MSS.
III. Chesterfield, Philip Stanhope, second Earl of, *Letters*, 1837, p. 106.
IV. Clar. S.P., vol. iii, p. 436.
V. Clar. S.P., vol. iii, p. 498.
VI. Clar. S.P., vol. iii, p. 514.
VII. Clar. MSS., vol. 61, f. 303.
VIII. Clar. S.P., vol. iii, p. 519.
IX. Clar. S.P., vol. iii, p. 529.
X. Clar. S.P., vol. iii, p. 530.
XI. Clar. S.P., vol. iii, p. 536.
XII. Clar. MSS., vol. 63, f. 237.
XIII. Clar. MSS., vol. 63, f. 135-6.
XIV. Clar. MSS., vol. 66, f. 24-24v.
XV. Clar. S.P., vol. iii, p. 646.
XVI. Hartmann, p. 10.
XVII. Camden Miscellany, vol. v, p. 14. (From an original holograph in the possession of the Marquess of Bristol.)
XVIII. Clar. S.P., vol. iii, p. 709.
XIX. Clar. MSS., vol. 71, f. 54.
XX. S.P. 18/221, f. 4.
XXI. S.P. 18/221, f. 4.
XXII. Clar. S.P., vol. iii, p. 735.
XXIII. Hartmann, p. 12. (Printed in Cartwright, pp. 54-5.)
XXIV. Clar. S.P., vol. iii, p. 745. Also in B.M. Sloane MSS. 1519.5, f. 201 (Copy).
XXV. Clar. MSS., vol. 62, f. 408.
XXVI. Hartmann, p. 14. (Printed in Cartwright, p. 57.)
XXVII. L.J. 1660-66, p. 48.

CHAPTER V

THE RESTORATION SETTLEMENT

I. Macray, pp. 22, 5, 6, 20, 7, 8.
II. L.J. 1660-66, p. 108.
III. L.J. 1660-66, p. 147.
IV. Macray, p. 11.
V. Macray, p. 21.

vi. Macray, p. 14.

vii. L.J. 1660-66, p. 236.

viii. Lauderdale Papers, vol. i, p. 39.

ix. Lauderdale Papers, vol. i, p. 92.

x. Macray, pp. 65, 52, 50.

xi. L.J. 1660-66, p. 240.

xii. Macray, p. 29.

xiii. L.J. 1660-66, p. 303.

xiv. H.M.C. Rep. 3, appendix, p. 423. From the MSS. of R. G. E. Wemyss, Esq.

xv. Davidson, L. C., *Catherine of Braganza*, 1908, p. 62.

xvi. L.J. 1660-66, p. 331.

xvii. Macray, p. 32.

xviii. Macray, p. 37.

xix. Macray, p. 40.

xx. Macray, p. 41.

xxi. Macray, p. 45.

xxii. L.J. 1660-66, p. 332.

xxiii. Hartmann, p. 35. (Printed in Cartwright, p. 110.)

xxiv. Hartmann, p. 36. (Printed in Cartwright, p. 111-12.)

xxv. C.J. 1660-67, p. 377.

xxvi. Macray, p. 67.

xxvii. Macray, p. 69.

xxviii. B.M. Lansdowne MSS. 1236, f. 124.

xxix. Hartmann, p. 43. (Printed in Cartwright, p. 120.)

xxx. H.M.C. Rep. (Heathcote), p. 28.

xxxi. B.M. Lansdowne MSS. 1236, f. 130.

xxxii. B.M. Lansdowne MSS., f. 132.

xxxiii. B.M. Lansdowne MSS. 1236, f. 128.

xxxiv. Hartmann, p. 54. (Printed in Cartwright, p. 121.)

xxxv. Macray, pp. 71, 73.

CHAPTER VI

FIRST APPROACH TO FRANCE

i. Hartmann, p. 57. (Printed in Cartwright, p. 124.)

ii. Hartmann, p. 60. (Printed in Cartwright, p. 125.)

iii. Macray, p. 78.

iv. Hartmann, p. 64. (Printed in Cartwright, p. 128.)

v. Hartmann, p. 68. (Printed in Cartwright, p. 132.)

vi. Hartmann, p. 70. (Printed in Cartwright, p. 133.)

vii. Hartmann, p. 70. (Printed in Cartwright, p. 133.)

viii. L.J. 1660-66, p. 478.

ix. Hartmann, p. 72. (Printed in Cartwright, p. 136.)

x. Hartmann, p. 73. (Printed in Cartwright, p. 138.)

xi. Hartmann, p. 73. (Printed in Cartwright, p. 138.)

xii. Hartmann, p. 74. (Printed in Cartwright, p. 138.)

XIII. C.J. 1660-67, p. 500.
XIV. L.J. 1660-66, p. 579.
XV. S.P. 44/15, f. 193.
XVI. Macray, p. 90.
XVII. Hartmann, p. 83. (Printed in Cartwright, pp. 147-8.)
XVIII. Hartmann, p. 87. (Printed in Cartwright, p. 149.)
XIX. Hartmann, p. 89. (Printed in Cartwright, p. 150.)
XX. Hartmann, p. 90. (Printed in Cartwright, pp. 151-2.)
XXI. Hartmann, p. 91. (Printed in Cartwright, p. 152.)
XXII. Hartmann, p. 93. (Printed in Cartwright, p. 153.)
XXIII. Hartmann, p. 95. (Printed in Cartwright, p. 228.)
XXIV. Hartmann, p. 96. (Printed in Cartwright, p. 154.)
XXV. L.J. 1660-66, p. 582.
XXVI. Hartmann, p. 97. (Printed in Cartwright, p. 157.)
XXVII. Hartmann, p. 99. (Printed in Cartwright, p. 137.)
XXVIII. L.J. 1660-66, p. 593.
XXIX. Hartmann, p. 100. (Printed in Cartwright, pp. 158-9.)
XXX. Hartmann, p. 101. (Printed in Cartwright, p. 160.)
XXXI. Hartmann, p. 105. (Printed in Cartwright, p. 161.)
XXXII. H.M.C. Rep. 13, appendix, part ii, p. 145. From the MSS. of the Duke of Portland.
XXXIII. Hartmann, p. 106. (Printed in Cartwright, p. 163.)
XXXIV. Hartmann, p. 107. (Printed in Cartwright, p. 166.)
XXXV. Hartmann, p. 108. (Printed in Cartwright, pp. 167-8.)
XXXVI. Hartmann, p. 111. (Printed in Cartwright, p. 171.)
XXXVII. Hartmann, pp. 112-13. (Printed in Cartwright, p. 171.)
XXXVIII. Hartmann, p. 114.
XXXIX. Hartmann, pp. 116-17. (Printed in Cartwright, p. 173.)
XL. Hartmann, p. 119. (Printed in Cartwright, p. 175.)
XLI. Hartmann, p. 121. (Printed in Cartwright, p. 175.)
XLII. Bromley, Sir G. *Collection of Original Royal Letters,* 1787, p. 283.
XLIII. S.P. 29/449, f. 43.
XLIV. Hartmann, p. 128. (Printed in Cartwright, p. 176.)
XLV. L.J. 1660-66, p. 624.
XLVI. Hartmann, p. 134. (Printed in Cartwright, p. 199.)
XLVII. Hartmann, p. 135. (Printed in Cartwright, p. 200.)
XLVIII. Hartmann, p. 138. (Printed in Cartwright, p. 202.)
XLIX. Hartmann, p. 139. (Printed in Cartwright, pp. 203-4.)
L. Hartmann, p. 142. (Printed in Cartwright, p. 205.)
LI. Hartmann, p. 143. (Printed in Cartwright, p. 206.)
LII. Hartmann, p. 144. (Printed in Cartwright, pp. 206-7.)
LIII. Hartmann, p. 149. (Printed in Cartwright, p. 209.)
LIV. Hartmann, p. 151. (Printed in Cartwright, p. 211.)
LV. Hartmann, p. 157. (Printed in Cartwright, p. 213.)
LVI. Hartmann, p. 160. (Printed in Cartwright, pp. 215-16.)
LVII. B.M. Sloane MSS. 1519, f. 192. (Printed in Ellis, *Letters in English History,* 2nd Series, vol. iii, p. 328.)

LVIII. From the Hinchingbrooke MSS. in the possession of the Earl of Sandwich.

LIX. Hartmann, pp. 165-6. (Printed in Cartwright, pp. 220-222.)

LX. Hartmann, p. 168. (Printed in Cartwright, p. 223.)

LXI. Hartmann, p. 171. (Printed in Cartwright, p. 223.)

LXII. Hartmann, p. 172.

LXIII. From the Hinchingbrooke MSS.

LXIV. L.J. 1660-66, p. 684.

LXV. Hartmann, p. 178. (Printed in Cartwright, p. 227.)

LXVI. Hartmann, p. 181. (Printed in Cartwright, pp. 236-7.)

LXVII. Birch, W. de Gray, *Historical Charters and Documents of the City of London*, 1884, pp. 124-30.

LXVIII. Privy Council Registers, vol. 59, f. 351. (At the Public Record Office.)

LXIX. L.J. 1666-75, p. 4.

LXX. Hartmann, p. 184. (Printed in Cartwright, p. 237.)

LXXI. H.M.C. Rep. ix, part ii, appendix, p. 235. From the MSS. of Sir R. A. O. Dalyell.

LXXII. L.J. 1666-75, p. 81.

LXXIII. L.J. 1666-75, p. 111.

LXXIV. S.P. 44/17, f. 241-2.

LXXV. S.P. 44/17, f. 243.

LXXVI. S.P. 44/17, f. 251-2.

LXXVII. Bromley, *Royal Letters*, p. 282.

LXXVIII. Hartmann, p. 193. (Printed in Cartwright, pp. 247-8.)

LXXIX. Seward, *Anecdotes*, vol. ii, p. 25.

XL. Hartmann, p. 196. (Printed in Cartwright, pp. 248-9.)

CHAPTER VII

THE SECRET TREATY OF DOVER

I. B.M. Add. MSS. 9796, f. 28.

II. Hartmann, pp. 200-1. (Printed in Cartwright, p. 255.)

III. Hartmann, p. 201. (Printed in Cartwright, p. 256.)

IV. Dalrymple, Sir John, *Memoirs*, vol. ii, appendix, pp. 7-8, ed. 1773.

V. Hartmann, p. 202. (Printed in Cartwright, p. 257.)

VI. Hartmann, pp. 202-3. (Printed in Cartwright, p. 257.)

VII. L.J. 1666-75, p. 181.

VIII. S.P. 29/235, f. 55.

IX. Hartmann, pp. 203-4. (Printed in Cartwright, p. 259.)

X. Hartmann, p. 206. (Printed in Cartwright, p. 261.)

XI. Hartmann, p. 207. (Printed in Cartwright, p. 262.)

XII. Hartmann, pp. 208-9. (Printed in Cartwright, p. 263.)

XIII. Hartmann, pp. 210-11. (Printed in Cartwright, p. 264.)

XIV. Hartmann, pp. 211-12. (Printed in Cartwright, p. 264.)

XV. Hartmann, pp. 216-17. (Printed in Cartwright, p. 268.)

XVI. Hartmann, pp. 217-18. (Printed in Cartwright, p. 247.)
XVII. Hartmann, pp. 218-19. (Printed in Cartwright, p. 269.)
XVIII. Hartmann, pp. 223-4. (Printed in Cartwright, p. 271.)
XIX. Hartmann, p. 225. (Printed in Cartwright, p. 272.)
XX. Hartmann, p. 227. (Printed in Cartwright, p. 274.)
XXI. Hartmann, pp. 228-9. (Printed in Cartwright, p. 275.)
XXII. Hartmann, pp. 229-30. (Printed in Cartwright, pp. 279-80.)
XXIII. Hartmann, pp. 236-7. (Printed in Cartwright, pp. 282-3.)
XXIV. Hartmann, p. 240. (Printed in Cartwright, pp. 283-4.)
XXV. Hartmann, pp. 241-2. (Printed in Cartwright, pp. 284-5.)
XXVI. Hartmann, p. 245. (Printed in Cartwright, p. 285.)
XXVII. Hartmann, p. 247. (Printed in Cartwright, pp. 287-8.)
XXVIII. Hartmann, pp. 249-50. (Printed in Cartwright, p. 264. Printed in part.)
XXIX. Hartmann, pp. 254-6. (Printed in Cartwright, pp. 288-90.)
XXX. Hartmann, pp. 257-8. (Printed in Cartwright, pp. 291-2.)
XXXI. Hartmann, p. 259. (Printed in Cartwright, p. 292.)
XXXII. Dalrymple, vol. ii, appendix, p. 35.
XXXIII. L.J. 1666-75, p. 251.
XXXIV. L.J. 1666-75, p. 287.
XXXV. Hartmann, pp. 292-5.
XXXVI. B.M. Stowe MSS. 142, f. 84.
XXXVII. S.P. 104/64, f. 1.
XXXVIII. Cardwell, E., *Documentary Annals of the Reformed Church of England*, 1839, vol. ii, pp. 282-6. (Original in Bodleian Library.)
XXXIX. Nijhoff, vol. iv, p. 10.
XL. B.M. Lansdowne MSS. 1236, f. 207.
XLI. B.M. Lansdowne MSS. 1236, f. 211.
XLII. B.M. Lansdowne MSS. 1236, f. 213.
XLIII. B.M. Lansdowne MSS. 1236, f. 139.
XLIV. B.M. Lansdowne MSS. 1236, f. 219.
XLV. B.M. Lansdowne MSS. 1236, f. 221.
XLVI. Lauderdale Papers, vol. ii, p. 228.
XLVII. B.M. Lansdowne MSS. 1236, f. 141.
XLVIII. Nijhoff, vol. iv, p. 12.
XLIX. Nijhoff, vol. iv, pp. 13-14.
L. Nijhoff, vol. iv, pp. 14-15.
LI. Nijhoff, vol. iv, pp. 15-16.
LII. L.J. 1666-75, p. 524.
LIII. C.J., vol. ix, p. 256.
LIV. L.J. 1666-75, p. 549.
LV. B.M. Lansdowne 1236, f. 195.

LVI. S.P. 104/64, f. 109.
LVII. B.M. Lansdowne MSS. 1236, f. 199.
LVIII. B.M. Lansdowne MSS. 1236, f. 201.
LIX. B.M. Lansdowne MSS. 1236, f. 156.
LX. B.M. Lansdowne MSS. 1236, f. 158.
LXI. B.M. Add. MSS. 38,849. (Also printed in H. T. Colenbrander, *Bescheiden uit vreemde archieven omtrent de groote Nederlandsche zeeoorlogen,* 1919, II, 288, from R.O. Admiralty, Secretary's Dept., Out Letters I.)
LXII. B.M. Lansdowne MSS. 1236, f. 170.
LXIII. B.M. Lansdowne MSS. 1236, f. 172.
LXIV. B.M. Lansdowne MSS. 1236, f. 178.
LXV. L.J. 1666-75, p. 588.
LXVI. L.J. 1666-75, p. 593.
LXVII. Lauderdale Papers, vol. iii, p. 2.
LXVIII. Lauderdale Papers, vol. iii, p. 13.
LXIX. L.J. 1666-75, p. 594.
LXX. Lauderdale Papers, vol. iii, p. 22.
LXXI. L.J. 1666-75, p. 616.
LXXII. L.J. 1666-75, p. 632.

CHAPTER VIII

STRUGGLE AND FINAL TRIUMPH

I. L.J. 1666-75, p. 653.
II. L.J. 1666-75, p. 725.
III. L.J. 1666-75, p. 729.
IV. S.P. 44/27, f. 68.
V. L.J. 1675-81, p. 4.
VI. S.P. 44/42, f. 20-2.
VII. S.P. 44/42, f. 34.
VIII. L.J. 1675-81, p. 36.
IX. L.J. 1675-81, p. 130.
X. S.P. 44/29, f. 247.
XI. H.M.C. (Hodgkin MSS.), 15th Report, part ii, pp. 194-5.
XII. Dalrymple, *Memoirs*, vol. ii, appendix, p. 192.
XIII. L.J. 1675-81, p. 221.
XIV. L.J. 1675-81, p. 252.
XV. H.M.C. (Finch MSS.), vol. ii, p. 42.
XVI. L.J. 1675-81, p. 293.
XVII. H.M.C. Rep. 14, appendix, part vii, p. 25. From the MSS. of the Marquis of Ormonde.
XVIII. L.J. 1675-81, p. 345.
XIX. L.J. 1675-81, p. 375.
XX. L.J. 1675-81, p. 447.
XXI. Davidson, *Catherine of Braganza*, p. 326.
XXII. Dalrymple, *Memoirs*, vol. ii, appendix, p. 260.

XXIII. L.J. 1675-81, p. 450.

XXIV. L.J. 1675-81, p. 530.

XXV. Clarke, James, *Life of James II*, vol. i, p. 557, ed. 1816.

XXVI. S.P. 44/164, f. 25.

XXVII. S.P. 29/412, f. 88.

XXVIII. S.P. 30. Case G.

XXIX. H.M.C. Rep. 14, appendix, part vii, p. 29. From the MSS. of the Marquis of Ormonde.

XXX. H.M.C. Rep. 14, appendix, part vii, p. 30. From the MSS. of the Marquis of Ormonde.

XXXI. L.J. 1675-81, p. 610.

XXXII. L.J. 1675-81, p. 716.

XXXIII. L.J. 1675-81, p. 745.

XXXIV. L.J. 1675-81, p. 756.

XXXV. Eachard, L., *History of England*, 1718, vol. iii, p. 62.

XXXVI. S.P. 389/4, f. 164v.-165.

XXXVII. Kennett, *History of England*, ed. 1719, pp. 408-10.

XXXVIII. *Archæologia*, Society of Antiquaries of London, vol. 58, part i, p. 176.

XXXIX. *Archæologia*, Society of Antiquaries of London, vol. 58, part i, p. 176.

XL. *Archæologia*, Society of Antiquaries of London, vol. 58, part i, p. 185.

XLI. *Archæologia*, Society of Antiquaries of London, vol. 58, part i, p. 186.

XLII. *Archæologia*, Society of Antiquaries of London, vol. 58, part i, p. 188.

INDEX

Morrice, Mr., 81
Munster, Treaty of, 175
Muscovy Company, letter to, 285
' Mutineers,' 304

NARBOROUGH, ADMIRAL SIR JOHN, 265,
270
Navy, Charles seeks to win over, 71,
74; expense of, 102-3; need for large,
214-15; bankrupt financial affairs of,
221; subsidy for increase of, 287; Act
for maintenance of, 297. *See also*
Fleet
Netherlands, Charles in, 45 *et seq.*, 78;
Charles leaves, 82; French victories
in, 209, 288, 293; Charles sends
troops to, 290; Charles saves, 294-6,
299; ports of, secured from French
occupation, 295; threat to, 298, 313;
Duke of York exiled in, 309; Louis
guarantees not to attack, 316
Neuburg, Duke of, 48
New Amsterdam, 168
New Delaware, 202
New Jersey, 202
New York, naming of, 168n.; secured
to England, 202
Newcastle, Earl of, letter to, 3
Newcastle, Marquis of, letter to, 160
Newmarket, Charles at, 226, 230, 234,
326; racing and hunting at, 231-2
Nicholas, Sir Edward, 17; left at
Brussels, 68
letter to, 18
Nicholls, Governor, 168n.
Nimuegen, Peace of, 295-6, 298
Nonconformists, Charles suspends laws
against, 247-9; enforcement of Acts
disqualifying, 309
Nore, Buoy of, fleet to repair to, 186;
refitting of ships at Buoy of, 250,
254-6
Norfolk, expected support for rising
from, 74; Justices of Peace for, 298
No-Resisting Bill, 281
North-East Passage, 284
Norway, trade from, 243

OATES, TITUS, 299; tries to involve
Queen in plot, 303
Oblivion, Act of, in Scotland, 107;
Charles's speech on passing of, 113.
See also Indemnity and Oblivion,
Act of
O'Neill, Daniel, 17, 41, 48; sent to
Don Lewis, 77; death of, 168
Opposition, creation of, 280; demands
of, 281; and dissolution of Parlia-
ment, 284; desires war with France,

288; accepts French bribes, 288-9;
starves Charles of supplies, 290-1;
and Popish plot, 299; strikes at
Catholic successor, 300; has majority
in Commons, 304; and legitimacy of
Monmouth, 304; given offices in
Council, 307; reaction against, 319;
in Corporation of London, 323
Orange, Prince of, Charles at court of,
6; helps Charles, 18, 21; death of, 21
letter to, 15
Orange, Princess Mary of, Charles expresses sympathy for, 21; and Jane
Lane, 25; Charles and, 30; at
Cologne, 38, 40, 42; in Paris,
50; supports Queen Mother against
Charles, 57; and Harry Jermyn, 58;
sees Charles embark, 92n.
letters to, 57, 58
Orleans, Duchess of. *See* Madame
Orleans, Duke of (Monsieur), 121, 170,
212, 214
Ormonde, Marquis of, in Ireland, 11;
defeated at Rathmines, 12; repudia-
tion of treaty of, 14-16; advised to
leave Ireland, 17-18, 20; sent to
fetch Duke of Gloucester, 32-3;
Charles's friendship for, 43; visits
Irish Army, 56; and Royalist rising
in England, 75; Lord Lieutenant of
Ireland, 98n.; plot directed against,
310; son of, 310, 313
letters to, 11, 17, 35, 45, 55, 204,
300, 313
Orrery, Earl of. *See* Broghill
Osborne, Sir Thomas. *See* Danby,
Earl of
Ossory, Earl of, 270, 310, 313
Ostend, 68, 291; Charles demands, 240;
danger of French occupation of, 297
Oxford, Charles I's court at, 4; Charles
visits, 147, 185; Parliament meets at,
187, 317, 321
Oxford, Earl of, 82

PANAMA plate-fleet, 40n.
Parliament, Charles expresses esteem
for, 85-6, 105, 155, 322; and religious toleration, 85, 122-4, 140, 260-
262; invites Charles to return, 90; and
Act of Indemnity and Oblivion, 100,
106, 110, 113; Charles appeals for
money to, 103, 119-20, 122-4, 142-5,
198, 241-2, 260, 271, 287, 289-90,
306; votes supplies, 103, 145, 261-
262, 287; Royalist reaction in, 110;
adjournment of, 115, 117; investi-
gates King's expenses, 144-5, 241;
votes money for Dutch wars, 169,